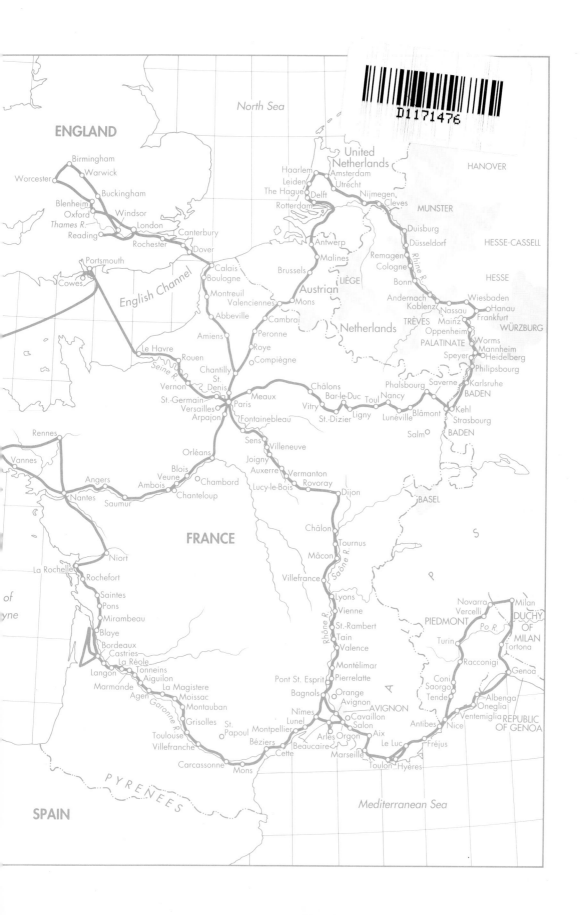

Thomas Jefferson's Travels
in Europe, 1784–1789

Thomas Jefferson's Travels in Europe, 1784–1789

George Green Shackelford

THE JOHNS HOPKINS UNIVERSITY PRESS
BALTIMORE AND LONDON

04 03 02 01 00 99 98 97 96 95   5 4 3 2 1

The Johns Hopkins University Press
2715 North Charles Street
Baltimore, Maryland 21218-4319
The Johns Hopkins Press Ltd., London

Frontispiece: *Vue du Port de la Rochelle*, ca. 1765, painting by
Joseph Vernet (1714–89).

Library of Congress Cataloging-in-Publication Data will be
found at the end of this book.

A catalog record for this book is available from the British
Library.

ISBN 0-8018-4843-1

To Grace

Contents

Thomas Jefferson's Travels
in Europe, 1784–1789

PROLOGUE:

An American for Paris

A WEALTHY AND OPTIMISTIC ANGLO-AMERICAN, THOMAS JEFFER-
son as a young man yearned to take the European grand tour, which in the
eighteenth century capped a cultivated Briton's education.[1] Not until 1784,
when he was more than forty years old, did he reach Europe, but he made the
most of it. That year the Continental Congress sent him to France as one of
three U.S. treaty commissioners. The other two were John Adams and Benjamin Franklin, the latter of whom was also minister to France. The three
republicans sought to enlarge French friendship with the fledgling United
States and gain trading concessions. When in 1785 Franklin retired to the
United States, Adams became minister to the court of St. James and Jefferson
succeeded Franklin at Paris. Jefferson did not return to the United States until
the fall of 1789. By that time this discriminating Virginian had so improved
his knowledge of the French language and had come to appreciate France so
deeply that to live there had become for him the only acceptable substitute for
residing at home.[2]

This is the first book to make a full, detailed examination of Jefferson's
residence and travels in Europe between 1784 and 1789. Its sharp focus
permits emphasis lacking in works that consider his whole career. On the
other hand, it traces a larger compass than does Howard C. Rice's superb
Thomas Jefferson's Paris.[3] Focusing on Jefferson the private man, it is a cultural rather than a political study. It says little about Jefferson's views on such
subjects as ideal and evil government, social-class conflict, or the French
Revolution—topics covered so well in Dumas Malone's and Merrill Peterson's life-and-times biographies of the third president.[4]

Our understanding of Jefferson the cultural tourist may not be as
important to public affairs, but it richly rewards close attention and even

calls for reexamination. When Gilbert Chinard published *Thomas Jefferson: Apostle of Americanism* sixty years ago, he popularized two incorrect and contradictory notions that linger to the present day: that Jefferson's interests, outlook, and goals were primarily American and that with regard to cultural matters he adopted a rigid standard of formal, classicist beauty before he went to Europe and never deviated from it.[5] The impression persists that Jefferson culturally and politically was *American*. Of course he was proud of the American republic, its people, and its rich and diverse countryside. Yet he was not a typical American of that or any other day. At no time after 1789 did anyone allege that he was a mere provincial. He had become an internationalist in the sense that his cultural horizons embraced all of the Northern Hemisphere. At the same time that this study recounts what and whom Jefferson saw in Europe, it seeks to assess how his European experiences influenced him.

BEFORE 1784 THOMAS JEFFERSON'S STYLISTIC PREFERENCES were for formality and symmetry in architecture, literature, music, painting, and sculpture. His grand models were epitomized by Versailles and Blenheim in building; by Cervantes, Milton, Pope, and Shakespeare in writing; by Lully and Purcell in music; by Raphael and Rubens in painting; and by Roman copies of classical sculpture. In the mid-1780s it became apparent to him that the Anglo-Palladian architectural models he once had admired were too grand in richness and in scale. His European experiences hastened, if they did not cause, the change in his aesthetic preferences to simpler styles that would continue for the rest of his life.

Jefferson's appreciation for high culture had been whetted by close acquaintance with a few sophisticated men, such as Virginia's Governor Francis Fauquier and Professor Charles Bellini, a Florentine teacher at the College of William and Mary.[6] Although these luminaries heightened his aesthetic sense and helped shape his early tastes, books had been his chief source of inspiration.[7] Judging from his considerable music collection, he preferred ballads and classical music scored for solos, duets, or small chamber groups. His chief authority on musical history and theory was Dr. Charles Burney, and his choice of composers included Bach, Handel, Lully, Mozart, and Vivaldi.[8] Claude Balbastre often is credited with having had a vague influence on Jefferson's musical tastes. I seek to show that Balbastre was one of the foremost musical arrangers of his day and that for almost a year he gave Jefferson's daughters weekly lessons at their Parisian home, when Jefferson doubtless engaged him in serious discussion.

As for fine art, Jefferson saw some good European paintings at Williamsburg and on early visits to Annapolis, Philadelphia, and New York;[9] his views on painting and sculpture were shaped in addition by readings in Joseph Addison's *Remarks on . . . Italy*, Edmund Burke's *On the Sublime and Beautiful*, William Hogarth's *Analysis of Beauty*, Lord Kames's *Elements of Criticism*, William Shenstone's *Works*, Daniel Webb's *The Beauties of Painting*, and Thomas Whately's *Observations on Modern Gardening*. In 1971 Jefferson expressed his artistic credo as follows: "Everything is useful which contributes to fix us in the principles and practice of virtue" and "If the painting be lively, and a tolerable picture of nature, we are thrown into a reverie."[10] As early as 1776 he was conversant with some of the art of the ancient world through Joseph Spence's *Polymetis: or An Enquiry Concerning the Agreement between the Works of the Roman Poets and the Remains of the Ancient Artists*, with its forty-one folio-size illustrations by L. B. Boitard.[11] He recommended to a relative François Perrier's *Segmenta nobilium signorum e statuarii. . . .*[12] It was probably while in Europe that he obtained copies of William Gilpin's *An Essay on Prints, Picturesque Beauty . . . and the Most Noted Masters . . .*, Jonathan Richardson's *Essay on the Theory of Painting*, Giorgio Vasari's *Delle vite de' piu eccellenti pittori, scultori et architetti*, Leonardo da Vinci's *Treatise on Painting*, and Horace Walpole's *Aedes Walpoliana: A Description of the Collection of Pictures at Houghton Hall*.[13]

Relying on his books and Professor Bellini's advice, Jefferson around 1781 compiled a list of paintings and statuary that he wished to have copied for Monticello.[14] At first he planned to hang there about a dozen canvases copied from Italian masterpieces and an equal number of statuettes, copied in terra cotta from Greek, Roman, or Renaissance works. He outgrew this list in the next seven years. Changes in his taste, not expense, were the reason why he did not have copies made of any of the pictures on his list. Nor did he ever purchase any of the sculpture that he listed. Even though he had noted Bellini's advice concerning landscape paintings, he included none on his early want list, and ultimately his collection included only one such oil painting. He did place on his 1782 want list some engravings by Francis Hayman and William Hogarth. Probably Hogarth's would have displayed the incisive social commentary for which that artist is famous. Hayman is perhaps as well known for being Thomas Gainsborough's teacher as he is for his own work, which included important views of landscape.

No one knows the title of the first architectural book Jefferson bought while he was a student at the College of William and Mary.[15] Millicent Sowerby's *Catalogue of the Library of Thomas Jefferson* attests to the fact that his library in 1815 contained a marvelous collection of books dealing with architecture, painting, and sculpture. But Jefferson owned few of these before he went to Europe in 1784.[16] Beforehand, when he remarked that Virginia's architecture was even "worse" than America's "bad" styles,[17] his benchmarks and ideas for substitutes or improvements were highly limited.

Students of Jefferson's early architectural taste have relied on his architectural drawings and specifications and emphasized the works of Andrea Palladio and his eighteenth-century English admirers, such as Robert Morris and James Gibbs, as the young Virginian's principal sources of inspiration. They point to both plans and surviving structures, especially Jefferson's 1779 sketches for remodeling the Governor's Palace at Williamsburg.[18] Yet Frederick D. Nichols and James A. Bear's guidebook for Monticello makes abundant reference to French architectural books as Jefferson's sources for the cornices, entablatures, and friezes in the rooms on the main floor of Monticello, particularly to Roland Frerard de Chambrai's *Parallèle de l'architecture antique avec la modèrne . . .* and Antoine Babuty

3

Desgodets's *Les Edifices antiques de Rome*.[19] So self-evident are the house's early Palladian sources that one easily misses the Louis Seize characteristics Jefferson imposed on it after he returned from Europe. The first professional architect with whom Jefferson became personally acquainted had the greatest impact on him. He was the Frenchman Charles Louis Clérisseau.

TO UNDERSTAND HOW JEFFERSON COMPLETED HIS EVOLUTION from talented provincial to traveled sophisticate, it is necessary to reconstitute his European journeys. Again, one cannot overestimate the importance of his books. In his writings Jefferson rarely commented directly or in detail on European works of architecture, art, or historic interest, because he had such good descriptions of them between covers. Jefferson's own library included the *Guide pour le voyage d'Italie en poste*, Joseph Addison's *Remarks On . . . Italy*, Carlo Bianconi's *Nuova guida di Milano . . . delle belle arti . . . e profane antichità*, Giacomo Brusco's *Beautés de Gènes*, Louis Dutens's *Itinéraire*, Thomas Shenstone's *Works*, and Thomas Whately's *Observations on Modern Gardening*.[20] Jefferson used these volumes not merely to get about from one place to another while in Europe but as long-term references about noted buildings and works of art. He kept them at Monticello, lent some for use in planning the city of Washington, and sold most of them to form the second Library of Congress.[21]

Yet we cannot understand the development of Jefferson's cultural sensibility without also knowing what he saw, heard, and felt. Making light of his sightseeing visits to châteaux and palaces, which then served as museums as well as residences, Jefferson wrote La Fayette that he welcomed the chance to "see what I have never seen before and shall never see again. In the great cities, I go to see what travelers think alone worthy of being seen; but I make a job of it; and generally gulp it all down in a day."[22] We must retrace Jefferson's steps in Europe and try to review or reenvision the sights he took in, the places where he lived, and the people with whom he spoke.

Thus the value of Jefferson's memoranda and account books[23] for the European adventure. Carefully kept though often sketchy, they provide the richest fund of information on how he responded to European châteaux, city plans, commerce, institutions, manufactures, monuments, palaces, people, theaters, and works of art. He consulted these notes before writing on these topics later. This book draws heavily upon them in reconstructing his itinerary and frame of mind, which necessarily had much to do with politics and unavoidably combined the personal and the public. In this volume I have employed modern English usage in capitalization, punctuation, and spelling. In his journeys Jefferson often imposed upon himself a timetable and itinerary tailored to America's agricultural, commercial, manufacturing, and scientific needs. He usually traveled in a private capacity, on leave time and at his own expense; whenever he combined the exploration of places of architectural or artistic importance with business, he tried to keep his public and private expenses distinct.[24]

It was disquieting to so resolute a republican and lover of liberty as

Jefferson to recognize that with the exception of the infant United States of America, monarchy and despotism were then almost universal. Like so many Americans of that day, he was too deeply embroiled in a love-hate relationship with Great Britain to be objective about its political institutions when he visited London, the Midlands, and southeastern England. He saw most of the great sights of the Low Countries and the Rhineland. Because he did not know German, he was never very specific about identifying the heritage from what he called the United States' second motherland after Great Britain. Knowing a fair amount of the Tuscan tongue, he delighted in everything that he observed in Italy, except the contemporary political and religious institutions of Turin and Genoa.

For Jefferson, the cultural monuments of European countries often were less significant as monuments than they were as examples of why the political and social institutions of those countries should be reformed. Because of his anticlerical views, he was concerned less with the architectural merit of Gothic cathedrals than with their relation to the human welfare of Englishmen, Frenchmen, Germans, or Italians. When he visited them, it was mainly to perceive from their heights the cityscape before taking the established tour of the "sights."[25]

In order to recount as fully as possible what Jefferson saw on his travels and to embellish the terse entries in his pocket account book of expenses, I have incorporated some descriptive passages from his guidebooks, his own letters, and the memoirs of such contemporaries as the Adams family, Dr. Samuel Johnson, and Mrs. Hester Thrale Piozzi.[26] This narrative also relies heavily for supplemental material on the travel journals of two men who visited many of the same places that Jefferson did in much the same manner and at much the same time: François de La Rochefoucauld-Liancourt, son of Jefferson's friend the Duc de Liancourt, and Arthur Young, the English agriculturist. Young's *Travels in France* became celebrated immediately upon their publication in 1792, but Liancourt's *Voyages* were not published for 150 years. Jefferson and young Liancourt probably knew each other, but in their surviving papers they do not refer to each other. Jefferson and Young seem never to have met, even though they were at Paris at the same time and consorted with many of the same people.[27] The American owned a copy of Young's great book and some of his pamphlets.[28] In addition to using written sources, I have visited almost every place that Jefferson went in Europe—pleasant pilgrimages to supplement his scanty testimony.

In considering Jefferson on the personal level, I have sought to link his new friends, such as Maria Cosway, with specific places, such as Marly. When Jefferson and Maria Cosway first met, he had been a widower, and she the wife of a childless marriage, for five years. He was forty-three and she was twenty-six. Writers have long speculated about Jefferson and Maria Cosway's relations. I interpret his correspondence with her not as love epistles but mock love letters that puzzled her then and have misled romantics ever since. I believe that I explain why any possibility of a passionate love affair between Thomas and Maria vanished during her 1788 visit to Paris. Long before learning of Mrs. Cosway's pregnancy late in 1789, Jefferson had dismissed any remaining romantic notions he might have had about her. Theirs was a friendship whose ardor had waned.

ALTHOUGH JEFFERSON WAS NOT A BLIND FOLLOWER OF FADS OR fashions, he rarely denied himself the comforts of life, large or small. Whether it was a question of cities to visit, curiosities to examine, houses to emulate, or furnishings or clothes to buy, he wanted the latest and the best for himself and his family. In closely examining his travels in Europe, one must note how greatly they changed his aesthetic views. After his return to America in 1789 Jefferson was its chief advocate of modern French architecture and decorative arts. He was also unshakably—perhaps unreasonably—optimistic about the likelihood of France's reformation.

1 *From Boston to the Champs Élysées*

THOMAS JEFFERSON WAS HAPPY TO GO TO EUROPE IN THE SUMMER
of 1784, even if he had to endure his customary seasickness to get there. He
had long wished to visit the Old World and to savor its cultural delights. He
had been a widower for almost two years, and there may have seemed little
point in his staying at Monticello to supervise the completion of the Palladian villa, which he must often have discussed with the woman he mourned,
Martha Jefferson. To the extent that Jefferson ever took serious account of
his financial abilities, he believed that he could well afford to improve his
mind and at the same time banish sadness.

Whether in the Commonwealth of Virginia or the Congress of the
Confederation, the lull in his interest in political affairs matched the lan-
guor of the country. Both national and state priorities were largely economic and reflective of those of other countries; two of the infant republic's
chief statesmen, Benjamin Franklin and John Adams, were in Europe seek-
ing trade treaties. Thus, for personal reasons and reasons of public service,
Jefferson determined to go abroad for several years.

He welcomed his appointment by the U.S. Congress as a member of its
Treaty Commission. He had come to know Franklin and Adams during
their service in the Continental Congress, and he was happy to join them
in Paris. He already had a harmonious working relationship with John Adams, but his wonderful friendship with John and Abigail Adams did not
begin until their diplomatic service coincided in Paris.

Jefferson booked passage from Boston to Cowes, England, for himself,

La Grille de Chaillot, ca. 1778, engraving by François Nicholas
Martinet. On the right is the Hôtel Langeac, which Jefferson
rented for the U.S. Legation from 1785 to 1790.

his twelve-year-old daughter Martha, who was called "Patsy," and his coach-man and slave James Hemings in Nathaniel Tracy's new brig *Ceres*, com-manded by Captain St. Barbe. Jefferson took not only their luggage but his Virginia-made phaeton, in which John had driven the Jeffersons from Vir-ginia to Massachusetts. Before embarkation, Jefferson sold his riding horse Assargoa and sent his groom Bob home with the pair of carriage horses, Odin and The Grey.[1]

On shipboard Patsy and her father shared a windowless cabin that was accessible from the open deck by a door so low that "one was obliged to enter on all four," with a floor space of three by four feet and two-doored bunks resembling coffins. Because the bunks were furnished with only a couple of blankets and no mattress, passengers slept in their clothes. They spent most of their time on deck or in the saloon. There were six other passengers, with all of whom Jefferson had a slight acquaintance; their acquaintance was improved by their consumption of four dozen bottles of wine that Jefferson prudently had brought with him for his first sea voyage. Besides watching the seascape, the diplomat read *Don Quixote* in Spanish, a language he was trying to master. Patsy, although a little seasick at first, declared that the Atlantic was as "calm as a river." Jefferson was able to write an acquaintance in Boston that his voyage was "as favourable as could have been asked." The *Ceres*'s passage of nineteen days was not uneventful. Off the Grand Banks of Newfoundland the passengers watched the crew catch cod, and they saw whales not far off. Two days out from the Isle of Wight they even saw what appeared to be a waterspout. Entering coastal waters on July 24, they vainly peered into heavy fog for ships headed for France, hoping to transfer to one rather than have to land first in England.[2]

On July 25, 1784, Jefferson and Patsy landed at Cowes, on the Isle of Wight. After distributing tips to the ship's stewards and leaving James Hemings and the phaeton at Cowes, the Jeffersons passed through cus-toms and breakfasted before crossing the Solent to Portsmouth, where they lodged at Bradley's Crown Inn. Because Patsy had caught cold and developed a fever, her father placed her under the care of a Dr. Meek and a nurse. Until July 31, when they were to sail from Cowes to Le Havre in Captain Grey's ship, Jefferson made a brief circuit of nearby villages in a rented chaise. Although Portsmouth was the Royal Navy's base for the home fleet and crowded with ships and sailors engaged in repair or refit or on leave, he did not comment on the great naval center. This was not so much because of his aversion to the sea as it was a reflection of his peace-loving, civilian character. At other times and places, he made more or less elaborate note of the number of ships, the proportions of those engaged in merchant or naval service, of American or of foreign registry, and their customary cargoes.

At six o'clock in the evening of July 31, Jefferson and Patsy boarded ship, carrying with them newspapers, pamphlets, cups, saucers, and a few vict-uals. Their Channel crossing was so rough that they had no use for the little delicacies they had bought for their voyage. They were relieved when at seven o'clock the next morning Grey's ship entered the harbor of Le Havre de Grace.[3]

Jefferson was in a hurry to get to Paris, where he wished to join his fellow treaty commissioners as quickly as possible. He looked forward to renewing his acquaintance with many French officer veterans of the American Revolution, especially General the Marquis de La Fayette. But the ordinary difficulties of an American gentleman entering a foreign country for the first time, encumbered with a young daughter, a rural black servant, a foreign carriage, and a lot of luggage, delayed Jefferson's arrival at Paris and taxed his ingenuity and patience.

When Jefferson's little party disembarked at Le Havre, there were discomforting and expensive negotiations for the American diplomat, who knew "very little French." The city then had a population of about twenty-five thousand, five thousand less than Philadelphia but more confusing to them because of the difference of language. A kind Irish stranger conducted them to Mahon's Hôtel l'Aigle d'Or. Jefferson paid a "broker" to assist in getting their possessions through customs. Patsy probably echoed her papa's grumbling about how foreigners cheated strangers and how it cost him almost as much to get their luggage from their ship to their hotel as from Philadelphia to Boston. In 1784 he did not inspect this busy port, as he was to do five years later.[4] During his stay at Le Havre, he began his practice of buying a map and guidebook at a new city. He called for a barber several times, and he purchased an umbrella. To while away the time and to calm himself, he ordered numerous cups of coffee and liqueurs. It was probably more for Patsy than for himself that he made a number of little purchases of fruits and nuts. By August 5 Jefferson and James Hemings had gathered together the Jeffersons' possessions, reassembled the phaeton, and bought luggage straps to assist in loading the vehicle with trunks and packages. Although he had his own carriage and coachman, for his journey from Le Havre to Paris Jefferson followed the custom of the country in hiring from the royal system of *relais de la poste et des chevaux* successive postilions and pairs of post horses at relay stations situated about twelve miles apart. Changing horses could be so lengthy a process that one of Jefferson's younger friends shot partridges at most of the posts between Calais and Paris.[5] At last Jefferson and his little party—James accompanied them on horseback—set out.

On the road to Paris, Jefferson was impressed by the five-mile-wide Seine estuary between chalk cliffs and by the many fine houses. As the harvest was beginning, he had ample opportunity to assess the farms along the way: "Nothing could be more fertile, better cultivated, or more elaborately improved." Patsy exclaimed that it was "the most beautiful country I ever saw in my life."[6] No matter how uninteresting this route might be to *habitués*, it was new and fascinating to the Jeffersons. Because their phaeton was very different from French carriages and because they were such innocents, they were surrounded by as many as nine beggars at every stop. Like almost all cities of that time, Rouen was ugly, stinking, and badly built. Because its provincial assembly had refused to register royal decrees limiting its authority, Rouen's Parlement House was "shut up, and its members exiled . . . to their country estates." Although Patsy was enthusiastic about the architecture, statues, and stained glass of Rouen's cathedral, neither she nor her father remarked upon its monuments to the dukes of Normandy and the kings of England. Jefferson's little party lodged at the Hôtel Pomme du Pin, where guests dined at a common table. Some Englishmen complained that the meals were too expensive and not bountiful enough, but an ordinary dinner consisted of soup, duck, chicken, veal, and salad; wine was extra. Often, meals were consumed so quickly that there was little or no conversation.[7]

Before leaving Rouen the morning of August 5, Jefferson bought some books, treated himself to coffee and Patsy to nuts, and bought a knife to cut fruit and a lock to secure his valuables. There were six relay stations before Triel, where he engaged quarters for his party to dine and spend the night at the Hôtel de la Poste. At the little city of Mantes, Patsy and her father paid for "seeing" the church of the monastic college of Notre Dame. She climbed to the top of its steeple and long remembered that it had as many steps as there were days in the year. The next day the Jeffersons did little more than glance from their phaeton at the town and château of St. Germain.[8] Having long been interested in the celebrated hydraulic works at Marly, Jefferson was happy to observe for himself how the water of the Seine was raised to provide for the king's châteaux at Marly and Versailles.[9] He was to return to Marly three years later, but he now pressed on, anxious to complete the two short stages remaining before their destination.

What excitement Jefferson and little Patsy must have felt when their carriage entered the gates of Paris. "Behold me on the vaunted scene of Europe!" How much meaning, how many meanings there were to Jefferson's oft-quoted pronouncement![10] The travelers planned to go to the commercial Hôtel d'Orléans. Because there were two hotels of that name in the French metropolis, the weary Jefferson could be excused for not going at once to the intended one, where most Americans lodged on their arrival at Paris. The next day he located the correct one, in the rue de Rivoli. Settling in, he bought a map of the city and a new hat for himself and ready-to-wear clothes, cambric, edging, and lace ruffles for Patsy.[11]

Although as a treaty commissioner and later as minister resident Jefferson conducted much official business at Versailles, he spent more of his time at Paris than had America's Revolutionary diplomats.[12] Throughout his stay in France, he lived close to the center of the city. It was not easy for him to find suitable quarters for the U.S. legation, because Congress had decided to reduce the salary and allowances for his position from the twenty-five hundred guineas Franklin had enjoyed to two thousand.[13] Indeed, Jefferson's household expenses as a diplomat forced him to incur private debt in order to keep up official appearances and satisfy his own aesthetic requirements.

Jefferson did not record his impression of Paris upon entering the city for the first time. It must have seemed to him very dirty, ugly, and crowded. We do not know whether he followed the advice he gave to young Americans that upon arriving they should climb to the top of a church tower, such as the cathedral of Notre Dame, in order to perceive the cityscape.[14]

On October 16, 1784, Jefferson leased from M. Guireaud de Talairac the Hôtel Landron, a three-story house on the Right Bank of the Seine at number 5, cul-de-sac Taitbout, just off the chaussée d'Antin. Although the neighborhood was crowded and built up, the house boasted a court, two gardens, and several small dependent structures.[15] It was not long before Jefferson determined that this house was inconvenient and unworthy of being the U.S. legation. In March 1785 he gave notice that he would vacate the premises in September. It is not clear whether the Hôtel Landron came provided with a staff or whether Jefferson recruited the five or six servants to run the establishment, but none of them seem to have been very satisfactory. Finding that it was more practical to have a French coachman than to use James Hemings in that capacity, Jefferson apprenticed the slave first to a caterer and then to the Prince de Condé's own chef before James assumed that duty for Jefferson.[16] Among the furnishings that Jefferson bought before March 1785 the most important were two sets of candlesticks, several comic busts, and twenty-two paintings, including an *Ecce Homo*.[17]

Not long after the battle of Yorktown, in 1781, Jefferson had met the Chevalier de Chastellux, now a marquis. Thanks to Chastellux's influence and Jefferson's own payment of the quarterly fee of six hundred francs, Patsy began attending an exclusive convent school in Paris, the Abbaye Royale de Penthémont on the rue de Grenelle. Jefferson was so pleased with the school that he later sent for his younger daughter, Maria, to come from Virginia to study there. Always apprehensive about his daughters' health, Jefferson had left Maria and her little sister, Lucy Elizabeth, in the capable and loving care of their aunt Elizabeth Wayles Eppes at Eppington in Chesterfield County. Its location above the Fall Line had not warded off the fevers of Tidewater Virginia, to which the youngest child and one of her little cousins had fallen victims. When in January 1785 Jefferson learned of Lucy Elizabeth's death, he immediately sent for Maria so that she might live under his scrutiny and obtain a fine education.[18]

In March 1785 Jefferson leased the *hôtel particulier*, or townhouse, of Comte Auguste Louis Joseph Fidèle Armand de Lespinasse Langeac. He may have done so through the good offices either of the comte's kinsman (and Jefferson's friend) the Duc de La Rochefoucauld, or of the Marquis de La Fayette, who was soon to buy the seigneurial rights to the village of Langeac.[19] The Hôtel Langeac was an up-to-date residence, of two full stories, a basement, and a mezzanine, located at the corner of the boulevard des Champs Élysées and the rue de Berri. Its lot also included stabling and an English garden of moderate size. Until 1787 it was adjacent to the Grille de Chaillot, a tollgate built in 1779 for the payment of municipal customs levied on goods entering the city. In 1787 the city's boundaries were extended, and a new pair of tollhouses were constructed further up the Champs Élysées at the Place d'Etoile, where the Arc de Triomphe later would be raised. The Hôtel Langeac had been designed in 1768 by Jean F. T. Chalgrin, whose architectural career spanned the reigns of Louis XVI and Napoleon I. Owing to complications of death and inheritance, this *hôtel particulier* was not completed until about 1780. At least two of its twenty-four principal rooms were oval-shaped, and it had a flush toilet.[20] In addition to the furnishings that Jefferson had acquired for his first house, he acquired for the larger one a considerable amount of new and used furniture. Besides providing for ordinary household items, he also commissioned a few specially designed pieces.

As his own attorney, Jefferson contracted for leasing both the Hôtel Landron and the Hôtel Langeac on terms that he did not perceive to be disadvantageous until later. On leaving the Hôtel Landron he discovered that French custom required the renter to pay annual municipal taxes.[21] He was mistaken in believing that he could terminate his three-year lease on giving ninety days notice, and eventually he had to negotiate a settlement. His purchase of his own horses and a new carriage necessitated a larger staff. In February 1786 he laid out a considerable sum for servants and animals, plus additional amounts to such suppliers as Messieurs Perrier for piped water.[22] From his old quarters Jefferson brought a lot of china, glassware, and ordinary household furniture, as well as some items that deserve special mention. Among these were fourteen pairs of window curtains of damask, lawn, and calico; a pendulum clock; and six armchairs and two easy chairs.[23] Perhaps in preparation for celebrating Christmas in 1786, he bought two expensive silver casseroles, a silver soup ladle, a personal silver goblet, and a *plateau de dessert*.[24]

On moving into the Hôtel Langeac, Jefferson incurred additional expenses for installing ironwork for security; outfitting the kitchen and pantry with a full line of linens, utensils, furniture, and supplies; painting walls and putting up wallpaper, bookshelves, and Venetian blinds; reupholstering furniture; and providing more andirons.[25] Unfortunately, he was more conscientious in keeping good household accounts than successful in reducing his expenditures. He attempted to budget sums for kitchen expenses, washing, and other household expenses, but unforeseen events always required him to spend more.[26] He had hard luck with servants. Some white domestics stole from him, whereas others loved him so much that their discharge was secured only upon payment of more than generous severance. While he was in France, he paid his slaves James and Sally Hemings monthly wages, plus the French New Year's present, the *étrennes*.

When Jefferson's younger daughter Maria, whom everybody called "Polly," came to Paris at the end of July 1787, her father had to buy a new bedstead and make a number of changes at the Hôtel Langeac. Her coming to Europe must have been traumatic for the nine-year-old, for she had a lifelong fear of strangers. When she arrived in Paris after a separation of three years, she remembered neither her father nor her sister. Polly had seen only strangers—except for her fifteen-year-old maid, Sally Hemings—since being tricked into boarding ship at Norfolk by the Eppeses' assurances that she was only going on a picnic. Delivered into the care of the Adamses at London, Polly had captivated Abigail Adams and was loath to leave, especially because her father had not come to London to meet her. He had sent his trusted major-domo, Adrien Petit, to bring the child to Paris.[27] Sally Hemings was possessed of only rudimentary training when she arrived in Paris, but there she learned the skills of a French headwaitress and parlormaid, which, to judge from later accounts of her service at Monticello, transformed her from a bothersome encumbrance into an accomplished servant.[28]

Jefferson wrote to relatives in Virginia that he had placed Patsy and Polly in the school of the Abbaye Royale de Penthémont, conducted by nuns of the Order of Saint Bernard, because it was the "best" school for girls, with the "best" teachers, in France, well worth its fees for room, board, and tuition. Its abbess, Madame Marie Catherine Béthisy de Mézières, impressed Jefferson most favorably. It was no doubt because of her stern high character that the Abbaye was not one of the church schools later terminated as part of the reforms of the early 1790s. Jefferson believed that under such leadership there could be no cause for religious fears, for there were "as many Protestants as Catholics" among the students, and "not a word is ever spoken to them on the subject of religion."

The Jefferson girls spent almost all their time, except for vacations, as boarding students at the Abbaye until spring 1789. When the impressionable Polly witnessed some of her older schoolmates becoming postulants for the nunnery and expressed interest in following suit, Jefferson withdrew the girls from school at once and engaged tutors to teach them at home. Polly had a Spanish master and a guitar teacher.[29] The piano and harpsichord teacher for both girls was Claude Balbastre, the organist of the Parisian Church of St. Roche, who was more noted for his "light and fanciful style as a performer" than as a composer of chamber or church music for harpsichord, horns, organ, and piano.[30] Patsy was studious by nature, but Polly was not. Patsy and her father seem continually to have been telling Polly what she must do. All three did homework at the Hôtel Langeac, necessitating the purchase of inkpots, fixing the "screw of [a] reading table," and "mending [a] secretaire." Whether for homework, entertaining, or display, Jefferson improved his lighting in December 1787 by buying silver-plated, three-branched girandoles. According to Gouverneur Morris, the Jefferson girls were not expected to help entertain their father's guests; instead, they demurely left the room after introductions were made.[31]

In the cold winter of 1787–88 Jefferson found that he had to buy four additional wool blankets for his enlarged family. The loving father tempered his sternness toward Polly by purchasing coils of wax tapir and "phosphoretic" matches to provide her a bedside light until she became accustomed to strange, new surroundings.[32] The shy Polly was not as brave as Patsy. Although he took quiet pride in being a good father and master, Jefferson believed that he did not indulge himself, his daughters, or his servants in luxuries. He spent more lavishly, however, than was prudent. Even though the three Jeffersons passed many quiet afternoons at the Hôtel Langeac during the spring and summer of 1789, Patsy and Polly found time to shop for much feminine apparel.[33]

If a stern head of the house expects servants or schoolgirls to be prompt, he must provide them with clocks and watches. This Jefferson did. He gave his trusted slave James Hemings a watch soon after they arrived in France. The pendule he bought in July 1787 must have been for a place of prominence, perhaps the entrance hall of the Hôtel Langeac so that the entire household could consult it in order to synchronize their more unreliable timepieces.[34] In 1788 Jefferson bought a large quantity of china and in 1789 several distinctive pieces from the Parisian silversmith Odiot—one coffeepot for himself and, at the expense of the Commonwealth of Virginia, another as a present for Charles Louis Clérisseau, in appreciation for his "assistance about the draughts & model of the Capitol prison." He also had Odiot make to his own design several silver goblets for himself.[35]

Celebrated still as the most hospitable of American presidents, Jefferson in Paris perfected his skills as a fashionable host. To entertain at the Hôtel Langeac in December 1787, he bought a large set of red china comprising three dozen plates, eight serving plates, and five compotes. He also bought tea-party paraphernalia for serving both hot and cold beverages that he, as a good father and host, may have thought appropriate for his daughters' use. It was only partly for their benefit that he sent for a London-made harpsichord with an up-to-date crank to modulate or swell the sound.

Jefferson and his secretary, William Short, devoted a lot of time to arranging for Jean Antoine Houdon to execute works of sculpture for the state of Virginia, in particular a bust of La Fayette to give to the Hôtel de Ville of Paris and a full-length, pedestrian statue of George Washington for the Virginia state capitol. Eventually, Jefferson commissioned the sculptor to make for use at Monticello plaster replicas of the busts of La Fayette, Washington, Franklin, John Paul Jones, Turgot, and Voltaire. (Carefully crated, these busts were part of Jefferson's baggage when he returned to Virginia in 1789.) He was pleased to take with him a wooden model of a Roman *askos*, or wine ewer, that he had admired at Nîmes in 1787 and once had intended to have copied in silver as a present to Clérisseau. In 1801 he had it copied in silver for himself at Philadelphia.[36] On the eve of Jefferson's departure from France, Philip Mazzei arranged to have copies of portraits of Columbus and other worthies painted at Florence, and John Trumbull purchased for him at London silver candlesticks to add to the four additional silver casseroles he had purchased in 1787.[37]

It would be simplistic to claim that Jefferson was so extravagant in outfitting and maintaining the Hôtel Langeac—largely at his own expense—that he contributed to his own eventual bankruptcy. But it nonetheless seems clear that he spent much more than he could afford. It is true that hidden and customary surcharges ran up the cost of his Parisian leases.[38] His expenditures in outfitting his legation and residence was by no means offset by later sales of some furniture at Paris and at Philadelphia. In 1790 most of Jefferson's furniture followed him across the Atlantic for his use at Philadelphia. In 1793 he sold a good deal of what he had shipped from Paris, mainly because he decided that it was too old-fashioned for Monticello, whither he dispatched the remainder in January 1794.[39]

2 The Paris Jefferson Knew

DESPITE HAVING PRAISED FARMERS AS "THE CHOSEN PEOPLE OF God,"[1] Thomas Jefferson was much more an urbanist than is usually recognized. If one considers the length of time that Jefferson spent in cities between the time he took his seat in the Continental Congress and when he retired from the presidency, one must question the literalness of his pretense that he was just a country gentleman. If, along with such populous places as Philadelphia, Paris, and London, one counts Williamsburg, Richmond, Annapolis, and Washington as cities, he resided in a city for some time during at least 276 out the 407 months between 1775 and 1809. In other words, up to the time when his presidential term ended he was a city-dweller for two-thirds of the years of his maturity.[2] When he counseled young Americans on how best to spend their time in Europe, he told them to spend two weeks in one city, five days in another, and two days in still a third.[3] Although he urged some to observe the making of Parmesan cheese,[4] he never advised visiting the Italian *campagna* during harvest time or the French province of Champagne during the *vendage*. He often is quoted to the effect that one should visit the houses of peasants, peep into the pot on their stoves, and observe the details of their life in order to discover the true character of a nation.[5] This Rousseau-like notion was so general in France in the 1780s that the abbés Arnoux and Chalut urged the prescription on Jefferson, as if to prove that simplicity was good, virtuous, and infectious.[6] Most of the time they were all content to see such "hovels" at a picturesque distance. It was not as

Vue de la Façade de la Nouvelle Eglise de Sainte Genviève, la Patronne de Paris, 1757, engraving by François Philippe Charpentier (1734–1817) after Jacques Germain Soufflot (1713–80). Jefferson owned this copy.

an afterthought that Jefferson urged young Americans to visit the urban palaces that then served as museums and concert halls so that they could admire works of art and architecture and hear good music. He told them to visit urban colleges and universities, where they could consult savants and visit libraries in order to read great works of literature.[7]

Although Jefferson was sincere in his celebration of the joys of the countryside and the role of the farmer as the provider and the good man, he reflected the ways of men of fashion at the end of the eighteenth century. Urban men of taste dressed very much as country gentlemen did except for court functions. They spoke frequently of their country estates at the very time that they were enjoying urban comforts of the body and mind. This was the age of the physiocrat, and polite urban society chimed in with the economic philosophers to say that agricultural production represented the true wealth of a nation and that farmers, healthier and happier than city folk, were the backbone of the country. Nobles and prosperous burghers were not completely hypocritical in paying at least lip service to the physiocratic creed. Most of the liberal nobles whom Jefferson knew owned a summer place in the countryside, usually on entailed land. The possession of land was important to their prestige, as well as for their income and health. It was also a safeguard against such governmental vagaries as inflation. Whether these men were true farmers or more familiar with the pleasure gardens of London or Paris, they spoke the international language of the gentleman farmer. In this avocation there was much competition: who gathered more bushels of wheat, who had the horses of greater speed and stamina, whose sheep had longer fleeces? Although Jefferson did not boast about his possessions, he did brag politely about how early his garden at Monticello produced peas for the dinner table.[8]

During the winter of 1785–86 the weather was so severely cold that Jefferson rarely was able to go out-of-doors. He blamed his physical indisposition on "extremely damp" air and "unwholesome" drinking water. By late spring, however, he was able to take daily walks of four or five miles in the vast Bois de Boulogne.[9] On its periphery he visited the Château de Madrid, once a trysting place for Louis XV, and in its midst the *folie*, now called the Bagatelle, which in 1777 the Comte d'Artois had commissioned the architect Francis Joseph Bélanger to build in sixty days in order to win a wager from Marie Antoinette.[10]

The American minister roamed all over Paris. He bought a new map of the city soon after its publication.[11] He observed the completion of the great structure now known as the Panthéon nineteen years after J. G. Sufflot designed it as the Church of Sainte Geneviève. Although Jefferson admired this domed neoclassical monument, he did not later express an opinion when the Constituent Assembly secularized it in 1791, but he did approve of its being used as a mausoleum for France's illustrious dead.[12] This amateur architect learned how creating the Panthéon's great stone vaults required professional engineering, not merely decorative skills. Ultimately, the United States profited from Jefferson's experience when he championed Benjamin H. Latrobe's plans for the south wing of the U.S. Capitol over those of Dr. William Thornton: the first was a professional engineer as well as a

professional architect, while the second lacked formal training in either architecture or engineering.[13]

Jefferson disliked the cathedral church of Notre Dame de Paris because
its thirteenth-century Gothic architecture for him represented a relic of the
barbaric Dark Ages, when superstition and despotism had joined church and
state to eclipse simple faith and ancient liberties. One of the occasions when
he visited Notre Dame was when he, together with John and Abigail Adams
and their daughter "Nabby," accompanied Madame de La Fayette to attend
the Te Deum sung on April 1, 1785, in thanks for the birth of the second son
of Louis XVI and Marie Antoinette. He later remarked sourly that the pompous ceremonies of that day were made up of more courtiers and functionaries
"than Gen[era]l Washington had of simple soldiers in his army."[14] The impressionable Nabby Adams, however, was awed by the procession of judges in
crimson robes and large wigs, lawyers whose long hair hung down on their
black costumes, ecclesiastics in purple robes with lace skirts, and great nobles
in cloaks embroidered with gold.[15]

Much more to Jefferson's taste was the architecture of the church of Saint
Philippe de Roule, but there is no record that he did more than pass by its
handsome façade. Because both the church and the Hôtel de Langeac were
located in the parish of Chaillot, Jefferson contributed to its fund for poor
relief. Years later he used this church as the model for the much-simplified
building he designed for an Episcopal church at Charlottesville.[16] In July and

St. Philippe de Roule was the parish
church of the faubourg in which Jefferson
rented his legation. Engraved by François
Denys Née (1732–1818). Designed by Jean
F. T. Chalgrin and completed in 1784, it
was the prototype for Jefferson's much
reduced Christ Church, Charlottesville.

August 1789 Jefferson twice visited the Bastille while it was being demolished. He contributed to a fund for the relief of the widows of those killed in the revolutionary assault on the prison-fortress.[17]

Jefferson was enthusiastic about all the municipal improvements that were being effected in Paris in the 1780s. When he arrived, the oldest of the city's two stone bridges across the Seine, Henry IV's Pont Neuf, was encumbered by what Jefferson called "rubbish"—shops and houses that gave it the medieval appearance still to be seen in Florence's Ponte Vecchio. At Paris these excrescences were demolished in 1787. In place of the dark and crowded bridge was now a broad and open one that appeared to soar above its great piers and vaults.[18]

On occasion he visited the Luxembourg Palace and its extensive gardens.[19] Built one and a half centuries earlier for Queen Marie de Medici, in the 1780s it was the Paris residence of Louis XVI's next younger brother, the Comte de Provence, later King Louis XVIII. Its museum gallery contained the famous series of pictures by Rubens celebrating Marie de Medici, who had ruled at the time of the massacre of Protestants on St. Bartholomew's Day.[20] It is not surprising that a Protestant and republican such as Jefferson did not admire these pictures.

As a dedicated gardener Jefferson did enjoy the Luxembourg's gardens. He also would have frequented the huge Jardin du Roi even if the great naturalist George Charles Louis Le Clerc, the Comte Buffon, had not been its intendant, as well as curator of the King's Museum, where gems and stuffed birds were exhibited. Although the American disagreed with some of the aged naturalist's pronouncements, he denied that Buffon was responsible for the mistaken belief that Europeans degenerated in America, correctly identifying the Abbé Raynal as the propagator of that canard. When Jefferson gave Buffon corrective artifacts, specimens, descriptions, and measurements, he happily renounced his belief that American dinosaur bones were those of the same family as elephants. Jefferson presented Buffon with a copy of *Notes On Virginia* and a diploma of membership in the American Philosophical Society, besides giving him bones, fossils, and skins of many American animals to convince him how un-European the fauna of the United States were.[21]

The American minister also made numerous visits to Le Nôtre's gardens at the Tuileries Palace. In the center of Paris, the Tuileries' fifty-acre garden and its open-air theater had become almost public. In fair weather the genteel could flirt, sit in hired chairs, or stroll under double rows of large, tall, trees beside pools fed with Seine water gushing from vases.[22] From the gardens of the Tuileries Jefferson delighted in watching construction of the Prince de Salm's town house across the Seine. He wrote to Madame de Tessé, La Fayette's aunt and a patroness of Americans, that he was so "violently smitten" with it that he went there almost daily to sit on a parapet at the river's edge to observe the work, even though he usually got an ache in his neck from twisting about in order to see

19

La Construction de l'Hôtel de Salm, ca. 1787.
Jefferson greatly admired this structure
from the Tuileries gardens, across the
Seine.

Marie Joseph Paul Yves Roch Gilbert
du Motier, Marquis de La Fayette, 1789,
painting by Joseph Boze (1744–1826).
This copy was commissioned by Jefferson.

more.[23] A young prince of the Franco-German borderlands, His Serene
Highness Frédéric Othon François Christian Philippe Henri de Salm-
Krybourg, had got the architect Pierre Rousseau to design for him this *hôtel
particulier.*

After graduation from the Collège de Louis Le Grand in Paris, the
Prince de Salm had served in the Austrian army before retiring to live at
Paris. An unchivalrous gambler, spendthrift, and voluptuary of superficial
charm and much bravado, he had succeeded in bilking bankers and tradesmen for years. In 1782 he bought a marshy tract on the Left Bank between
the rue de Bourbon and the rue de Bellechasse. On it he built a beautiful but
sound structure that has resisted many floods. Although disgruntled creditors were unable to limit Prince Frédéric's lifestyle, they protracted construction of his *hôtel.* Successively a high-flying partisan of the queen, a
follower of the Duc d'Orléans, and a liberal who renounced his seigneurial
rights, he became a battalion commander in the National Guard in 1789.
Although he was unsuccessful in trying to sell his *hôtel,* he attempted to flee
the country to avoid arrest for being an aristocrat, taking with him the two
children of his friends Alexandre and Josephine de Beauharnais. Alexandre
overtook them and persuaded them to return to Paris. Later, the Committee for Public Safety sent both Salm and Beauharnais to the guillotine as
enemies of the people.[24]

Jefferson and La Fayette had known one another in Virginia during
the American Revolution, but they did not become steadfast friends until
1785. In Paris, Jefferson and his daughters went frequently to the Hôtel La

Fayette, on the rue de Bourbon (now 119, rue de Lille), on the Left Bank. There young George Washington and Virginie de La Fayette sang American songs for guests, and the marquis explained why there was in his study a large blank placard hung beneath a copy of the U.S. Declaration of Independence: "It is there so that the Declaration of French Rights may be written on it."[25]

On the Right Bank, some distance inland from the Seine, the market building known as the Halle aux Bléds was then one of the greatest curiosities of Paris because it met "the most demanding engineering challenge of its day." Located near the present-day Centre Pompidou, the structure had been designed by Le Camus de Mezières in brick and stone, so that its body was virtually fireproof. It was a double-aisled, circular building whose bays tapered inward to Tuscan columns supporting flat vaults. The central court had a diameter of 150 feet, almost as great as that of the Pantheon at Rome, and it possessed twin oval stairways whose interweaving "up" and "down" flights were strong enough to support the weight of men carrying heavy bags of grain. In 1766 Jacques Guillaume Le Grand and Jacques Molinos completed the Halle with the world's first dome of alternating panels of wood and glass.[26] Jefferson called it a "wonderful piece of architecture" and suggested to Maria Cosway that it was "worth all [else] you had yet seen in Paris!"[27] Jefferson sometimes went to the Louvre Palace, which Louis XIV had substantially completed almost a century before. The portion of the immense complex that the American most admired was the classical colonnade of its most recent addition, Claude Perrault's 548-foot-long east wing.[28]

21

Vue de la Halle aux Bléds et don bel Dôme, ca. 1788, engraving by Guiget after Courvoisier.

Exhibition dans le Salon du Louvre en 1787,
drawing and engraving by P. A. Martini.
Jefferson attended this biennial show.

Changes in architecture were matched by changes in painting and in the manner of displaying art. In the late 1770s the king's directeur général des bâtiments, Charles Claude de la Billarderie, Comte d'Angiviller, received royal approval for a comprehensive scheme to bring order and direction to French art. (Some who unjustly believed him to be old-fashioned and stodgy referred to him as "the elephant.") Angiviller designated the disused Louvre Palace to become the central repository for the exhibition, conservation, and storage of paintings and statues. Not only was he authorized to move thither pictures from the Luxembourg Palace and other royal châteaux but he was empowered to buy great pictures at home and abroad in order to enhance the collection. What was most important, the collection would be hung for public inspection. Although the Louvre was not opened as the first modern art gallery until 1793, its conceptual planning was all but complete before 1789 under the leadership of Angiviller and the artist Hubert Robert.

Robert had risen through the normal route of patronage to become the king's landscape architect, especially charged with redesigning the Bassin d'Apollon in the gardens of Versailles. In the late 1780s he became the first modern museum conservator in the world and began the Louvre's purchases and conservation of works of art. Robert assigned and arranged space for the collections, but it was Angiviller who assigned living quarters and ateliers to

Marble bust of Thomas Jefferson, 1789,
by Jean Antoine Houdon (1741–1828).

about thirty artists, musicians, and sculptors. Besides Robert and his wife, Jean Antoine Houdon and Jacques Louis David also lived at the Louvre. Jefferson went to Houdon's studio to pose for a portrait bust that was later exhibited in the Salon of 1789,[29] and he accompanied John Trumbull to visit David's atelier. Hubert Robert found it convenient to use the Louvre's twelve-hundred-foot-long gallery as a partial source for his paintings of Roman ruins, but he also struggled with the problems of how to light, subdivide, and arrange it as the heart of the future museum. Ironically, the Louvre was first opened as a gallery while Robert was imprisoned during the Reign of Terror; however, he later resumed his residence and functions as conservator.

IN THE DECADE BEFORE THE FRENCH REVOLUTION ONE PART OF the Louvre open to the general public was the Salon Carrée, for showing paintings and statues at biennial exhibitions of new works by the members of the Académie française of Painting and Sculpture. This practice gave to the French word *salon* its special artistic meaning.[30] The exhibited works were chosen from portraits, landscapes, and works on mythological, patriotic, and religious themes. Soon after Jefferson attended the opening of the Salon of 1787 on August 25, he urged John Trumbull to hasten from London to see it. The "best thing" exhibited, he said, was David's *Death of Socrates*. Among other works that were "much approved," he liked greatly Roland de La Porte's oil painting *The Crucifixion*, which imitated sculptured relief; Hubert Robert's pictures of the Pont du Gard, the Maison Carrée, the Temple of Diana at Nîmes, and of the Arch and Amphitheatre at Orange; and Madame Vigée Le Brun's portrait of Madame Dugazon in the title role in *Nina*, as well as her self-portrait with a daughter.[31] Although Jefferson was later to write that he did not "feel an interest in any pencil but that of David,"[32] he was temporarily overwhelmed by a famous picture by Jean Germain Drouais, *Marius in Prison*. He modified his excessive praise of it after discussing its merits and demerits with Madame Sophie de Tott.[33]

Le Mort de Socrate, 1787, painting by Jacques
Louis David (1748–1825). Everyone, including
Jefferson, agreed that this was the most
important picture shown in the Salon of 1787.

Few scholars, if any, have remarked on how important the sophisticated
artist and art lover figured in Jefferson's friendships with ladies in France and
how they shaped his artistic views quite as much as did John Trumbull. They
were women of superior education, experience, and talents. Jefferson treated
them as his intellectual equals. In society their sophistication enabled them
to speak up and show their conversational charms. That the sophistication
of some of them was not only mental but also sexual was not unusual in high
English or French society in the 1780s.

One of these women was Maria Cosway, of whom I shall say more later.
Another of Jefferson's lady friends in Paris who had great cultural influence
on him was Sophie Ernestine de Tott. She was the only daughter of an
impoverished baron who had been an amateur painter and musician in the
Near East for twenty-three years before returning to France in 1779 a poor
widower. Sophie worked as a semiprofessional artist, living at first in a convent and later in the Hôtel de Tessé. Although she had no dowery, the Baron
de Tott and the Comtesse de Tessé tried to arrange a "suitable" marriage,
which she spurned because she had fallen in love with a penniless, blind
painter named Charles de Pougens, who was also a protégé of the comtesse.
Madame de Tessé broke up this unsatisfactory romance, sent Pougens packing, and assumed responsibility for Sophie Ernestine as a permanent member of her entourage. Whether it was because of Jefferson's innate courtesy

or because Sophie had an illegitimate daughter, he always addressed her as "Madam," although she was not a married lady. Their correspondence on artistic affairs usually passed first through the hands of the domineering comtesse.[34]

Just before leaving France, Jefferson accompanied Gouverneur Morris to view the Salon of 1789, in which Hubert Robert's *Bastille during the First Days of Its Demolition* was the centerpiece. Also in the 1789 Salon was David's *Love of Helen and Paris*, as well as Madame Vigée Le Brun's portrait of Hubert Robert.[35] There were other reasons for Morris to frequent the Louvre during his years at Paris, 1789-94. Although he did pose there for Houdon so that the sculptor could model his full-length statue of George Washington after Morris's torso, he also carried on there an affair with Madame de Flahaut, whose favors he shared with Talleyrand, then the Bishop of Autun. Amicable without being close friends, Jefferson and Morris were frank in their disagreements over the latter's attempts both to get for Robert Morris a monopoly on French importation of American tobacco and to buy cheaply certificates representing France's loans to the United States. It is a credit to both men that they got on as well as they did, because in conferring with Foreign Minister Montmorin concerning trade and finance Gouverneur Morris was almost an unofficial rival of the U.S. minister. When Morris "hinted" to Jefferson that the minister should present him to the *corps diplomatique* of the court of Versailles, Jefferson astutely replied that they were not worth becoming acquainted with.[36]

Besides learning more about art, Jefferson was able to indulge his fondness for music. He attended a series of concerts in the Salle des Machines of the disused Tuileries Palace that included both religious and secular music. From the *Journal de Paris* we know that a typical performance included a Hayden symphony, a harp concerto by Krumpholtz, and a violin concerto by its composer, Rudolphe Kreutzer.[37] Among the musical works that Jefferson bought at Paris were some by Balbastre, one of which was probably his setting for *Ça Ira*, and four pieces by Wolfgang Amadeus Mozart—*Trio pour le Clavecin . . . [et] Violon*, the overture to *Symphonie III* for keyboard instruments, and the arias "Batti, Batti" and "Fin Ch'han del vion" from *Don Giovanni*. The most outstanding musician whom Jefferson ever met was Niccolo Piccini, who advised him at Paris on buying a harpsichord for Patsy. Jefferson attended his opera *Didon* and bought copies of its arias "Que je fus bien inspirée" and "C'est une charme suprème qui suspendra mon torment," as well as "Jours Hereux" from his *Dardanus*. Helen Cripe, the foremost authority on Jefferson and music, concludes that after breaking his wrist in 1787, Jefferson played the violin some, but not often, until about 1800. Because of their personal acquaintance, however, it was Claude Balbastre who had the greatest musical influence on Jefferson in France. Balbastre was a composer, teacher, and master of the piano and organ. Because Jefferson employed him to give Patsy lessons at the Hôtel Langeac, he saw the musician frequently during the first eight months of 1789. Helen Cripe lists twenty-one of his compositions as having been in the music library at Monticello. Balbastre held remunerative posts as an organist at the Church of St. Roche and later at Notre Dame. If today he were given the credit due him,

Salome with the Head of John the Baptist, a copy after Guido Reni's *Salome con la testa del Battista* in Galleria Nazionale d'Arte, Rome. When Jefferson bought this picture at auction, it was described as an original by the 17th century French artist Simon Vouet.

he would be noted most for his orchestration of Roget de Lisle's *La Marseillaise* in the 1790s.[38]

Jefferson often attended the opera and the theater in Paris. Three times in the first week of September 1784 he attended either the Comédie Italienne or the Comédie Française. After such performances he would go for light refreshment and cabaret entertainment to the Palais Royal, the new, commercial complex that the Duc d'Orléans had built on the site of his Paris residence after the latter burned in 1781.[39] It included shops, coffeehouses, and a music hall decorated with paintings, statuary, fountains, and colonnades. Among its many fine pictures were *The Judgement of Paris* by Rubens, in which Juno's peacock pecks at Paris's leg, Titian's *Mars and Venus,* and Raphael's *Mother and Child.*[40]

The Odéon, called the Théatre Français when its architects Wailly and Peyre completed it in 1782, is the only Parisian theatrical or opera house of the 1780s still standing. There Jefferson saw plays by Racine, Molière, and Beaumarchais.[41] Jefferson enjoyed French opera, despite the glitter and clamor of its intermissions. Beaumarchais's play *Figaro* was so popular that it enjoyed an extended run after its premiere in April 1784, and Parisian women carried fans with Beaumarchais's verses on them.[42]

The Comédie Italienne was housed in a fine building and had good scenery, costumes, decoration, and dancing. Jefferson may have attended

Gluck's opera *Alceste* there. He thought that its second lead, the sixteen-year-old Mademoiselle Renard, "sings as nobody ever sung before." With Mrs. Adams he discussed Marmontel and Piccini's new opera *Penelope*, in which Mademoiselle Renard achieved so great a personal success that Jefferson declared her to be "now all in all"; the opera itself, while critically acclaimed, proved to be only moderately popular.[43] Indirectly, Jefferson's experiences in the Odéon's semicircular auditorium may have influenced the United States to adopt this style, rather than the British parliamentary style, for seating legislative bodies.

Most of the advances in Parisian architecture during the reign of Louis XVI, however, were expressed in residences of modest scale. Off the rue et chausée d'Antin, Jefferson saw an example of such French modern architecture that was to influence him greatly. This was the small house designed by Claude Nicholas Ledoux in 1770 for Mademoiselle Guimard, the opera dancer. When Jefferson designed the University of Virginia, he included among a baker's dozen of neoclassical buildings one modern building, Pavilion IX, a much simplified version of Madame Guimard's house.[44]

In Jefferson's day Ledoux was hailed by some as famous and by others as infamous for his design of forty-seven tollhouses for the collection of taxes on goods entering the city of Paris. Ledoux had the genius to conceive of these little buildings as elegant *propylaea*, or entrance portals, to the capital, rather than as merely utilitarian buildings. Jefferson exclaimed

27

Maison de Mlle Guimard, située a la chausée d'Antin, ca. 1770, drawing by Claude Nicholas Ledoux (1736–1806). Jefferson admired this house and later used it as a prototype for a pavilion at the University of Virginia, Charlottesville.

Propyléea de Paris, situé dans la plaine de Monceau, ca. 1784, drawing by Claude Nicholas Ledoux (1736–1806).

William Short, 1806, painting by Rembrandt Peale (1778–1860). Jefferson called Short his "adoptive son" and took him to France as his secretary.

Charlotte Alexandrine Sophie de Rohan-Chabot, Duchesse de La Rochefoucauld d'Enville, ca. 1810, engraving by Manxi, Joyant & Co., Paris.

that they were "magnificent."[45] Ledoux's reinterpretations of Roman temples may have been pure geometry, but they were not historically pure. In his plans for model towns, he was more akin to Giambattista Piranesi than to conventional city planners. Later, blind revolutionary anger destroyed some of these tollhouses, but the two at the Place d'Etoile on the Champs Élysées were torn down as late as 1865. Of his *propylaea*, there remain a circular, templelike one in the Parc Monceau; a pair of square buildings with mannered rustication at the old Porte d'Orléans, now called the Place Denfert-Rochereau; a pair of tollhouses adjoined by gigantic columns at what has been variously called the Barrière du Trône, the Porte de Vincennes, and the Place de la Nation; and the large, round rusticated and pedimented structure at the old Porte de la Villette, now called the Place Stalingrad.[46]

A number of young Americans enjoyed Jefferson's hospitality at the Hôtel Langeac. First and foremost of these was William Short. A young relative of Mrs. Jefferson, he was such an intimate of the Monticello family that Thomas Jefferson referred to him as his "adoptive son,"[47] advised him on his college and legal education, launched him in Virginia politics, and appointed him as his secretary at Paris, where Short became chargé d'affaires. Short received an adequate salary, first out of Jefferson's pocket and then from the U.S. government. He lived at the Hôtel Langeac gratis and enjoyed most of the minister's social life but paid for his meals. Although Jefferson gave Short the opportunity to become America's first career diplomat, between 1789 and 1802 he fruitlessly urged his protégé to return to the United States to refresh his Americanism. Before Jefferson returned to

America in 1789 Short had commenced a love affair with Charlotte Alexandrine, the beautiful young Duchesse de La Rochefoucauld, whom everyone called Rosalie. If Jefferson ever admonished Short on that subject, he did not do so directly in writing, although he persistently advised Short of the political necessity of returning to the United States.[48]

Thomas Lee Shippen dined at the Hôtel Langeac twice a week during his lengthy stay in Paris.[49] When Jefferson was in England in the spring of 1786, John Adams introduced him to John Trumbull and other young American art students.[50] When Trumbull came to Paris in August 1786, he accepted Jefferson's invitation to stay in the Hôtel Langeac[51] while arranging for his paintings *Battle of Bunker's Hill* and *Death of Montgomery* to be engraved and sold.[52] At the same time, the diplomat helped him secure appointments to sketch the principal French officers present at the British surrender at Yorktown for eventual use in his painting of that subject. He also helped Trumbull gain admittance to see art collections at Paris and Versailles.[53] Although he took pains not to appear to pretend to be a "connoisseur" of art, Jefferson declared his belief that Trumbull was "superior to any historical painter of the time except David" and that his subjects were "monuments to the taste as well as of the great revolutionary scene of our country."[54] During this visit, Trumbull painted what was the second portrait of Jefferson.

A year earlier, Mather Brown had depicted Jefferson at London in a costume that was at the time appropriate for a statesman, a courtier, or a dilettante. By mid-1787, however, Jefferson was no longer willing to be seen thus, except during obligatory attendance at Versailles. Just as the court of Versailles was becoming increasingly irrelevant, so was the dress of the courtier. Although the idealism of the author of the Declaration of Independence was genuine, most aspects of his taste were consonant with fashion. Nowhere is the transition from the old to the new conventions of dress clearer than in the contrast between Brown's and John Trumbull's portraits of Jefferson (see pp. 46 and 74). For the Virginian the shift to more "natural" costume and a more natural way of wearing one's hair allowed him to combine his ideals with his observance of fashion. He now wore his graying sandy hair without powder, and he soon stopped curling the ends. Following his usual practice, Trumbull painted a miniature portrait of Jefferson that he later copied in his large picture *The Signing of the Declaration of Independence*. In that famous canvas he portrayed most of the signers in powdered hair or wigs. One may wonder whether in painting Jefferson's hair *au naturel* Trumbull engaged in a republican symbolism that was premature for 1776; nevertheless, posterity has agreed that it was Trumbull's unpowdered Jefferson, not Brown's powdered Jefferson, who wrote the Declaration. Convention in dress had changed so greatly that it was no longer possible to reconcile a courtier's appearance with the inner stern, moral purpose expected of a chaste republican.[55]

Jefferson's residence at Paris gave him the opportunity to savor at first hand the gamut of the modern culture of his age. At this time he saw and inspected the age's greatest expressions of state, church, and private architecture and of both large formal and small private entertainment, as well as the age's greatest performances of classic theater, opera, and concerts. All of these urban cultural advantages combined to provide him with the calm assurance of experience that enabled him later to set the mold for an American republic of virtue and talent.

There were, of course, at least two other French worlds with which Jefferson became familiar in the 1780s. The first of these was the world of the court and government, most of which was based upon Versailles but some of which followed the king to such of his seats as Fontainbleau.

3 Court and Country: Versailles, Fontainbleau, and La Roche-Guyon

THOMAS JEFFERSON BEGAN HIS SERVICE AS CO-TREATY COMMIS-
sioner with Benjamin Franklin and John Adams at the end of August 1784.
When Franklin presented him to the foreign minister Charles Gravier,
Comte de Vergennes, on September 15, Jefferson's official position was
either nonexistent or, as Jefferson himself put it, "obscure." It was not until
May 17, 1785, when as minister resident he handed his credentials to Louis
XVI, that he was presented to the court of Versailles.[1] Two hundred years of
change in the Château de Versailles make it difficult for people of nowadays
to visualize what it was like in the 1780s. Jefferson was not merely reticent
about the "magnificence" that so many writers have attributed to the château;[2] he considered it old-fashioned and went there only when he had to.

Louis XIV had established the court's etiquette a century before.[3] On
Tuesdays were held royal *levées*, at which a minister or an ambassador could
introduce distinguished citizens of his country in a ceremony that some
Americans thought was cloaked with "oriental splendor" but Jefferson considered only "tedious." Those to be presented arrived in carriages at half past
ten in the morning and went first to the office of the secretary of state for
foreign affairs in one of the second range of buildings in the southwestern
part of the complex. This handsome structure had been built in 1759–62 to
house both the ministry of foreign affairs and that of marine. Until the
foreign minister concluded an hour of private conferences, everyone engaged in small talk, during which Europeans were apt to question an Ameri-

L'Escalier des Ambassadeurs, Versailles, until 1830, engraving by
M. Cheviot. Like other diplomats, Jefferson ascended these stairs
to Louis XVI's reception rooms.

can about his emerging country and the oddities of the New World. When the foreign minister entered the reception hall, foreign diplomats introduced their countrymen to him. At noon the foreign minister led those to be presented to the king across the entrance court to the "golden doors" of the east wing of the château, where they ascended a fine staircase to the Salle des Ambassadeurs, in which they could admire large pictures of the royal family, drink coffee, chocolate, or wine, and read the papers of the day. Under the direction of the grand master of ceremonies, the Marquis de Dreux-Brézé, an announcer and several ushers introduced newcomers to senior members of the diplomatic corps.

Among his fellow diplomats, Jefferson became most friendly with Baron Friedrich Melchoir von Grimm, whose official position was minister of Saxe-Gotha but whose additional and unofficial role was private correspondent of Catherine the Great of Russia. Baron von Grimm visited the Hôtel Langeac frequently enough for Jefferson to say that he knew him "intimately" and considered him the "pleasantest and most conversable member of the diplomatic corps . . . a man of good fancy, acuteness, irony, cunning and egoism. No heart, not much of any science, yet enough of every one to speak its language; his forte was belles-lettres, painting and sculpture. In these he was an oracle. . . . Although I never heard Grimm express the opinion directly, yet I always supposed him to be of the [atheistical] school of Diderot, D'Alembert, [and] D'Holbach."[4] Jefferson did not follow the example of his friend of Albemarle days the Italo-American Philip Mazzei in forming an intimacy with the Comte de Samour, who was the minister of Saxony, the Marquis de Spinola, who was the minister of Genoa, or Signor Favi, the chargé d'affaires of Tuscany.

After a while, Grand Master Dreux-Brézé ushered the foreign minister, diplomats, and guests into Louis XVI's ceremonial office for presentation. Such meetings were almost always perfunctory. If the king was not yet ready, "the file of ambassadors, envoys, ministers in full dress" was admitted to the king's state bedroom while attendants were still helping Louis XVI put on his ceremonial clothes. A young American whom Jefferson presented thought it was shameful that those attending paid such "obsequious adulation" to the king, who ungraciously addressed "three words to a few of the ambassadors and two to a German prince" before leaving. The procession of diplomats and their guests then passed to other rooms to be presented to the queen, the king's aunts, brothers, sister, and sisters-in-law, as well as the four secretaries of state. Usually Jefferson was not "done with bowing" until two o'clock in the afternoon. It is not surprising that the republican Jefferson had so low an opinion of the pomp of a royal *levée* at Versailles and that he later set diametrically opposite standards for the executive branch of government in the United States.

Regardless of whether foreigners were there in an official or an unofficial capacity, the minister of foreign affairs customarily invited all who had been presented to dine with him at three o'clock. Until then, one usually walked in the gardens, which had been designed by André Le Nôtre and Jules Hardouin Mansart a century before. In bad weather one might inspect in Mansart's Orangerie its twelve hundred orange and three hundred other

varieties of trees. At the appointed hour there were in the foreign ministry's
reception hall thirty "long and hungry faces." After fifteen minutes of des-
ultory conversation, the company went upstairs to join in a "superb feast."
According to one young American, "They were all hungry and . . . rejoiced
at the very splendid and plentiful *repast*." After dinner the company could
drink coffee and chat while newcomers were introduced "very formally" by
all their titles of nobility or office to the Comtesse de Vergennes and her
daughters. Most Frenchmen believed that the Americans' simple elective or
appointive offices were important, hereditary ones.[5]

It is remarkable that Jefferson, an inveterate concert- and theatergoer,
seems never to have attended a performance in the château's magnificent
opera house, which had been built between 1740 and 1778 according to
plans by Jacques Ange Gabriel and redecorated by him in 1768–69. Doubtless Jefferson would have done so if he had had quarters nearer the court.
Both Jefferson and Gouverneur Morris disliked the grandiose style of the
Château de Versailles, left over from the previous century, but only the
former disliked its pompous ceremonies.[6] All agreed that the garden front
was "by far the most beautiful" of Versailles' aspects achieved by Mansart's
enveloppe, by which he had expanded the château. Only the most fastidious

complained that the whole so lacked architectural unity that it was merely "an assemblage of buildings; a splendid quarter of a town, but not a fine edifice." Admitting the fineness of the Hall of Mirrors, which measured 235 feet in length, 35 feet in width, and 46 feet in height, they recounted the themes that Charles Le Brun painted on its ceiling and the matching of its seventeen great windows with seventeen great mirrors. Arthur Young did not consider its other public rooms "remarkable." In general, he was offended by the too-public character of the château, complaining that, with the exception of Mansart's 1699 chapel, it was "open to all the world." Indeed, it was only at the very door of the king's dining room that guards turned sightseers away.[7]

In a somewhat similar vein Mrs. Piozzi scornfully observed that the queen of France enjoyed no more privacy and convenience than any other French woman: "[She] has only two rooms in any of her houses—a bed chamber and a drawing room. In the first she sleeps, dresses, prays, chats, sees her sisters or any other . . . who is admitted to her intimacy, lives . . . in a bustle hardly to be supported. . . . She has no second room to run to for solitude, nor even a closet to put her close stool in, which always stands by the bedside." Remarkably, Mrs. Piozzi complained that there was no "prospect" to be seen from the windows of the château, and she dismissed both the Grand and the Petit Trianon from serious consideration as royal residences, saying that they were only "elegant summer house[s]." With mistaken patriotism this Englishwoman declared that Mansart's chapel at Versailles was about the same as Sir Christopher Wren's chapel at Greenwich. Because she was a devotée of the theater and a member of Johnson's literary circle, one can take more seriously her acknowledgement that Versailles' theater was a most admirable creation, even though she blanched at how much a performance cost. She did not give the king much credit as a collector of paintings, saying that the French nobility were "never weary of representing to themselves their own Magnificence. Pictures of their palaces, or of beautiful spots in their gardens are the only pictures one ever sees except now and then a ceiling by Mignard with all the Gods and Goddesses paying homage to the King of France."[8]

Jefferson once told William Short that the "only bureaux" to which the U.S. minister ordinarily could "apply with propriety or without offence" were the secretariat of foreign affairs and the ministry of finances.[9] Jefferson believed that Vergennes, although "wary and slippery" with "those whom he knew to be slippery and doublefaced themselves," was always "honorable, and easy of access to reason" with him because the French statesman knew that the American "practiced no subtleties, meddled in no intrigues, [and] pursued no concealed objects." After the death of Vergennes in February 1787, Comte Armand Marc Montmorin de Saint-Hérem succeeded him and, except for an intermission in 1789, served in that capacity until 1792. Although Jefferson wrote in his autobiography that Montmorin was "one of the most honest and worthy of human beings," he confided in a coded letter to James Madison that the new foreign minister was lazy and not to be trusted. The U.S. minister to Spain, William Carmichael, who had known Montmorin when the latter was French ambassador there, wrote Jefferson an ambiguous appraisal of him, saying that he was "a much honester man than ministers are generally supposed to be" but, nonetheless, was a man who, behind a liberal and noble manner, was quite "capable of finesse" in dealing with adversaries.[10]

Besides business with the minister of foreign affairs, Jefferson occasionally had to deal with various civilian departments of the Maison Domestique du Roi. This institution extended so far beyond the affairs of the court that in many ways it resembled a ministry of the interior. Its head in 1789 was the grand chamberlain, the Duc de Bouillon. Just below him in precedence was the grand master of the king's wardrobe, the Duc de La Rochefoucauld-Liancourt, whose authority included the licensing of physicians, purveyors to the court, and operators of mineral baths throughout the country. Although Bouillon had nominal authority over Liancourt and a voice in the conduct of royal ceremonies from which both their positions had evolved, the actual conduct of those ceremonies was under their subordinate, the grand master of ceremonies, the Marquis de Dreux-Brézé. From time to time, Jefferson dealt also with officials of several other governmental bureaux who were practically autonomous of the four secretariats of state. One was the directeur général des bâtiments, Charles Claude de la Billarderie, Comte d'Angiviller, who had authority over the construction, maintenance, and furnishing of the royal châteaux—a post once graced by André Le Nôtre and Jules Hardouin Mansart. Another was the director general of royal horse farms, posts, and relay stations. By 1785 the combined postal and relay service in France had so outgrown the old system of farming out its franchise that this office was created within the Maison Domestique, but in fact it was virtually independent of its hierarchical parent. It possessed twelve hundred eighty-four bureaux and three thousand relay stations, employed twelve thousand employees, and carried thirty thousand letters in 1789.[11]

One of the court ceremonial occasions at which custom required Jefferson's attendance was New Year's Day. On that day all diplomats were expected not only to pay respects to the king but also to present *étrennes*, or New Year's gifts, to the functionaries employed by the minister of foreign affairs. Such gifts were not inexpensive. Jefferson gave presents of cash to the foreign minister's *valet de chambre*, three Swiss Guards, liveried servants, and a *garçon de bureau*. In addition, it was customary for a diplomat to distribute tips in the Salle des Ambassadeurs to its two coffeemen, two Swiss Guards, and servants of the announcers and secretary. When the axletree of Jefferson's carriage broke on the way from Paris on New Year's Day of 1788, he was not able to make his appearance or pay his *étrennes* on time, but he did so on January 2. When Jefferson went to Versailles on business, he usually visited only the secretariat of foreign affairs. Only periodically did he make visits to the offices of other officials, such as to the grand master of ceremonies in order to obtain tickets for seats at ceremonies, places in processions, or parking spaces for sedan chairs.[12]

During Jefferson's day, there was a ceremonious gift of portraits of

Louis XVI and Marie Antoinette to the U.S. Congress.[13] For about three years Jefferson thought the king was a good-hearted though ineffective ruler; before 1789, however, he concluded that Louis XVI not only was weak of will and mind but was developing a drinking problem.[14] From beginning to end, Jefferson disliked the character and manner of Marie Antoinette, although he usually was predisposed toward pretty ladies. Ultimately, he concluded that "had there been no queen, there would have been no revolution."[15] His antipathy toward her limited his opportunities to inspect the modern features she had commissioned the architect Richard Micque to institute at the Petit Trianon in remodeling its interior, originally designed by Jacques Ange Gabriel for Madame de Pompadour. Aided by Louis Carrogis, known as Carmontelle, Micque also redesigned its hundred-acre park into an English-style garden with winding paths and a lake in which a circular temple-summerhouse was set on an island. Jefferson professed not to admire Micque's picturesque *hameau*, or peasant village, built to relieve the ennui of the queen's intimates,[16] and he may have agreed with Arthur Young that her *jardin anglois* was more Chinese than English and owed more to "effort and expenditures than to nature and taste." If he also considered the grand canal at Versailles so small and in such bad repair that it resembled a "horse pond,"[17] Jefferson did not say so. He disliked the formal contrivance of the celebrated fountains of Versailles, and it was not he, but Madame de La Fayette, who took Patsy Jefferson to spend an August afternoon viewing the "rare" and "beautiful spectacle" of these waterworks.[18]

Usually the court followed the king to Fontainbleau for a month in the early autumn so that he could hunt the region's quail and hares. Jefferson wrote to the Reverend James Madison, the president of the College of William and Mary, that the town of Fontainbleau, located about forty miles southeast of Paris, swelled from five thousand to twenty thousand inhabitants at such times. Because it was not "indispensably required" that a foreign diplomat reside there, Jefferson did not lease a house at Fontainbleau, particularly since its rental would have exceeded his salary. He stayed there a week in 1785 in order to attend a royal *levée*.[19] Most foreigners who stayed in the town at such times found their lodgings in the town "wretched."[20]

Then, as now, it was almost impossible to deduce which were the older or newer parts of the palace that had been begun by Francis I two hundred years before. Some thought its gardens less remarkable than its many large, tame carp. Although Young thought that most of its rooms suffered from an "extremity of ornament" and gilding,[21] Jefferson admired the "exquisite" Queen's Suite, recently redecorated by Micque and the artist Hubert Robert.[22] Jefferson must have forgotten that among the works of art in the château were pictures by Francisco Primaticcio and sculptures by Benvenuto Cellini. Although watching royal dinners was a free spectacle for gentlefolk, the town's innkeepers made up for it by charging ten livres for an indifferent dinner. When the court was in residence, one could attend a rollicking comedy in the town or an opera at the château. The latter presented as glittering a spectacle as could be had when the opera house was lit by "a chandelier of only sixteen candles" and the packed house was filled with heat and stench. On some evenings, after a day of hunting on horseback,

Queen Marie Antoinette did not change her clothes before going to the opera and sitting incognito elsewhere than in the royal box.

One evening Dr. Johnson and the Piozzis were presented to the king and queen and later watched the royals dine. Johnson laconically remarked that "the king fed himself with his left hand as we [do]." The housekeeper in Mrs. Piozzi observed not only that the king and queen's damask tablecloth was of only medium fineness but also that it was the only cloth on the table, contrary to the genteel English custom of using separate cloths for each of five customary courses. Although the royal family's plates, knives, and forks were gilt, Mrs. Piozzi thought that the silver serving dishes were not as clean or bright as they would have been in England. Because the king and queen and the Comte and Comtesse de Provence did not speak with one another during their stately meal, but only to lords in waiting, Mrs. Piozzi pronounced that they were like "people stuffed with straw." Neither Jefferson, Dr. Johnson, nor the Piozzis commented on the hermitage at Fontainbleau, designed by the architect Gabriel in the 1740s for Madame de Pompadour. Although he was a city man, Johnson inveighed against the king's "filthy" kennels and "cool" stables.[23]

Whether at Versailles or Fontainbleau, Jefferson avoided all but the most obligatory appearances at the French court. He was desirous of becoming familiar with that third French world of the 1780s, which lay beyond Paris and the royal châteaux.

Although Jefferson was a great list maker and quantifier, he never compiled a list of the names of the famous persons whom he hoped to meet or did meet at Paris, that capital of eighteenth-century Enlightenment. Not long after he arrived in France he met the La Rochefoucauld family, noted as patrons of scholars: the dowager duchesse, Marie Louise Nicole Elisébeth Le Tellier de La Rochefoucauld d'Enville, her son Duc Louis Alexandre de La Rochefoucauld d'Enville, and her nephew Duc Frédéric de La Rochefoucauld de Liancourt. The aged duchesse was usually referred to as Madame d'Enville, and the two first cousins as the Duc de La Rochefoucauld and the Duc de Liancourt. Together with La Fayette the dukes became leading spokesmen for a thoroughgoing constitutional, economic, and social reform of France.

Jefferson became friendly with both dukes and their families, but especially with Duc Louis Alexandre, his mother, and his wife, Rosalie. The La Rochefoucaulds believed that Madame d'Enville's late husband, Admiral the Duc d'Enville, had been blamed unjustly for the loss of his squadron in a severe storm in 1745 while trying to relieve the British siege of Louisbourg on Cape Breton Island, Canada. They did not frequent Versailles, but divided their time between their *hôtel particulier* in Paris and their three great estates, La Roche-Guyon in Normandy and La Rochefoucauld and Verteuil in Angoulème.[24] The Hôtel de La Rochefoucauld, in Paris, was a large structure on the Left Bank set amid dependencies, gardens, and service courts, all of which have since been absorbed by the Sorbonne. Judging from its near twin, the Hôtel de Liancourt on the rue de Varennes, to maintain the *hôtel particulier* required a staff of about thirty persons, plus food, upkeep, and stabling.[25] In giving Jefferson advice about prominent Parisians,

Virginia's one-time agent Philip Mazzei said that the La Rochefoucaulds' house was "devoted to philosophy and their garden to experiments for the improvement of knowledge."[26]

Interested in a wide variety of things, Duc Louis Alexandre was so admired that both John Adams and St. John de Crevecoeur called him "the pearl of all dukes."[27] The sixth duc de La Rochefoucauld, he was the great-great-great-great-great-grandson of the seventeenth-century author of the celebrated *Maximes*. He and his cousin Liancourt had traveled in England in 1768. Both were agricultural reformers, but it was Liancourt who became the friend and patron of the English agriculturalist Arthur Young. By 1789 both dukes were advocates of a limited constitutional monarchy for France. Duc Louis Alexandre translated into French the fourteen constitutions of the United States and Adam Smith's *Wealth of Nations*.[28] To serve French needs, he expanded Virginia's Bill of Rights from sixteen to eighteen articles by adding a prohibition of ex post facto laws.[29] Not only did Jefferson make no complaint but he gave La Rochefoucauld one of the first of the twenty-odd copies of *Notes on Virginia* and also copies of Virginia's Act for Religious Freedom, Bill of Rights, and Constitution of 1776.[30] Because of La Rochefoucauld's agricultural, rural, social, and urban interests, he was an ideal leader of the French reformers of 1789. To the tenants on his and his mother's farms he was so good and popular a landlord that, unlike many other nobles, he suffered no destruction of barns, rent-rolls, or châteaux between 1789 and 1792. Reserved and austere, he reflected the detached and generalized humanitarianism of the Enlightenment.

After the death of his first wife in a riding accident, the duke had married Charlotte Sophie Alexandrine de Rohan-Chabot, the younger sister of his brother-in-law Antoine August, Duc de Chabot. An old family name, Rosalie, became her *précieuse* name. Although she was fairly well educated, she was in most respects a follower of stronger spirits. Love of nature was her strongest characteristic. The two participated together in the salon of his mother, Madame d'Enville.

Minister Jefferson and his personable secretary were frequent guests at both the Hôtel de La Rochefoucauld in Paris and the Château de La Roche-Guyon in Normandy. In the summer of 1785 the two Americans first visited La Roche-Guyon as members of a house party made up of philosophes and liberal nobles. The château seemed to have a wing or tower to mark every role members of the family had played in French history. High on its chalk cliff stood a ninth-century Norman tower, connected by a staircase with the château, sited on a terrace about fifty feet above the Seine. Partly French Renaissance and partly eighteenth-century neoclassical, the château represented over three hundred years of building. On a still lower terrace, on a level with the highway, was a great eighteenth-century riding hall and stable complex that rivaled the Prince de Condé's at Chantilly. Many of La Roche-Guyon's elegant furnishings had been specially commissioned at the end of the seventeenth century by Madame d'Enville's father, François Michel Le Tellier, Marquis de Louvois, the great minister of war and of public buildings in the reign of Louis XIV. In it were great sets of tapestries woven on

Louis Alexandre, Duc de La Rochefoucauld d'Enville, 1790, engraving by Le Tellier after Labadye.

Garden of the Hôtel de La Rochefoucauld, Paris, ca. 1776, drawing by George Louis Le Rouge. Jefferson was a frequent guest at the Hôtel de La Rochefoucauld, on whose site part of the Sorbonne now stands.

the looms of Arras and of the Gobelins, a profusion of eighteenth-century furniture of all styles, and a great library.

The *doyenne* of these occasions was Marie Louise Nicole Elisébeth de La Rochefoucauld. She and her late husband, Jean Baptiste Louis Frédéric de La Rochefoucauld, had been distant cousins.[31] Upon their marriage in 1732, Louis XIV had created him Duc d'Enville. An educated and scholarly woman, as well a great heiress, she sometimes was called the most learned woman in France.[32]

Her wealth and patronage helped win for her protégé, Nicolas de Caritat, the title of Marquis de Condorcet and the positions of inspector of

Le Chateau de La Roche-Guyon, ca. 1776, painting by Hubert Robert (1733–1808). Jefferson visited his friend the Duc de La Rochefoucauld here.

the mint and perpetual secretary of the Académie française. He was, of course, a member of the house party at La Roche-Guyon in the summer of 1785. One of the last of the great eighteenth-century philosophes, Condorcet was a self-confident man whose specialty was mathematical applications but who moved in the borderland between moral and natural philosophy. Because he realized that the constitutional knowledge of most Frenchmen was "more intense than informed" and limited to maxims drawn from *L'Esprit de lois*, some of which were "more ingenious than sound, more dangerous than useful," he tried to inform them by publishing in 1789 *Sur les fonctions des Etats-généraux et des autres assemblées nationales.*[33] It pleased Jefferson that Condorcet praised Virginia's freedom of religion and social welfare,[34] and he took pleasure in presenting the French scholar with a membership in the American Philosophical Society. While he was U.S. secretary of state, he may have been secretly relieved when his intelligent French friend Condorcet supplanted his indecisive friend, La Fayette, as a leader of the French government.[35]

Most scholars have alluded to Jefferson and Condorcet's friendship without specifying its bases. That both men were wont to speculate on how constitutional, legal, and administrative acts affected society was given proof in a complicated series of events just before the American left

Paris in 1789. Jefferson's physician, Dr. Richard Gem, gave him a memorandum that provoked an important discussion of moral and political principles. Gem stated that one generation of men has "no right to make acts to bind another," that "the earth and all things whatsoever . . . belong to the living," and that a nation can refuse to pay debts incurred by its past "ambitious and corrupt" rulers. In agreement, Jefferson cautiously framed a letter as if he were addressing James Madison on how French precedents might be useful in the United States. Because he did not wish to offend diplomatic proprieties by meddling in French domestic affairs, he ostensibly sent only a copy to Dr. Gem. From the concept that the earth belongs to the living, he proceeded to declare that "no society can make a perpetual constitution, or even a perpetual law," and that posterity is free to repeal laws or constitutional provisions. Uncompromisingly, he denied that the "present generation" in France was obliged to pay for the "dissipations" of Louis XV. He proposed that in order to achieve an ideal republic, all contracts, constitutions, and laws ought to become void a generation, or nineteen years, after their adoption. Accepting the theory that there was an unnamed recipient, I conclude that he was the Marquis de Condorcet. To speculate upon the duration of a generation was a congenial topic for men such as Jefferson and Condorcet.[36]

The Duc de Liancourt was somewhat on the periphery of Madame d'Enville's circle, even though he was the friend of and heir presumptive to the childless Duc Louis Alexandre. Liancourt lived much of the time at court. As master of the king's wardrobe, he supervised Louis XVI's official rising and retiring. Lacking the intellectuality of Madame d'Enville's intimates, he was an agricultural reformer celebrated for having founded a school to teach his tenants agricultural and mechanical arts on his seigneurial estate northeast of Paris. He provided his son, the Chevalier François Armand Frédéric, an excellent education by his tutor, the Franco-Polish savant Maximilien de Lazowski, and he encouraged their travels in France, England, Ireland, and Switzerland before the young man entered the French army in 1789 at the age of twenty-four.[37]

Thanks to Madame d'Enville and La Fayette's aunt the Comtesse de Tessé, Jefferson met many of the great and lesser figures of the Enlightenment.[38] One of these savants was the Abbé de Morellet, whom he already knew by reputation as the author of the articles on religion for Diderot's *Encyclopédie*.[39] Possessing so biting a wit that Voltaire referred to him as "L'Abbé Mord-les," Morellet had been imprisoned in the Bastille for two months in 1760 on charges on having libeled a patroness of the author of a scurrilous play. Elected to the Académie française in 1785 and interested in economics, he was associated with those who wished to reform the Parlement of Paris. After Jefferson met Morellet at La Roche-Guyon in the summer of 1785, he sent the abbé a copy of *Notes on Virginia*. The Frenchman's thanks were effusive, and he begged permission to translate and publish the book.[40] To avoid a "surreptitious" and faulty French edition, Jefferson agreed.[41] Later, the American confided to a colleague that Morellet had so "changed" the text and made so many "typographical errors" that it became "a different book, in some respects a better book, but not mine."[42]

For this French edition of the *Notes*, Jefferson received neither royalties nor even reimbursement for paying to have its map engraved.[43]

Two minor philosophes whom Jefferson met in the summer of 1785 were the abbés Arnoux and Chalut. They were, to use Jefferson's words, "most useful acquaintances, . . . unembarrassed with families, uninvolved in form and etiquette, frequently learned, and always obliging."[44] Chalut was about seventy-five years old, a Knight of Malta and of the order of St. Louis. The sixty-year-old Abbé Arnoux was considered a man of vivacity, wit, and pleasantry. Although they were "totally destitute of the English language," they helped Adams learn French.[45] Soon they were well enough acquainted for them to invite Jefferson to dine at their villa at Passy and for him to ask them to his Fourth of July dinners. They provided acorns of the cork oak for germination at Monticello, and he later sent them from New York some of the herb *balsamum canadense*.[46] Their greatest favor was to furnish him letters of introduction to friends along the way of his journey in southern France and northern Italy during the spring of 1787,[47] which they encouraged, saying that he thus would receive proof that bad government was the cause of vice: "We are what our laws have made us. Pity our old nation and give thanks for the virtue and youth of yours."[48]

Before Jefferson could explore the French countryside outside the Ile-de-France, diplomatic business required that he go to England.

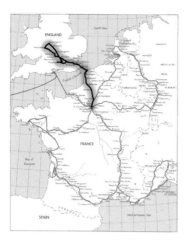

4 In England

BECAUSE JEFFERSON AND JOHN ADAMS HOPED TO MAKE A TREATY with Great Britain to safeguard American seamen, ships, and cargoes, Jefferson visited England in the spring of 1786. His anticipated three-week sojourn stretched into two months.[1] Since his and Adams's business became attenuated, Jefferson did a considerable amount of sightseeing, in the course of which he also intended to achieve some useful purposes.

On March 6, 1786, Jefferson left Paris for Calais in his own carriage, accompanied by his valet, Adrien Petit, and John Adams's secretary of legation, Colonel William S. Smith, who was soon to marry Adams's daughter, Nabby. Their first night on the road, they lodged and supped at Chantilly, without making written comment on the Prince de Condé's famous château and stables. They sped through the countryside without recording, as Arthur Young did, that French women plowed the crop fields.[2] They supped and lodged at Breteuil, proceeded the next day to Abbeville, and reached Calais on the eighth in time to dine at Dessein's Hotel, where he left his carriage. Jefferson then had to wait thirty-six hours for the English Channel to become calm enough for them to embark.

A poor sailor, Jefferson was glad to see the cliffs of Dover after nine and one-half hours on the Channel. Solicitously, Smith exclaimed: "I know of no gentleman better qualified to pass over the disagreeables of life than Mr. Jefferson."[3] They traveled by post chaise to London, changing horses at Canterbury, Maidstone, Rochester, and Greenwich. Past hop barns and through unfenced crop fields, they bowled along smoothly on sandy roads. They probably dined at Chatham, where, three years before, Abigail Adams had enjoyed a "very elegant inn" whose powdered waiters offered her eight different dishes besides vegetables. Jefferson and Smith were calmer than

The Canterbury-Dover Fly Descending a Steep Hill, ca. 1785–1800, watercolor by Thomas Rowlandson (1756–1827).

Mrs. Adams, who had learned there that a highwayman had stopped and robbed a chaise just ahead of hers. Presumably Jefferson's party, like Mrs. Adams, arrived in the metropolis at about eight o'clock at night. They went at once to 9 Grosvenor Square, the U.S. legation and residence for the Adamses and Colonel Smith. Mrs. Adams welcomed Jefferson as her own friend and as her husband's esteemed colleague.[4]

Jefferson rented rooms for himself and Petit from a Miss Conners at 14 Golden Square, not far away. This peaceful, pleasant square, with its iron street lamps and fenced gardens, gave no hint of having been a site of the Gordon Riots six years before, when anti–Roman Catholic mobs had marched to petition the House of Commons and to burn Newgate Prison.[5] After making himself comfortable, Jefferson engaged both a chariot and a coach, two horses, and a coachman named John. Bending to their duties, Adams and Jefferson signed a most-favored-nation trade treaty with Chevalier Louis de Pinto de Souza of Portugal. Although they conferred over coffee and hookahs several times with the Tripolitanian ambassador, Abdrahaman, the latter's demands for tribute money were so great that the Americans allowed this project to die.[6] Because Adams and Jefferson's powers as treaty commissioners would soon expire, they hastened to propose a trade treaty with Great Britain, a venture for whose success they had few illusions.[7]

When in the spring of 1786 Thomas Jefferson explored the capital of the British empire, the sights provided most of the contradictions of the eighteenth-century world: poverty and wealth; slums in the East and fashionable localities in the West End; sinkholes of depravity and pleasure gardens; the police escorting miscreants to the gallows at Tyburn and the Royal

Society discussing contributions to knowledge; the East End's boisterous docks and manufactories and the sedate banking and political institutions of the City and Westminster. Despite Britain's defeat in the American War of Independence, she possessed great optimism. Most Englishmen were confident that their country, not France, would lead the world from the dark ages into a golden age. Only a few, like Joseph Priestly and Horace Walpole, prophesied that "the next Augustan age will dawn on the other side of the Atlantic."[8]

So that they could give exchange portraits, Jefferson and Adams commissioned the American-born artist Mather Brown to paint their likenesses. Brown and two other young Americans, Matthew Pratt and John Trumbull, were then students of Benjamin West. Some did not consider Brown's a good likeness of Jefferson, then aged forty-three. Perhaps he did not sit often enough for this, his first portrait.[9]

While at London, Jefferson bought many things. For himself there were books, boots, boot garters, chess sets, a copying press, gloves, harness, a hat, maps, pistols, pocketbooks, lots of scientific paraphernalia, stockings, tools, toothbrushes, travel trunks, a walking stick, and watch chains; and he had a tailor make him some new clothes. He bought calico, pocketbooks, shoes, slippers, trinkets, and yard goods for his daughters and sisters. He went to Mr. Broadwood's shop to discuss the latest improvements in harpsichords before ordering one for his daughters.

Also while at London, he bought sealing wax and had a seal ring cut with the Jefferson coat of arms, with which he attested his signature to the Portuguese treaty that he and John Adams proposed. He did not have to go to the College of Heralds to learn about his family's coat of arms, because he had gotten a friend to do so in 1771. The reason why he did not use the ring later was probably not because of ultrademocratic beliefs, as some have suggested; rather, it was probably among the articles stolen from his Paris house a year later.[10] Despite purchasing his ring and attending to some family business concerning John Wayles's debts,[11] Jefferson was not the sort to look up distant relatives or to investigate his "roots." Had he been, he might have visited St. Paul's Church in Shadwell Parish, London, where his grandmother, Jane Randolph, had been baptized while her parents, Isham and Jane Rogers Randolph, lived on Shakespeare's Walk, next to the church.[12] Although Jefferson opposed sending young Virginians to England for their education, two of Mrs. Jefferson's Skipwith nephews were then there for that purpose. He saw one of them, Fulwar Skipwith, at London, but he made no effort to see Sir Peyton Skipwith's son Grey.

On Wednesday afternoon, March 17, John Adams presented to the court of St. James Mr. Jefferson, who had bought a pair of gloves for the occasion and tipped the flunkies at the door. Although Adams's own presentation a year earlier had been friendly, King George III was so churlishly "ungracious" to Jefferson that the American was convinced that "the ulceration in the narrow mind" of the "mulish" king justified the charges against him in the Declaration of Independence. With justifiable peevishness, Jefferson declared, "They require to be kicked into common good manners." Nor was the Marquess of Carmarthen, the minister for foreign affairs, more

45

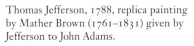

John Adams, 1788, replica painting by Mather Brown (1761–1831) given by Adams to Jefferson.

Thomas Jefferson, 1788, replica painting by Mather Brown (1761–1831) given by Jefferson to John Adams.

than faintly cordial. Jefferson interpreted "the distance and the disinclination which he betrayed in his conversation [and] the vagueness and evasion of his answers" as proof that the British government was averse to doing serious business with the American diplomats.[13] When Adams and Jefferson proffered the draft of their trade treaty on April 4, they suspected that Carmarthen would pigeonhole it, but they could only wait.

Jefferson did much sightseeing, but he complained that he also wasted time in exchanging ceremonious official visits. Besides those to Carmarthen and Abdrahaman, he exchanged calls with fourteen diplomats and a dozen prominent Britishers, led by the Marquess of Lansdowne and Sir John Sinclair. He had conversed with Sinclair in Paris about abolishing slavery, and the two were congenial. Among more than a dozen Americans with whom Jefferson consorted in London was Dr. Edward Bancroft.[14] The American-born doctor was a member of the Royal Society and had interceded with Adams and Jefferson to seek a financial settlement of the Virginia estate of his fellow member John Paradise and his wife, Lucy Ludwell Paradise. Jefferson may have visited Bancroft at his quarters in the York Buildings at 12 Villers Street. Neither Jefferson nor Adams suspected that Bancroft long had spied on Americans for the British government.[15]

Jefferson viewed the great monuments of London with much ambivalence. Here he had the opportunity to compare actual structures with his remembrance of their illustrations. Even though he had been the prime mover in Virginia's separation of church and state, he was always interested in tolerant religion and good preachers. He never claimed relationship to the sixteenth-century John Rodgers, who had preached at the old St. Paul's until Bloody Queen Mary beheaded him, but it is likely that he had heard from his mother's family about this martyr.[16] Thus, it was for multiple reasons and with mixed emotions that he inspected the new Saint Paul's, the masterpiece by Sir Christopher Wren. One may wonder whether he contemplated the statue of Queen Anne in front of the cathedral. Where now was the happy union it celebrated of England, Scotland, Wales, and America? The Tower of London and Westminster Abbey were distasteful to Jefferson the enlightened eighteenth-century man because they symbolized the barbarism, cruelty, superstition, and tyranny of England's Norman conquerors. Generally, he subscribed to the tastes of his day, which looked for its models to the Greek and Roman republics of antiquity and to the Florentine republic of the Renaissance. But he also avidly sought evidence of the Anglo-Saxon liberties that he imagined to have existed before 1066.[17]

Jefferson probably reserved judgment on the architectural merits of the great complex of buildings that housed the War Office and the Admiralty, which William Kent had built in the 1750s on the site of the old Whitehall Palace. Their baroque architecture never appealed to Jefferson, who preferred the more chaste neoclassic of Inigo Jones's nearby Banqueting House. Although he may have lingered a moment while passing the prime minister's residence at 10 Downing Street, he surely saw it as a conventional urban house, architecturally no better than those in Golden and Grosvenor squares and considerably inferior to Brooks's and Boodle's celebrated clubs, which he observed near St. James's Palace. He must have admired the front of Somerset House, that great bureaucratic office complex along the Thames, for which Clérisseau's student Sir William Chambers had been the architect.

While he was in London, Jefferson attended the theater and opera three or four times at Covent Garden, Drury Lane, and the Haymarket. He must have admired Covent Garden, whose overall plan by that hero of early English classicism, Inigo Jones, united into one ensemble a church, an opera house, a marketplace, and a range of structures having shops below and rooms above. Since Mrs. Adams had attended a performance of *Macbeth* there a few days before Jefferson's arrival, she undoubtedly urged him to see its star, the celebrated actress Mrs. Siddons, whom she declared "interesting beyond any . . . I have ever seen." On March 13 he attended her performance in the new tragedy *The Captives*, which was followed by the afterpiece *The Gentle Shepherds*, in which highland reels were danced. He returned to see her as Portia in *The Merchant of Venice* on the twentieth and two days later as Lady Macbeth. He attended a double bill at Covent Garden on April 19, *The Mourning Bride* and *The Two Misers*, and at the Theatre Royal in the Haymarket he attended a royal command performance before the Prince of Wales of the opera *La Scuola de Gelosi*, one of the forty-one operas of Antonio Salieri, the rival of Wolfgang Amadeus Mozart and the court composer for the Holy Roman Emperor Joseph II.[18]

Like all tourists, Jefferson visited eating establishments that had been recommended to him. He supped at London Tavern on Ludgate Hill, which was "famous for its Turtle and immense wine cellars." It had been a favorite of Benjamin Franklin a decade before and was still frequented by the chemist and defender of the American Revolution, Joseph Priestley. He also went to Dolly's Chop House in Queen's Head Passage between Paternoster Row and Newgate Street, an establishment noted for hot beefsteaks served fresh from the grill, but not inexpensively, according to Gouverneur Morris. It had been a favorite haunt of literary giants since the previous century—Defoe, Dryden, Fielding, Smollett, and Swift.[19]

Especially hospitable to Jefferson were John and Lucy Ludwell Paradise at their house at 28 Charles Street in Cavendish Square. Mr. Paradise was the long-suffering husband of the flighty daughter of a great Virginia family. He undertook to teach Jefferson modern Greek, which was Paradise's mother's native tongue.[20] On March 30, 1786, the Paradises entertained at dinner the Russian ambassador and two of his aides, the Venetian minister, Dr. Bancroft, Jefferson, and the Adams family. Afterward, they all attended the "uncommonly splendid" ball of the French ambassador, Comte d'Adhémar, at his embassy facing St. James's Park. The ballroom was hung with gold tissue, arches, garlands of flowers, and cornucopias spilling out oranges and sweetmeats. The Prince of Wales and his morganatic wife, Mrs. Fitzherbert, came late to the ball, whose throng numbered between two hundred and three hundred. It is possible that Jefferson may have danced a minuet with Lucy Paradise, but he certainly did not join in gambling at cards. Instead, he probably joined John Adams in conversation with the Marquess of Lansdowne, the Earl of Harcourt, and Sir George Yonge. Adams professed that such Englishmen showed an "awkward timidity" because of their "guilt and shame" over their government's duplicity in not giving serious attention to the American trade proposals after having raised American expectations of reconciliation by the peace treaty of 1783. Although the London *Chronicle* reported that the French ambassador's ball was brilliant, the Adams ladies did not enjoy themselves. On the pretext that Nabby Adams had a cold, the Adamses and Jefferson made their adieux before the supper was served at one o'clock. Defensive about her daughter, Mrs. Adams complained that the dance floor was too small and that the whole affair was inferior to those of the court of France and even of America! As for the women of London society, she loyally declared that "not all their blaze of diamonds set off with Parisian rouge c[oul]d match the blooming health, the sparkling eye, the modest deportment of our dear girls of my native land."[21] The Paradises entertained often and well at London, but they did not introduce Jefferson to their friend Maria Cosway. The activities of the Cosways' set were far too lively for the sedate Adamses.[22]

On April 18 Jefferson visited the queen's house, or as it was more usually called, Buckingham House.[23] Since no part of it was open to the public, he undoubtedly followed John Adams's example in securing permission through Benjamin West to view its great rooms. Located on a thirty-acre tract adjacent to St. James's Park, Buckingham House comprised three principal buildings constructed in the early eighteenth century. On the same axis as the Buckingham Palace of today, its grand entrance was through a wrought-iron screen into a squarish court, in the middle of which was a fountain representing Neptune. Connected to the central bloc by arcades were two-story dependencies devoted to kitchens, laundry, servants' quarters, and stabling for forty horses. The two-story

mansion in the center was of rubbed brick with Tuscan over Corinthian pilasters that reached up to a flat roof, from whose pediment lead statues of demigods and heroes recently had been removed for the safety of mortals below. Inscribed over the entrance front were the words *Sic Siti Laetantur Laures*, "The household gods delight in such a sight," while the western, or garden, front bore the words *Rus In Urbe*, "The countryside in the city."

Jefferson entered Buckingham House through a large, paved hall, admirable for its Corinthian columns and for pictures in the style of Raphael. The next room was a paved parlor with murals by Ricci, an artist whose work Jefferson once had admired but soon was to consider too florid and pompous. One of the most famous features of the palace was its painted staircase, which was in a room fifty-five feet high, forty feet wide, and thirty-six feet long whose lower walls were decorated in bas-relief. The forty-eight steps of Portland stone, ten feet in breadth, ascended to a platform, divided, and turned back. The walls were painted with the story of Dido, while the ceiling depicted Juno begging help from Venus and a host of gods and goddesses. At that time these paintings were attributed to Antonio Verrio, but today this attribution is in question. One next entered the salon, or *saloon*, as the British perversely termed it, which was about thirty-five feet wide, thirty-five feet high, and forty-five feet long. On its ceiling the artist Orazio Gentileschi had painted a round picture of the Muses playing in concert for Apollo, who reclined somewhat uncomfortably on a cloud bank. This room was remarkable in that it had an upper row of windows to admit light in such a way as to "drown the glaring" on the pictures, which at that time included Raphael's cartoons for the tapestries of the Sistine Chapel at Rome. Also here was Rubens's *Summer and Winter,* along with Gerrit Honthurst's portrait of the family of the Duke of Buckingham. Besides pictures he inherited, George III had commissioned West to paint for Buckingham House *The Return of Requlus, The Death of Epaminondas, The Death of Bayard,* and *The Death of General Wolfe.* Later, his son moved to elsewhere many furnishings and pictures, but three decades later there remained at Buckingham Palace three by Sir Anthony Van Dyke, two by Claude Lorraine, and at least one each by Poussin and Guido Reni. There was a large octagonal room for George III's rare books, now in the British Museum, and two smaller, oval rooms housed his barometers, clocks, and models of warships and dockyards. Despite their artistry and variety, Jefferson did not comment on the contents of Buckingham House.[24]

Accompanied only by his coachman John, Jefferson made several jaunts west and south of London. He visited London's famous pleasure gardens— the Vauxhall, the Pantheon, and the Ranelagh. On March 22 he visited Windsor Castle, concerning which he noted only his expenses, even though he probably saw from a distance the royal family's lodge and strode upon the castle's terrace, where on Sunday afternoons the king and the royal family often showed themselves to their subjects. Unlike Mrs. Adams, he left neither a description of the queen's bedchamber, on whose walls were Benjamin West's "very handsome" portrait of the queen, along with miniatures of her fourteen children, nor one of its ceiling depicting the story of Diana and

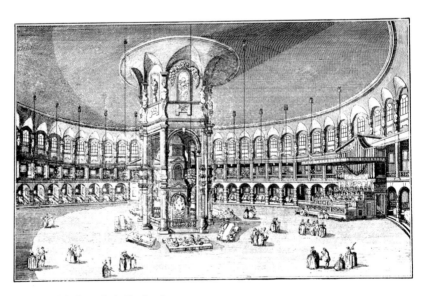

Intérieur de la Rotonde des Jardins de Ranelagh, ca. 1776, drawing by George Louis Le Rouge after Antonio Canaletto. Jefferson visited this London pleasure garden in early 1786.

Endymion over a state bed with pea-green curtains and white satin counterpanes.

On April 2 Jefferson set out in his coach for Chiswick, Twickenham, and Hampton Court on the north side of the Thames and Woburn Old Farm on the south side.[25] It was appropriate that this gentleman-architect visit leisurely and alone at Chiswick, the magnificent villa built by Richard Boyle, Earl of Burlington, who a generation earlier had been the patron of the architects William Kent and Giacomo Leoni. Jefferson owned a copy of Leoni's 1715 English edition of *The Architecture of A. Palladio* and of Kent's 1727 edition of *The Designs of Inigo Jones . . . With Some Additional Designs*, of which nine designs were by Burlington.[26] The elegant suburban villa of Chiswick was now owned by Burlington's great-nephew, the Duke of Devonshire. Although it had stimulated the rage for the Palladian style in the mid-eighteenth century and was in some ways a prototype for Monticello, Jefferson considered that its octagonal dome had an "ill effect, both within and without." He complained that William Kent's garden about the villa showed "too much artifice," that one of its two obelisks was "of very ill effect," and that the other, "in the middle of a pond," was "useless." Although the shallower octagonal dome that Jefferson built at Monticello may have been more pleasing aesthetically than Burlington's, neither could be justified functionally. Jefferson never attempted to realize at Monticello or elsewhere the obelisk and *tempietto* that he sketched at Chiswick.[27]

Because he long had possessed copies of Alexander Pope's poems and translations, Jefferson was pleased to have an opportunity to inspect the poet's three-and-one-half-acre estate on the bank of the Thames. With the help of Charles Bridgeman and William Kent, Pope had crowded its gardens with an obelisk, a grotto, an orangery, a vinery, a kitchen garden, a wilderness, and a grove. Jefferson also went to Hampton Court Palace to see the favorite royal residence from Henry VIII's reign to that of George III. He was not interested in its Tudor quadrangles, and he did not admire the south wing, the *allées*, the parterres, the canals, the fountains, and the topiary, which were in the old-fashioned style of Versailles.

After Jefferson made a preliminary survey south of the Thames, Adams joined him in a lengthy tour of stately homes and gardens. On April 4 they began in Surrey a circuit of the great triangle of the English Midlands, whose northern apex was Birmingham and whose western corner was Oxford. They planned to visit places praised by the reigning authority on gardens, Thomas Whately, with whose book *Observations on Modern Gardening* Jefferson said he "always walked." They did not have clear plans how far or how long they would go, but both made notes of their expedition. Adams's notes were mainly historical. Jefferson prefaced his with the caveat that "my enquiries were directed chiefly to such practical things as might enable me to estimate the expense of making and maintaining a garden in that style." Following his usual practice, he did not repeat descriptions available in Whately's book. Sharing expenses, the Americans hired a fresh pair of horses and a postilion at relay stations at ten- or fifteen-mile intervals. The English system of relays gave priority to royal mail coaches in the rental of horses and service by postilions, but it also accommodated commercial passenger coaches and private equipages. Generally, the stations were maintained by coaching inns, through whose arched gateways vehicles entered a large yard. While passengers waited, ate, or drank in public rooms, hostlers and postilions put fresh teams of horses between the shafts, inspected harness, and renewed the greased packing of axles.

Jefferson and Adams passed through Richmond, Cobham, and Weybridge before reaching Esher Place, the seat of the Pelham family since the beginning of the century. The house and its park occupied about forty-five acres of hilly and bottom land of the Thames Valley. Forty years earlier, Lancelot "Capability" Brown had improved its grounds with trees planted in "clumps" that Jefferson termed a "most lovely mixture of concave and convex" and made beautiful what Whately said would otherwise have been "trifling." Jefferson found the nearby estate Claremont to be "nothing remarkable." Although Claremont's original structure had been designed by its owner-architect, Sir John Vanbrugh, subsequent owners had left only his arcaded dependency, with bold, masculine quoins and keystones and a detached three-storied belvedere. Jefferson must not have visited the latter, because he surely would have noted with admiration its panoramic view of the Thames from Windsor to St. Paul's.

Three landscapists in succession had designed Claremont's gardens and park. The first of these was Charles Bridgeman, who had installed there an amphitheater of turfed terraces and a bowling green. Two generations later, Capability Brown had obliterated these with plantings of trees and *Rhododendron ponticum*. Meanwhile, William Kent had enlarged Bridgeman's lake and added a cascade, a grotto, and a pavilioned isle. Considering what has survived, today's visitor must agree with Horace Walpole that Kent sought to use artistic illusion to improve upon nature. Claremont is one of the places said to have been the birthplace of Bridgeman's ha-ha, that moatlike fence which helped create the illusion "that all nature was a garden." Jefferson employed this device at Monticello, even though he felt that both Kent and Brown usually presented too tame a nature.[28]

The two Americans next visited Painshill, a house and garden belonging to a Mr. Hopkins, which Charles Hamilton had created after 1738 on a crown lease of 250 acres along the Mole River. Painshill's garden was then one of the most celebrated in England. Noting that it had been created from sandy, commonplace terrain, John Adams considered it the "most striking piece of art" he had seen. Jefferson termed the now vanished classicist mansion "incorrect" and objected to an overabundance of evergreens on the grounds. Commending the beauty of its now vanished Doric Temple of Bacchus, he may not have known that some its architectural details were of papier mâché. He did not seem to know what to think of its Gothic "temple," situated at the end of a lawn and facing *allées*. At the end of one was a copy of Giambologna's statue *The Rape of the Sabine Women*. Through the ogival arches of the Gothic temple there is a splendid view of the lake, around which were located a Gothic ruin, a rustic mill, a cascade, and a grotto. Jefferson considered building near Monticello a *folie* in the form of a Gothic tower. Although the little summer house that Jefferson later built on his

garden wall has been recreated in brick with sashed windows set in round-headed frames, akin to the arcaded loggias of the mansion house, its site and vista have something in common with the Gothic Temple at Painshill.[29]

In *Observations on Modern Gardening* Thomas Whately gave such an enthusiastic description of Lord Loughborough's Woburn Old Farm that Jefferson visited it twice. This was an estate of about 135 acres, of which about 35 were given over to a garden that was "adorned to the highest degree." Its attraction was not its buildings, although these included a "neat" thick structure among its curiosities, but its combination of ornamental and functional landscape gardening into what the French called *une ferme ornée,* whose objective was to "bring every rural circumstance within the verge of a garden." A wavy path of sand and gravel bordered by a broad belt of shrubs and flowers communicated to meadows and arable fields. To enhance the effect, there were little seats, alcoves, bridges, and even a menagerie of ordinary farmyard beasts and fowl. Jefferson often recalled Woburn Old Farm as the finest he ever had seen of its type, and he made such careful note of the tenant houses that he must have examined everything in detail before tipping Lord Loughborough's servants about half again what he had tipped the servants at Hampton Court and Chiswick. He found that three teams of four persons tended the farm, the pleasure garden, and the kitchen garden. As attorneys, Jefferson and Adams had a professional interest in visiting Loughborough's seat. He was then Lord Chief Justice of the Court of Common Pleas and was soon to become Lord Chancellor, despite, or because of, the fact that he was known more as a politician than as a jurist. Jefferson may have had additional interest in the fact that before George III raised Loughborough to the peerage in 1778, he had been plain Alexander Wedderburn, bearing the same name as a tavernkeeper at Williamsburg.[30]

Jefferson and Adams spent the night at Weybridge before recrossing the Thames to Reading. They admired views toward Windsor through great, tree-lined avenues. On April 5 and 6 they drove through the villages of Wallingford and Thame to visit the Viscount Cobham's estates at Wotton and Stowe before spending the night in the village of Buckingham. The first of these Jefferson found "much neglected," with only two men detailed "to keep the pleasure grounds in order." Considering his own troubles in securing an adequate water supply at Monticello, he must have envied Wotton's lake, river, and basin, which he calculated comprised seventy-two acres and produced "2000 brace of carp a year."

At Stowe the architect William Kent had created an immense garden that made extravagant use of water. Fifteen men and eighteen boys maintained its three hundred acres of walled park, divided into meadows and woods by ha-has. After approaching the mansion along a mile-long avenue, one reached a Corinthian arched gateway sixty feet high and sixty feet across, which Jefferson disliked because the avenue did not pass through the "useless" arch, which thus became only "an obstacle to a very pleasing prospect." By the time of Jefferson's visit, Stowe had lost some of its initial

The House and Gardens at Woburn in Surrey as laid out by Philip Southcote, 1798, engraving by L. Walker after painting by William Wollett (1735–85).

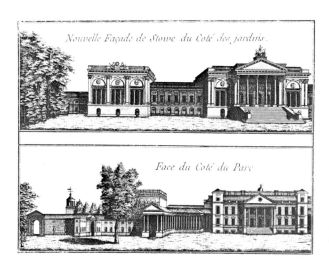

Nouvelle Façade de Stowe du Côte des Jardins, ca. 1776, drawing by George Louis Le Rouge.

complement of Kentian invention—an Egyptian pyramid, two rotundas, and a grotto. Three temples were left, however, to embellish the park, a circular one dedicated to Ancient Virtue and two rectangular ones dedicated to Venus and to Concord and Victory. If the latter were more like the Maison Carrée at Nîmes, about which Jefferson was to be so rhapsodic a year later, than the Virginia state capitol was, Jefferson never said so. Nor did he remark on Kent's tribute to his heroes of civilization—Homer, Plato, Socrates, and the like—with whose busts on a curving wall was one of the father of English architecture, Inigo Jones, Latinized into "Ignatius" Jones.[31] Jefferson bought some books at Buckingham, and the party spent the night there before they continued their progress to Stratford-on-Avon.

55

Jefferson did not comment on the battlefield of Edgehill, through which they passed, even though one of his Randolph forebears had fought there for the king's cause in the first large engagement of the English Civil Wars. His friend and cousin Thomas Mann Randolph, Sr., then owned an Albemarle County estate named Edgehill, which later became the property of Thomas Mann Randolph, Jr., and Martha Jefferson upon their marriage.[32] John Adams, however, had a lot to say about Edgehill. He was so moved by having stood on the ground where "freemen had fought for their rights" that in the next town, Worcester, he exhorted the "ignorant and careless," saying: "And do Englishmen soon forget the ground where liberty was fought for? Tell your neighbors and your children that this is holy ground; much holier than that on which your churches stand. All England should come in pilgrimage to this hill once a year." Adams professed that his stump speech "animated" and "pleased" his auditors.[33]

They journeyed on to Stratford-on-Avon, where they spent the night in an inn that was only three doors from Shakespeare's birthplace. Jefferson recorded in his account book expenditures for lodging, dinner, breakfast, postilions, horses, and tips to servants for showing him the bard's house, tomb, and effigy. That he wrote little else about his visit there was not because he did not care for Shakespeare. He owned copies of Shakespeare's works, which he recommended that all young people read in order "to learn the full powers of the English language." He approved of the moral instruction in Shakespeare's depiction of the "villainy" of Macbeth's murder of Duncan and the nobility of Cordelia's "filial duty" to King Lear. Not long after his visit to Stratford, Jefferson asked John Trumbull to help him get likenesses of Shakespeare in oils and in a sculptured bust. When Monticello assumed its final form in 1809, Shakespeare's portrait hung in company with portraits of others of Jefferson's heroes—Columbus, Galileo, Newton, and Locke.[34] John Adams wrote with unapologetic candor of their visit to Shakespeare's "small and mean" birthplace: "They showed us an old wooden chair in the chimney corner where he sat. We cut off a chip according to custom."[35]

Adams and Jefferson spent the next night at Birmingham. They walked around the town and inspected a "manufactory of paintings upon paper." There Jefferson visited a hairdresser and bought some books and a candlestick, presumably for night reading in country inns. Following Whately's advice, he and Adams went to see Leasowes, as the poet William Shenstone had named his 150-acre farm after the nearby Anglo-Saxon village of Halesowen. The poet had been dead twenty-three years, and the new proprietor had erected a new house in the garden. Believing that Nature was no "raw goddess" who needed to be improved upon, Shenstone had been one of the originators of the natural, English garden that became the international rage of the second half of the eighteenth century. He had combined the use of rustic seats in natural bowers with classic urns, a copy of the Medici Venus, and both neoclassic and Gothic "ruins." There was even a piteous cast-iron tombstone Shenstone had erected to his dog Rover, bearing the inscription "The Most Faithful." Neither Jefferson nor Adams remarked on any of these features, although the Virginian did say that Leasowes's prospect was "fine." No longer the *ferme ornée* of Shenstone's time, the estate's superb natural setting on Mucklow Hill provided a panoramic view of the Malvern Hills to the south and the Wrekin on the west that still inspires contemplation on the immortality of nature and the mortality of man. Jefferson the landscape gardener found there as much to disappoint him as to please him. Although the garden was "small," he thought its two cascades "beautiful." While the estate once may have justified the designation "ornamented farm," it now was "only a grazing farm" with a few "umbrageous and pleasing" paths through the woods and only occasional seats and inscriptions. "Architecture," he opined, "has contributed nothing. The obelisk is of brick." Jefferson seems to have been blind to how the transitory character of Shenstone's accomplishments posed a warning of what he and Monticello might suffer, but he wrote that Shenstone had "ruined himself by what he did to this farm. It is said that he died of the heartaches which his debts occasioned him."[36]

The party spent the night at Stourbridge before visiting Hagley Hall, the seat of Sir William Henry Lyttleton, who had been governor of South Carolina a generation earlier.[37] The mansion and most of the other buildings were the work of the Warwickshire gentleman-architect Sanderson Miller. One may disagree with Sir John Summerson's condemnation of the mansion as "a Palladian building of no particular importance" and yet agree that Miller was an originator of the Gothic movement because of his sham castle in Hagley's park.[38] Although Jefferson did not describe Hagley Hall,

Principal Front of Hagley, 1771, engraving by F. White. Of all the houses Jefferson saw, this probably most resembled one by Palladio.

it was the purest example of Palladian architecture that he ever saw. He had not seen a plan or picture of this house before going there, but he did own books that illustrated its prototypes, especially Andrea Palladio's design for the Villa Schio. Unlike Palladio, Miller did not incorporate into his noble residence a farmhouse, stables, haylofts, or grain bins. The Villa Schio had only two towers to "nobilitate" it, but Hagley Hall had four stubby ones. The Italian villa's suite of three large principal apartments *en suite*, plus two staircases and a stair chamber on the *piano nobile*, became in England a gallery, seven principal apartments, and two stairs and passageways lighted by skylights. Both the Italian villa and the English hall are set on generous rusticated basements.[39]

Hagley Hall was also of interest to Jefferson because it was the seat of the Lyttleton family. In the fifteenth century Lord Thomas Lyttleton had compiled his important legal tome *On Tenures*, the basis for English property law, which Jefferson had studied and of which he owned at least two seventeenth-century editions.[40] The Sir Edward Lyttleton who built Hagley Hall had served in the 1750s as Chancellor of the Exchequer. He had been a friend of Pope, Fielding, and Shenstone, the last of whom helped him develop the grounds of Hagley Hall in the picturesque style. Hagley's park boasted a grotto, a Palladian bridge, a sham castle, a statue of Venus, and a great obelisk commemorating Lyttleton's patron, Frederick, Prince of Wales. No stately home that Jefferson visited anywhere had a site as similar to that of Monticello. Both commanded almost a 270-degree vista of higher mountains and a plain. Jefferson made no remark about the English house, but he praised its grounds, saying that farm, garden, and park were well "blended" and that pathways were so skillfully located on contour lines that they could be "scarcely gravelled." They became a prototype for Monticello's roundabouts. In the park there were both fallow and red deer. In the hollow between two arms of Mucklow Hill that accommodated a garden and small trout ponds linked by rivulets, Jefferson was charmed to discover "a *Venus pudique*, turned half round as if inviting you with her into the recess." Unfortunately, there was only enough water to permit occasional transformation of the rivulets into cascades. In the park is a triangular Gothic sham castle with round towers at its angles. This structure, built by Sanderson Miller in 1748, so pleased Horace Walpole that he said that it seemed to possess "the true rust of the Barons' Wars." Jefferson admired it enough to sketch its plan, something he did only three or four times in his European travels, but he had nothing to say about Miller's fine stone church near the mansion.[41]

After spending nights at Worcester and at Moreton, Jefferson and Adams reached Woodstock, where they slept after viewing Blenheim Palace. Blenheim! What must Jefferson, the resolute republican who did not like Versailles, have thought of this extravagant, grandiose, and sumptuous palace that Vanbrugh had created for the Duke and Duchess of Marlborough! As Abigail Adams said, it requires "a week to view it and a volume to describe it." Both Jefferson and Mrs. Adams appreciated the fact that this, the part of the royal manor of Woodstock that Queen Anne gave Marlborough, included the site of Henry the Second's palace and of the romantic bower where Shakespeare and others said the king visited Rosamund, the most comely of his wife's ladies-in-waiting. Jefferson and the Adamses were dismayed that the Duchess Sarah had "taken down" and "leveled" its ruins. Jefferson noted that of the estate's twenty-five hundred acres, two hundred were devoted to ornamental gardens, twelve to kitchen gardens, thirty to park, one hundred fifty to water, and the remainder to pasture, woods, and crop fields. He reckoned that to keep these in order it was necessary to employ two hundred persons, of whom about fifty worked exclusively on the pleasure grounds, which they mowed once every ten days in the summer. In the park there were about two hundred fallow deer and two thousand to three thousand sheep.

Capability Brown had swept away the original parterres at Blenheim and moved fifty-foot trees in order to create a natural, English garden in the 1750s. The most remarkable thing he had done, however, was to raise the level of its lake, even though doing so flooded part of Vanbrugh's lovely bridge. Jefferson was so enchanted by the river, lake, and cascade that he was not content with Whately's printed description and wrote in his memorandum book that "the water here is very beautiful and very grand. The cascade from the lake [is] a fine one." But he considered that its garden had "no great beauties. It is not laid out in fine lawns and woods, but the trees are scattered thinly over the ground, and every where and there [are] small thickets of shrubs, in oval raised beds, cultivated, and flowers among the shrubs. The gravelled walks are broad. Art[ifice] appears too much; There are but few seats in it, and nothing of architecture [, such as a temple or grotto]. . . . There is no one striking position in it."

Jefferson made no comment about the interior of the palace. One wonders whether he, upon coming into the great stone entrance hall, envied the duke his bronzes of the Medici Venus and Faun or whether he already had abandoned his old desire to place copies of those sculptures at Monticello. Having recently commissioned at Paris the reupholstery of his own furniture in blue and red fabrics, and about to order a lot more, he must have looked with a speculative eye at how the drawing room was fitted out with white brocade. Did this fashionable man wonder if he had ordered the wrong color? We can only guess. We do know that in 1793 he sold at Philadelphia much of his French furniture because he deemed it inappropriate for a country house like Monticello. The great portrait at Blenheim that Sir Joshua Reynolds had painted of the current duke, duchess, and their six children was displayed in the dining room, clashing with its famous murals. Jefferson must have envied the duke's library of twenty-four thousand volumes and his observatory, whence the duke, an amateur astronomer, sent visual "signals" to the great Sir William Herschel at Windsor.[42] Like everyone else, the American tourist must have recalled the famous couplet by the little-known Abel Evans on Vanbrugh's death: "Lie heavy on him, Earth, for he / Hath laid many a heavy load on thee."

By the time Jefferson and Adams reached Worcester, it had become clear that they would have to accelerate their homeward journey. Although they passed through the countryside quickly, they found time to see some of the colleges at Oxford, where Jefferson tipped the doorkeepers handsomely.[43] The two Americans pressed on to High Wycombe, where they spent the night after visiting the Dashwoods' estate, but not the Hell Fire Caves, which once had beguiled Benjamin Franklin. They may have been overnight guests of Sir Francis Dashwood. The next day, the party was back in London.

After their return to the metropolis, Jefferson alone visited the Enfield Chase, a remnant of what had been a royal hunting preserve before the English Civil Wars, on the northern periphery of London. One part had become the site of the Enfield Grammar School, whose master was said to have been the first to plant a cedar of Lebanon in England. In the mideighteenth century the Earl of Chatham had bought and improved another portion with a garden of about sixty acres. Its tenant in 1786 earned Jefferson's reproach for neither keeping it in good repair nor "extending the walks &c. to the principal water at the bottom of the lawn."[44]

Nearby was Moor Park, in Hertfordshire, a two-story mansion that Sir Lawrence Dundas had employed Robert Adam to improve in the 1760s by adding curving colonnades that terminated in small, one-story pavilions. One of these housed an octagonal tea room decorated to give the illusion of a tropical garden with palm tree columns and fronds at the corners, for which Adam may have designed some fine Louis XVI chairs. One may infer that Jefferson's reason for going to Moor Park was to inspect the neoclassical improvements by his friend Clérisseau's student. He must not have known that the new owner, Thomas Bates Rous, was pulling down Adam's colonnades and wings. Nonetheless, the Virginian admired the portico's four Corinthian columns at the front, a broad terrace at the back, and what was left of the colonnades.[45] Not far off was Forty Hall on Forty Hill, a Dutch-looking building of three stories dating from the 1620s that was wrongly attributed to Inigo Jones. When Jefferson went there, it was for sale and could be inspected at leisure. It is unlikely that its heavy quoins and window surrounds or its delicate little Corinthian porch misled Jefferson to believe that Forty Hill was Jones's work.[46]

Jefferson made one last visit to London's southern periphery. Although he may have caught glimpses of Kew previously, he did not visit there until April 14. The palace, or Dutch House, had been built by a London merchant in the 1630s. A century later, the royal family had commenced using it as a country house. Once the residence of George III's older sons and their tutor, it had become Queen Charlotte and King George's favorite residence near London. Like most royal estates, it was often open to the genteel public. It is not surprising that Jefferson did not comment on the Dutch House, both because of its style and because of its royal character. Thanks to the queen's enthusiasm for gardening, there were at Kew roses, carnations, pinks, and orange, lemon, and tea trees.[47] Jefferson did not comment on the palace or its garden, but only contented himself by making notes of Kew's model of Archimedes' screw for raising water, sketching the device, and copying its mathematical formula. He does not seem ever to have put these sketches to use in America. Certainly the elevation of Monticello Mountain was too great to thus raise water from the Rivanna. Alas, Monticello's supply of water was so little and so unreliable that its flowers, shrubs, trees, and vegetables had to rely mainly on rainwater.[48]

On April 20 Jefferson and the Adams family made a last excursion to the west of the metropolis of London. Their objective was to view two great houses that had been remodeled by Sir William Chambers and Robert Adam. They went first to Osterley Park, which a former owner had engaged Chambers to transform from an Elizabethan to a neoclassical mansion.[49] By 1786 Chambers's rival Robert Adam had reworked the house into an advanced example of his own style. John Adams commented on its exterior in prosaic terms, but Horace Walpole had called it "the palace of palaces" and rhapsodized on how its new double portico filled the space between the Elizabethan towers "as nobl[y] as the Propyleum of Athens." Although Adams exclaimed over the cherries, plums, roses, and strawberries grown in its "curious" greenhouse, he unconsciously agreed with Walpole in not liking the pleasure grounds. "The beauty, convenience and utility of these country seats," said he, are "not enjoyed by their owners. They are mere ostentations of vanity." Servants denied Jefferson and the Adamses access to Osterley Park's magnificent interior because the owner, Lady Childs, was away and they had "no ticket." Disappointed at not seeing its famous rooms by Adam, Jefferson wasted no ink on Osterley Park beyond recording his tips to the servants for showing him about the park and its dependencies.[50]

The Adamses and Jefferson then "called to see Syon House, belonging to the Duke of Northumberland." In comparing its park with others, John Adams observed that it was merely "a repetition of winding walks, gloomy evergreens, sheets of water, clumps of trees, green houses, hot houses, etc." Like most people then and since, he acclaimed as "beautiful" the great entrance gate designed by Robert Adam. Presumably the Americans were denied admission for the lack of a note of introduction, because none of them made any record of its superb Adam interiors, whose lavish recreation of Roman decoration vastly exceeded in richness anything Clérisseau ever attempted and were unlikely to please Jefferson. As it was, he only noted in his accounts that he gave the servants modest tips.

Doubtless Jefferson agreed with his friend John Adams that they had "seen Magnificence, Elegance and Taste enough."[51] He had been away from his post at Paris for almost six weeks. As there seemed no hope of successful negotiations for a British trade treaty, it was time for him to go back to France. Traveling in a new chariot that he had purchased in London, Jefferson left London on April 26 for Dover, with Petit and John on the box and the learned John Paradise as his fellow passenger to Greenwich, the first posting station. Although Mrs. Paradise, née Ludwell, of Williamsburg, was troublesome to her friends and a virago to her husband, John Paradise was a mild-mannered, scholarly, impractical man with whom Jefferson had great rapport.[52] Protracting the usual brief delay for changing horses, Jefferson took the opportunity to visit the famous Greenwich Observatory, with Paradise, a member of the Royal Society, as his cicerone. From this eminence they could also study the exterior of the villa that Inigo Jones had designed for Queen Henrietta Maria and scan hurriedly Sir Christopher Wren's Greenwich Palace, which had been converted to a hospital for naval pensioners. Jefferson and Paradise did not make a hurried tour of the Naval Hospital. Three years later Gouverneur Morris wrote that it was "a noble building and extremely well kept," but he complained that the twenty-three hundred pensioners were given "too much" food considering "the little exercise which many of these disabled men can possibly take." Although Morris walked through the park, he mentioned neither the queen's house nor the observatory. Instead, he wrote in his diary of having observed just beyond the park "the Goff ground of Black Heath," where some of the

The Landing at Greenwich, ca. 1795–1800, watercolor by Thomas Rowlandson (1756–1835). Jefferson and John Paradise visited Wren's palace, which by then had been converted into a naval hospital.

"Greenwich Lads" caddied for "the Players, for which they each get one shilling."[53]

Failing to encounter either golfers or highwaymen on Black Heath, Jefferson, Petit, and John continued their journey down the Dover Road without incident. Jefferson did not tarry at Dartford, Rochester, Sitting-bourne, or Canterbury longer than to pay for post horses and postilions. We cannot know whether he agreed or disagreed with Mrs. Adams in thinking Rochester "a pretty town" in the shadow of its ruined keep, still watching over a busy shipping trade where the Medway meets the Thames. Probably he would have assented if she had asked him whether he shared her strictures on Canterbury:

> It contains a number of old Gothic cathedrals, which are all of stone, very heavy, with but few windows, which are grated with large bars of iron, and look more like jails for criminals, than places designed for the worship of the Deity. One would suppose, from the manner in which they are guarded, that they apprehended devotion would be stolen. They have a most gloomy appearance, and really make me shudder. The houses, too, have a heavy look, being chiefly thatched roofs, or covered with crooked brick tiles.[54]

Jefferson got to Dover a little before midnight. He probably lodged at the Royal Hotel Inn, kept by Charles Mariee, whose establishment was built into the cliffside.[55] It turned out that the American had hurried unnecessarily, because bad weather prevented his crossing the straits for a day and a half. To occupy his time Jefferson saw what little there was of the town and paid to tour Dover Castle. He settled up his account with his coachman, John, sent him off to London, paid for the portage of his own baggage, passed through customs, and took passage for himself and Petit on Captain Payne's ship for France. After an "excellent passage of three hours only," Petit took one of the carriages on the road, while Jefferson rode in the other with postilions. They arrived at Paris on May 3.[56]

Whereas Jefferson was an optimistic man and John Adams was a cantankerous one, they both enjoyed rural delights and simple ways. Both were inclined to be skeptical of the pretensions of the English and French aristocracy that often cloaked an idle luxury on their country estates. Four days after he returned to Paris, Jefferson wrote to John Page in Virginia that his seven-week sojourn in England "fell short of my expectations." He praised most the English pleasure gardens, saying that they surpassed all others. He considered English laborers better off than their French counterparts, and he believed English agricultural lands to be better than French ones, not because of soil or method of cultivation, but because they were "better manured" by tenants on long leases. In a burst of patriotism, he declared that "London, tho' handsomer than Paris, is not so handsome as Philadelphia. Their architecture is the most wretched stile I ever saw, not meaning to except America where it is bad, nor even Virginia where it is worse than in any other part of America, which I have seen." There was an important fact that Jefferson did not tell Page: he had been frustrated in his efforts to see some notable examples of the architects Sir William Chambers and Robert

Adam, namely, the interiors of Osterley and Syon and those parts of Moor Park that had been demolished.

In writing to Page how "the mechanical arts in London are carried to a wonderful perfection," he gave as an example the application of steam to a grist mill where he saw thirty grinding stones worked by steam in sets of as many as eight.[57] Like most of the founders of the American republic, Jefferson was suspicious of Great Britain. He and John Adams were made more so by being rebuffed in their efforts to renew good relations in 1786. Jefferson felt personally affronted by George III and his ministers, while Adams was only slightly less repulsed. Both U.S. statesmen believed that the leaders of Great Britain were guilty of perverting political principles common to Anglo-Saxon peoples.[58] What concerned Jefferson most was the abiding enmity of Britain's hereditary and elective rulers. Writing to a French friend about the "growling temper" of the English people, he remarked that "the splendor of their shops" was all that was worth seeing at London.[59] In his letter to Page he concluded: "That nation hates us, their ministers hate us, and their king [hates us] more than all other men. They have the impudence to avow this, tho' they acknowledge our trade important to them. . . . Our overtures of commercial arrangements have been treated with a derision which shews their firm persuasion that we shall never unite to suppress their commerce or even to impede it. I think their hostility to us is much more deeply rooted at present than during the war."[60]

5 *Marly and Maria Cosway*

A LITTLE MORE THAN THREE MONTHS AFTER HIS RETURN TO Paris from England Jefferson met Maria Cosway. She provided a charming excuse to make leisurely visits to some of the great sights of Paris and its environs. On the first of these little excursions, John Trumbull was the leader, and both Jefferson and Richard Cosway were tourists. Soon, however, the forty-three-year-old American minister arranged for the young American artist to sketch French celebrities, while he himself conducted Maria about in his handsome new carriage, with his fine pair of horses and a well-clad coachman. Although there was much for them to see and do in the city, it was the verdure and coolness of the royal parks that most attracted them.

The royal retreat of Marly, near Versailles, was in the 1780s still an object for the curious to visit, even though its century-old "machine" for lifting water from the Seine to the little plateau of Versailles and Marly, which Jefferson had seen in 1784,[1] had ceased to excite wonder. Elsewhere in the complex was the king's house, with its eight flanking pavilions, which had been designed by Mansart for Louis XIV a century earlier, and the adjacent pavilion at Louveciennes, which Claude Nicholas Ledoux had designed for Louis XV's mistress, the Comtesse du Barry. In 1786 Jefferson took Maria Cosway to see the whole complex and its paintings and also to enjoy a picnic.

The great upper cascade of Louis XIV's day, the so-called *rivière d'eau*, had been removed a half-century earlier, but Guillaume Coustou's magnifi-

La Terrasse de Marly, ca. 1783, painting by Hubert Robert (1733–1808). Thomas Jefferson and Maria Cosway picnicked beneath the bowers of Marly.

cent statues of the Numidian Horses still adorned its park.[2] Gouverneur Morris was pleased by the château's garden, but he thought Mansart's complex of structures only "tolerable" and their furniture "indifferent."[3] Whether or not the royal quarters could be viewed except from a respectful distance, Thomas and Maria seem to have devoted their time to the park and to inspecting the nearby Pavilion de Musique at Louveciennes, which Claude Nicholas Ledoux had designed *en grande luxe* for Madame du Barry.

This elegant villa scorned both the strict Palladian and the ornate rococo style of the mid-eighteenth century, so anticipating the Louis XVI style that a later commentator said that when Louis XV sat down at Madame du Barry's, he sat in Louis Seize chairs. The structure comprised a main floor for entertainment and madame's bedroom, a mezzanine of two skylighted bedrooms for servants or guests, an ample basement for service facilities, and a subbasement. The house is a triple cube of white stone; the central block is smooth white ashlar, and the ends are finished in horizontal bands, broken by windows, over which there are carved stone panels. A parapet concealed a roof that was almost flat. On the entrance façade are four Ionic columns, topped by a plain frieze about the whole. Behind them is an inset, semicircular portico pierced by a pair of French doors between niches. On the side overlooking the Seine there is a shallow, rectangular balcony. The pavilion's great oval vestibule is sheathed in marble, with sixteen colossal pilasters with gilded Corinthian capitals, a patterned floor, and a magnificent ceiling, painted by Restout. Madame du Barry also commissioned Jean Honoré Fragonard to paint for the walls of the square salon four scenes known as the Loves of the Shepherds, but they were never installed.[4] Above

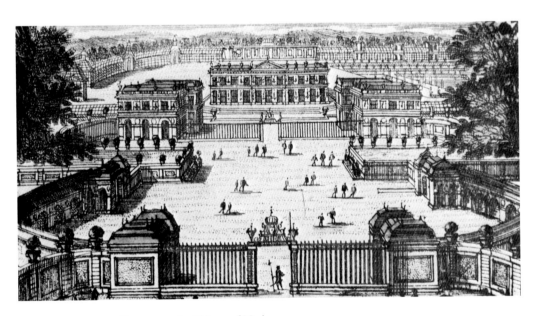

Entrance to the Château of Marly,
ca. 1750, engraving. Jefferson took Maria
Cosway to inspect this little château
overlooking the Seine.

the winding river and the deep shade of the forest of Marly, the pavilion commanded a noble prospect of Paris. According to Gouverneur Morris, from Louveciennes it seemed as though "the bells from a thousand steeples at different distances murmur" and combine with "the fragrance of the morning" to create a "vernal freshness of the air."[5]

On September 16, 1786, Jefferson and Maria Cosway visited a remarkable garden in the "natural" style adjacent to Marly. This was the ninety-acre Désert de Retz, belonging to François Racine de Monville. It was not a desert in the infertile, bleak, or desolate sense; the term *désert* meant that it was a private place for contemplation. Monville's garden and structures were the result of his own amateur talents, but he was heavily influenced by the architects François Barbier and Etienne Boullée and by the painter Hubert Robert. The gate to the Désert was rusticated on the side facing the road, but it resembled a giant's mouth on the side facing the park. In the evening a pair of statues in the form of satyrs held lighted torches to aid—or terrify—guests. Besides a pyramidal icehouse, there were a real, ruined Gothic chapel; a neoclassical Temple of Pan; a Chinese pavilion; and a turfed amphitheater. The central feature was Monville's residence, a five-story truncated building in the shape of a large column, whose fluted, plaster exterior had both square and circular windows. Besides presenting a startling appearance to visitors, the Column House had a minimum of straight lines to conflict with the sinuous paths and roads of the Désert.[6]

Jefferson seems to have enjoyed only Marly among the royal châteaux,[7] primarily for its privacy, forests, waters, and vistas. While Jefferson sent his coachman to lunch in the village, he and Maria enjoyed a romantic picnic "under the Bowers of Marly."[8] This was a magical moment to which Thomas and Maria both often referred, but one they never relived.

Although Jefferson was contemptuous of the "profligate" Prince of Wales,[9] he accepted the mores of European society of the 1780s in condoning most extramarital liaisons. Not only did worldly philosophers such as Voltaire and Rousseau provide real-life models for promiscuity, but excuses for gallantry were provided by the arranged marriages of many of Jefferson's friends: the Houdetots, the La Fayettes, the La Rochefoucaulds, the Noailles, and the Tessés. Besides Maria Cosway, the five French ladies who were Jefferson's best friends were Mesdames de Bréhan, de Corny, d'Houdetot, de Tessé, and de Tott. At least four of them had romantic affairs with men other than their husbands. Educated privately or in convent schools, they were interested in literature and political science. One of them was knowledgeable about botany, and two were painters.

Rocher Vué de l'Intérieur du Jardin Faisant
l'Entrée du Désert par le Forêt de Marly, ca.
1776, drawing by George Louis Le Rouge.

Mrs. Maria Hadfield Cosway seems to have been the lady in whom Jefferson had the greatest romantic interest after Martha Jefferson's death in 1783.[10] Born at Leghorn, Italy, in 1759, the daughter of a successful English hotelier and an Italian lady, Maria had been educated in music and painting at Florence, where she had become one of the very few feminine members of the prestigious Accademia di Firenze.[11] She also had studied for a little more than a year at Rome, where she frequented the atelier of one of the greatest painters of that day, Pompeo Batoni. After her father's death in 1781 Maria moved to London, where Angelica Kauffmann championed her. A year later, when the Hadfield family had almost exhausted their inheritance, Mrs. Hadfield urged her poor daughter to accept the proposal of Richard Cosway, who, as a court painter to the Prince of Wales, was a rich man. They were married in 1782.

Thereafter Maria placed her works in the biennial exhibitions of the Royal Academy, of which Richard Cosway was a member. He was a dwarflike man who cut a figure that was at best quixotic. Because of his early sponsorship by the Prince of Wales, his fashionable success was assured; and his talent as a miniaturist has never been surpassed. Richard and Maria's marriage was not exactly an arranged one, but it is clear that it was one of convenience. Richard seems to have been more complaisant about Maria's admirers than he was accepting of her artistic career. He rarely permitted her to accept commissions for portraits other than from nobles so great that he dared not object. Consequently, her oil paintings were usually landscapes, religious scenes, still lifes, or illustrations for reproduction as prints or in books. The Cosways entertained much in their elegant quarters in

Maria and Richard Cosway in costume,
ca. 1780, drawing by Richard Cosway.

Schomberg House on Pall Mall. Maria often sang to her own piano or harp accompaniment for the fashionable, if racy, company of the Prince of Wales and his early *amour*, Perdita Robinson. Up until 1788 Maria seems to have given scandalmongers no cause to assert that she was sexually promiscuous, but no matter how virtuous, a lady as beautiful as she who conducted a salon, most of whose guests were friends of the dissolute prince, eventually would inspire such gossip. Eventually Maria proved the gossipers were correct. The Cosways' marriage was childless until the birth of a girl in the summer of 1790.[12]

The sophisticated ladies whom Jefferson accepted on their own merits without prudish qualms were unusual women, representing a false dawn of feminist expression. They were much more than good conversationalists; they were educated, and they commanded respect in their special fields of endeavor. Besides physical beauty and charm of manner, Maria Cosway's special talents were in music, painting, and the education of young girls, topics especially interesting to Jefferson.

It was in early August 1786, when Trumbull was a guest at the Hôtel Langeac, that he introduced Jefferson to Richard and Maria Cosway. Soon

Trumbull wrote that "Mr. Jefferson joined our party almost daily."[13] On one such occasion they all visited the Luxembourg Palace to inspect its works of art. While Trumbull was busily executing portraits, for which Jefferson had secured appointments, Jefferson escorted Mrs. Cosway about Paris and its environs to see examples of art, to hear varieties of music, and to enjoy the beauties of the countryside. They visited the newly redecorated Palais Royal to see the celebrated Orléans art collection and to visit its restaurants and entertainment halls, whose "subterranean circus" he already knew. He took her to Ruggieri's Vauxhall cabaret and later to hear the great harpist, Johann Baptiste Krumpholtz. On other days, the two visited not only the Louvre Palace but also the royal châteaux of Fontainbleau, St. Germain, and Versailles, as well as the Bagatelle in the Bois de Boulogne.[14] They went primarily to see the paintings that were hung at these places but also to be refreshed by the cool of their parks. Since Jefferson's position as a diplomat gave him easy entrée, nothing could have been more natural for two such persons, both of whom found pleasure in art, music, and nature, than to enjoy them together at and about Paris. On their excursion to Marly they traveled in Jefferson's carriage, crossed the Seine by ferry at Surennes, and sent his coachman Petit to lunch in a nearby tavern so that they might enjoy an intimate picnic that was more in the manner of the artist Watteau's *fête galante* than of a nineteenth-century *déjeuner sur l'herbe*. In mid-September Jefferson was strolling with Maria down the Champs Élysées between the Hôtel Langeac and the Place Louis Quinze when he lost his footing, fell, and broke his right wrist.[15] After several days his great pain subsided, but he was unable to write with his right hand for several months.[16]

To commiserate about his broken wrist, Maria Cosway wrote to Jefferson, partly in Italian and partly in her own faulty English: "I have appeared a monster for not having sent to know how you was, the *whole day*. . . . Oh, I wish you was well enough to come to us tomorrow to dinner and stay the evening. I won't tell you what I shall have, temptations now are too cruel for your situation. . . . I would serve you and help you at dinner, and divert your pain after diner by good music." So captivated that he must have thought his injury less severe than it was, Jefferson went to the Cosways' for dinner, enduring the discomfort of his carriage bumping over cobblestoned streets. He spent the rest of that night "in so much pain" that he had "not closed my eyes" and had called for a surgeon. Assuring Maria that he wished to see her before she and Richard Cosway left Paris, he bade her "Addio, Addio." In reply, she lamented that she had to go back to England and thanked him for the "charming days we have past together." She assured him that she would come back to Paris in the spring of 1787.[17] To bid the Cosways good-bye, Jefferson rose from his sickbed to accompany them in their coach as far as Saint Denis.[18]

About a month later he was able to write Maria a lengthy epistle that he entitled "Dialogue Between My Head and My Heart."[19] It would be an exaggeration to call it, as Julian Boyd does, "one of the most notable love letters in the English language."[20] Instead, it exemplifies the eighteenth-century conceit of an imaginary dialogue and lends itself to either an amorous or a platonic interpretation. When Jefferson's Head warned him that friendship with Maria was a threat to his own tranquility, his Heart replied that they merely shared interests in architecture, art, and music. The Heart admitted that he falsely had used official business as an excuse to break an engagement at the Hôtel La Rochefoucauld so that they might lunch together, visit St. Cloud, sup at Ruggieri's restaurant, and hear a concert by Krumpholtz. The Head admitted joyous recollection of a day "as long as a Lapland summer day," when they viewed together the beautiful hills along the Seine.[21] Among the sites of greatest pleasure had been the rainbows created by the machine at Marly, the château, gardens, and statues of Marly, the Pavillon de Musique at Louveciennes, and the *folies* of the Désert de Retz. Sternly the Head admonished the incorrigible Heart, saying, "You were imprudently engaging your affections" with a lady more for her beauty than for her talents. The Heart replied that in America "the lady, who paints landscape so inimitably" would find "subjects worthy of immortality to render her pencil immortal": Niagara Falls, the Passage of the Potomac through the Blue Ridge Mountains, the Natural Bridge of Virginia, Monticello. In mock-romantic tone, Jefferson's Heart referred to his lonely state as a widower and wondered whether anyone might be able to console him. Soberly and ominously the Head admonished that his most effectual antidote was to retire to intellectual pleasures, since "Friendship is but another name for an alliance with the follies and the misfortunes of others." But the Heart responded with feeling: "How grateful is the solace of our friends!

The Birth of the Thames, ca. 1800, engraving by P. W. Tomkins after painting by Maria Cosway at the Cosway Foundation, Lodi, Italy. Mrs. Cosway's portrait of her daughter Louisa Paolina Angelica Cosway served as the model for the infant Thames.

Armand Louis de Gontaud, Duc de
Lauzun et Duc de Biron, as Colonel of
Lauzun's Hussars, ca. 1787.

. . . When Heaven has taken from us some object of our love, how sweet is
it to have a bosom whereon to recline our heads, and into which we may pour
the torrent of our tears!" Ardently, it recalled their August days to prove that
"Friendship is precious." Then "the sun shone brightly! How gay did the face
of nature appear! Hills, vallies, châteaux, gardens, river, every object wore
its liveliest hue! Whence did they borrow it? From the presence of our
charming companion. They were pleasing, because she seemed pleased.
Alone, the scene would have been dull and insipid: the participation of it
with her gave it relish."[22]

On the same day that he posted this letter to Maria Cosway, Thomas
Jefferson also fulfilled his promise to send her sheet music of Antonio Mario
Gasparo Sacchini's air "Jours Hereux," from *Dardanus*, the opera about the
founder of Troy. He appealed to her: "Bring me in return its subject, Jours
heureux! Were I a songster I should sing it all to these words 'Dans ces lieux
qu'elle tarde a se rendre!'"[23]

More than capable of making only a "baffled and ineffectual response"
to Jefferson's dialogue,[24] Maria displayed agility in presenting an enigmatic
face to so enigmatic a suitor. How should one reply to a mock love letter?
People of today might infer that Jefferson was more clever than committing.

Maria had every right to ask him, "Why do you say so many kind things?"[25] The gentleman was not straightforward with the lady. He never became more specific about his intentions. What was a lady to think on reading the following:

> Were the hand able to follow the effusions of the heart, that would cease to write only when this shall cease to beat. . . . When sins are dear to us, we are but too prone to slide into them again. The act of repentance itself is often sweetened with the thought that it clears our account for a repetition of the same sin. . . . Heaven has submitted our being to some unkind laws. When those charming moments were present which I passed with you, they were clouded with the prospect that I was soon to lose you: and now, when I pass the same moments in review, I recollect nothing but the agreeable passages, and they fill me with regret. . . . I am determined, when you come next, not to admit the idea that we are ever to part again. But are you to come again?[26]

Maria replied on New Year's Day of 1787 that at London "pleasures come in search of me." If this was a hint that Jefferson should visit London, he did not acknowledge it. In mid-February she wrote him again: "Are you to be painted in future ages sitting solitary and sad, on the beautiful Monticello tormented by the shadow of a woman. . . . Oh! how I wish myself in those delightful places! Those enchanted grottoes! Those magnificent mountains, rivers! . . . If I should be happy enough to come again in the sum[mer of 1787 to] Paris I hope we shall pass many agreable days, [but] I am in a millio[n] fears about it."[27]

It was only after returning from his excursion into the "Elysium" of Italy that Thomas informed Maria of his journey thither in the late spring of 1787. Yet he disingenuously declared: "Why were you not with me? So many enchanting scenes which only wanted your pencil to consecrate them to fame." Understandably annoyed by such cavalier treatment, Maria tartly replied: "Oh! if I had been a shadow of the *Elysium* of yours! How you would have been tormented!"[28]

Although Maria and Richard Cosway were now partially estranged, there were many reasons that she and Jefferson did not see much of one another when she finally returned to Paris in the autumn of 1787, even though he insisted to John Trumbull that it was the "mere effect of chance" that each usually was out when the other called.[29] She was the guest of the beautiful Franco-Polish Princess Aleksandra Lubomirska and consorted with nobles whose interests were more pleasure-seeking than high-minded. Nonetheless, Jefferson invited Maria to bring the princess and some others to an elegant dinner party.[30] The most important reason for the coolness between them, however, was that Armand Louis Gontaud, the Duc de Lauzun, had become a serious rival for Maria's attention.

At Yorktown and Williamsburg in 1782, the duc had been known by Virginians as the Duc de Lauzun. A spendthrift, he wasted his patrimony. In the late 1780s he inherited another fortune and the title Duc de Biron, but he was called Lauzun as often as he was called Biron. According to his *Mémoirs*, Lauzun's amatory career rivaled Cassanova's, and he scandalized France by claiming that Marie Antoinette had succumbed to his charms. A

Thomas Jefferson, 1788, painting by
John Trumbull (1756–1843), miniature
given to Martha Jefferson Randolph.
Jefferson also gave one each to Angelica
Church and Maria Cosway.

Marly and
Maria Cosway

74

portrait of him in an egret-plumed shako that John Trumbull later included
in his *Surrender at Yorktown* is considered a good likeness of this handsome
rake of a cavalry officer. This profligate soon ran through his second fortune,
lost his *hôtel particulier*, which today houses the Musée Rodin, and became
for a while a pensioned adherent of the Duc d'Orléans. Because in 1787
Richard Cosway grudgingly allowed Maria to accept the commission to
paint the Duchesse d'Orléans's portrait,[31] he inadvertently provided opportunities for Maria and Lauzun to meet often in the duchesse's salon. Whereas Jefferson gave her a miniature portrait of himself by their mutual friend
Trumbull, the Duc de Lauzun gave her a life-size portrait bust of himself in
marble. Suffice it to say that Maria gave Jefferson very little of her time
during the summer of 1788.[32]

By November 1788 Jefferson and Maria very likely equivocated in their
heads, if not their hearts. Perhaps one should sympathize less with Thomas
than with Maria, who had not understood how Jefferson's primness limited
his sophistication. When Jefferson wrote Maria his first letter from America in June 1790 he did not reprove her directly for not confiding in him, but
merely stated: "They tell me that you are going to have a child." Terse in
felicitating her, he sent no word of congratulation to the father. Sternly, and
with a degree of the self-righteous assurance of a virtuous American facing
a sinful Europe, he admonished Maria "as a mother to come and join us" in
the United States.[33]

The conclusion of the story of Maria Cosway and Thomas Jefferson
provides neither a happy ending nor a noble tragedy. If there was ever a time
when a fiery romance and consummated passion was possible for them, it
was at Marly on an August afternoon in 1786.

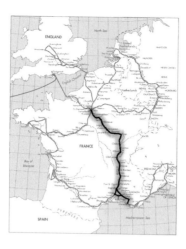

6　*From Paris to Marseilles*

AFTER A WEEK'S DELAY CAUSED BY THE DEATH OF VERGENNES AND
the succession of Montmorin as secretary of state for foreign affairs, Jefferson set out from Paris on February 28, 1787, on a twelve-hundred-mile journey that lasted until early summer.[1] He traveled east to Dijon, south to Marseilles, east to Genoa by way of Turin and Milan, west from Marseilles to Bordeaux by way of the Canal Royal de Languedoc between Sète and Toulouse, north from Bordeaux to Nantes, and east to Paris by way of the Loire valley.[2] Those who have written about Jefferson's travels usually have attributed to him only agricultural and economic reasons for these journeys. Yet he made it plain to his secretary and confidant, William Short, that "architecture, painting, sculpture, antiquities, agriculture [and] the condition of the labouring poor fill all my moments." He traveled in the capacity of a private gentleman from Virginia, not as a minister of the United States. He rode in his own one-seated, enclosed carriage, which he called a chariot. He was so jealous of his privacy that he left his regular servants in Paris, intending to hire postilions and valets in the cities he visited. However, Petitjean, the *valet de place* he hired at Dijon, was "so good" that he kept him for the whole trip, adding local valets where he stayed for more than a day.[3] Petitjean's chief duty was to deal with hostlers and innkeepers in their own *argot*, engaging postilions and pairs of horses at the *relais de poste et chevaux*— the combined postal, livery, and hotel system that the royal government maintained throughout France in the days of the ancien régime. Relay stations were about a dozen miles apart. Jefferson traveled so light that one small trunk held all his clothes, even though he did have a lot of washing done on the way and bought occasional extra clothes, such as canes, gloves, hats, and stockings.

English Diligence, 1788. Jefferson's carriage may have resembled this one, owned by the Marquis de Thomassin, Grand Bailly d'Epée de Vitry-Le-François.

Thus equipped, Jefferson passed between Ledoux's toll houses at the Porte d'Orléans, on the south side of Paris. He had traveled only as far as Fontainbleau when he was delayed for two days while the wheels of his carriage were repaired.[4] Such repairs were to be a recurring problem. It was not that the roads were bad or that Jefferson had an old-fashioned or poorly built carriage; rather, the humped-back roads of the day threw the weight of the carriage against the "off," or outboard, wheels, which also were the most likely to strike fallen boulders. Furthermore, the wheel assemblies of all carriages required constant greasing, packing, and tightening of carriage nuts and cotter pins in order to assure enough play, but not too much, where the wheel bore upon the extremity of the axle.

At Sens and at most places where he later stopped, Jefferson earnestly recorded in a journal of expenses what he paid for lodging, meals, and tips. His only other notation at Sens was for paying to see its "handsome and vast cathedral." Following his own advice to Americans traveling in Europe, he climbed to the top of the cathedral's tower in order to perceive the location of the town's principal buildings. It is highly unlikely that Jefferson was interested in the plaques stating that Saint Louis was married here or in the white marble mausoleum of Louis of France, the dauphin from 1729 to 1765, who was the son of Louis XV and the father of Louis XVI.[5] He then crossed to the Yonne River at Villeneuve and proceeded to Auxerre through unfenced rolling country that he said resembled the "rich mulatto loam" of the Virginia Piedmont. He surmised that intermittent rain was why the people appeared to be so "illy clothed," but it does not seem to have occurred to him that the reason why he saw no cattle, sheep, or swine—only some "fine mules"—was that farmers may have moved their best livestock to shelter.[6]

This Anglo-American country gentleman was quick to complain that the rural people of France were "gathered into villages . . . where they are less happy and less virtuous than they would be [if they were] insulated with their families on the ground they cultivate." As he was to do in every country he visited except England, he condemned women's and children's carrying heavy burdens and laboring with the hoe and plow: "This is an unequivocal indication of extreme poverty. Men, in a civilised country, never expose their wives and children to labour above their force or sex, as long as their own labor can protect them from it."[7]

The Yonne flows through a verdant countryside of vineyards and wheat fields interspersed with clumps of trees.[8] Entering the medieval gates of Auxerre, Jefferson visited its fine Gothic cathedral without enthusiasm. He may have been more interested in the nearby Hospice of the Knights Templar of Jerusalem, who had helped introduce hospitals to western Europe after the Crusades. On the road to Dijon he passed villages and half-timbered manors and admired newly planted wheat and occasional flocks of sheep on the rolling hillsides. The boredom of straight, long avenues of trees was only occasionally interrupted by sighting near the road a château, such as at Vermenton.[9]

Jefferson was fatigued by the time he passed over a deep moat and through a gauntlet of league-long walls to enter the city of Dijon, where the most important thing that he did was to hire Petitjean as his valet. He stayed three nights at the Hôtel de Condé, had a barber shave him, and bought boots, slippers, and an oilcloth poncho. He paid guides to show him the sights, especially the former palace of the dukes of Burgundy. He climbed to the top of its medieval tower to enjoy what Henry James later called the "tortured vistas" of the cityscape. Jefferson did not note that he visited the adjacent church of St. Beninge to see its fine tapestries and stained glass, but he usually followed such a customary route of tourists. It is probably just as well that he did not comment on the now-destroyed Sainte-Chapelle, whose holiest relic was three drops of blood said to have been gathered when Christ was subjected to flagellation by the Jews. In the eighteenth century the architects Mansart and Gabriel had rebuilt the ducal palace into what was called the king's house, even though it would have been more accurate to call it the provincial governor's. In the 1780s this was the official residence of the Prince de Condé whenever he presided over the provincial estates in their nearby assembly hall. The interiors of the king's house were considered very grand and well arranged. The principal unaltered room of the old Burgundian palace was its banqueting hall, whose colossal Gothic chimney piece and cavernous fireplace were needed to heat such a large, high chamber. Jefferson must have admired the way parts of the old palace had been adapted for use by academies of painting and music. He probably visited the Academy of Sciences, where there were busts of such of Dijon's worthies as the Comte de Buffon. Jefferson, an amateur city planner, gave only a general commendation to the semicircular Place Royal, probably because neither the streets nor the buildings elsewhere in the city had been improved similarly.

Jefferson turned south and reached the walled town of Beaune for a one-night stay at the Ecu de France, whose poor service and high prices provoked him to exclaim, uncharacteristically, "Cher Dieu!" He may have been appalled by the Romanesque porch and tower of Beaune's cathedral. Predictably, he was interested in the city's two *hôtels Dieu*, through which church and state ministered to the bastards, the needy, the old, the sick, and the widowed. But it was the celebrated vineyards near Beaune that most excited this oenophile. He hired an old peasant woman and two mules to make a circuit of the region's "most celebrated vineyards, going into the houses of the laborers, the cellars of the *vignerons*, and mixing and conversing with them as much as I could." After visiting the vineyards of Chambertin, Mersault, Montrachet, Nuits-Saint-Georges, Pommard, Romanée, Vosne, Volnay, and Vougeot, he recorded that red wines were made from vineyards where there was not too much gravel and that they not only were less prone to seasonal failures but also could "bear transportation" better than the whites. He noted that of the reds the Chambertin, Vougeot, and Vosne were the "strongest, and will bear transportation and keeping," while the best of the whites, Montrachet, fetched only one-eighth the price of the reds. As a religious skeptic, Jefferson doubtless would have agreed with the adage that in the wine country the sites monks chose for their monastic establishments "show what a righteous attention they give to things of the spirit." Judging from Jefferson's orders then and afterward from these famous vineyards, he concurred in the opinion that "the soil and the care given by the inhabitants" earned for them "the greatest reputation" in Burgundy.[10]

Beaune is a great depot of wines. It is a "drowsy town, . . . very old and ripe," whose crooked streets and steep roofs create oblique vistas. Its ancient Hôpital St. Esprit has high, pointed gables and a slate-covered spire containing chimes. Set in a windowless wall, its portal is shielded by a large hood with a star-spangled, blue ceiling.[11] Jefferson employed his innkeeper, M. Parent, to buy wine and grape slips to be delivered to the back door of the Hôtel Langeac, in order to avoid paying the toll levied by the City of Paris on goods passing through the internal customs post at the Grille de Chaillot en route to Jefferson's front door. Jefferson made careful observations of Burgundian methods of

> planting, pruning and sticking their vines . . . in gutters about 4 feet apart. As the vines advance, they lay them down. They put out new shoots, and fill all the intermediary space until all trace of order is lost. They have ultimately about one foot square to each vine. They begin to yield a good profit at five or six years old and last 100 or 150 years. A vigneron at Voulenay carried me into his vineyard, which was about 100 arpents. He told me that [in] some years it produced him [15,000 bottles of wine and in other years not more than 750 bottles]. The wine is better in quality and higher in price in proportion [when] less is made: and the expences at the same time diminish in the same proportion. . . . In very plentiful years they often give one half the wine for casks to contain the other half. A farmer of about 10 arpents has about three laborers engaged by the year. He pays 4 Louis to a man, and half as much to a woman, and feeds them. He kills one hog and salts it, which is all the meat used in the family during the year. Their ordinary food is bread and vegetables.

Jefferson took careful note of how the red, sandy soil along the eastern slopes of the Burgundian hills, called the Côte de Beaune, became increasingly gravelly as one ascended to the rocky little summits of this five-league-long site of superb vineyards. Never successful in his efforts to establish vineyards of consequence in Virginia, he may have hoped that the adage that if land is not ideal for grape culture, it is good for growing wheat, was true.[12]

Following the fast-flowing Saône River, which in this area was as large as the Seine at Paris, Jefferson passed quickly through Chagny, Chalonssur-Saône, and Sennecy, to spend the night at Tournus in the Hôtel du Palais

Royal. Jefferson delighted in Beaujolais's "fine plains of . . . dark rich loam," partly in meadow and partly in wheat. He compared the merits of the region's white cattle against those of Anglo-Virginian breeds. He was pleased to see that more of the region's peasants lived on farms than in villages and that roofs were sheathed in tile instead of thatch. At Mâcon, where the Rhône and the Saône almost girdle the town, Jefferson lodged at the Maison Blanche. Whereas many travelers here turned off the main road to inspect the monastery of Cluny, Jefferson, the oenophile, turned off to visit the Château de Laye Epinay and the vineyards of St. George de Renan. Since his carriage needed repair, he engaged riding horses for himself and his valet, Petitjean. It was to the Comtesse de Laye Epinay that he presented a letter of introduction from his friends the abbés Chalut and Arnoux, because her husband was, as usual, at Paris or Versailles. It was she, not her lord and master, who coped with the overseers of the fifteen-thousand-acre seigneury planted in vine, wheat, and wood. Hoping to learn here some of the charms of making wine in the manner of Mâcon, Jefferson was a guest at the château for three days. Madame de Laye entertained him "with a goodness and ease which was charming" even though she suffered from a severe cold and "a constant tempest" kept him indoors for the first day of his visit. His generous tips to the servants of the château and estate showed his satisfaction in having made leisurely inspections of the estate's diversified farm, vineyards, and cellars in order to learn the practical aspects of viticulture. He enthusiastically concluded: "This is the richest country I ever beheld." It was, he said,

79

> thick sown with farmhouses, châteaux and the [vacation houses] of the inhabitants of Lyon. The people live separately, not in villages. The hillsides are in vine and [wheat]: the plains in [wheat] and pasture. The lands are farmed either for money or on half-stocks. . . . When lands are rented on half [shares], the cattle, sheep &c. are furnished by the landlord. They are valued and must be left of equal value. The increase of these, as well as the produce of the farm, are divided equally. These leases are only from year to year. They have a method of mixing beautifully the culture of vines, trees and [wheat]. Rows of fruit trees are planted about 20 feet apart. Between the trees, in the row, they plant vines 4 feet apart and espalier them. The intervals are sowed alternately in [wheat], so as to be one year in [wheat,] the next in pasture. . . . The women do not work with the hoe; they only weed the vines, the [wheat], and spin. . . . The husbandry seems good, except they manure too little. This proceeds from the shortness of their leases. The people of Burgundy and Beaujolais are well clothed, and have the appearance of being well fed. But they experience all the oppressions which result from the nature of the general government, and from that of their particular tenures, and of the seignorial government to which they are subject. What a cruel reflection that a rich country cannot be a free one.

Besides its fine agricultural estate, the Château de Laye Epinay possessed at least one example of the fine arts that Jefferson coveted, "a *Diana and Endymion*, a very superior morsel of sculpture by Michael Angelo Slodtz, done in 1740."[13]

Jefferson arrived at Lyon on March 11, lodged at the Hôtel du Palais

Royal, and departed on the fifteenth. He hired a *valet de place*, called in a barber, and had some laundry done. At the bank of Messrs. Fingelin Cie. he drew on his letter of credit from his Paris banker, Ferdinand Grand. He bought for Petitjean a cloak and a cheap saddle so that the valet could ride as a second postilion instead of sitting inside the one-seated carriage with him. Jefferson so enjoyed the city's delights of "architecture, painting, sculpture and antiquities" that he did not visit any of its manufactories. Although he was disappointed to note that the city's Roman antiquities consisted of "feeble remains of an ampitheatre of 200 feet diameter and of an aqueduct in brick," he appreciated the beauty and utility of the city's main bridge, the Pont d'Ainay, which had nine arches of forty-foot spans. He justified his devoting time to sightseeing by saying that a knowledge of the factories and economy of Lyon would be "useless, and would exclude from the memory other things more worth retaining."[14]

At Lyon the Rhône possessed great "picturesque," or natural beauty, which mankind had enhanced by good bridges and quays. Perhaps bad weather prevented Jefferson's seeing from them the distant Mont Blanc. If he had been there four months later, he could not have forgone comment on how the Lyonnais warded off summer heat by *jets d'eau* and pleached trees. He did not remark upon the industriousness of Lyon's tradesmen.[15] The city's population of two hundred thousand was confined to the long, stiletto-shaped triangle between the Saône and Rhône. In the oldest section, the Quartier des Terreaux, "opulence and extreme misery lived side by side." Elsewhere, the city's streets were straight and narrow, bordered by large, tall, well-built houses that were often divided into one-floor flats that were either owned or leased. The newest section was about the Place Bellecour, where streets were wider and houses finer. At its center was a bronze equestrian statue of Louis XIV by the Lyonnais sculptor Lemot, flanked by figures representing the Saône and Rhône by Nicholas and Guillaume Coustou. The city's quay facing the Rhône, eight feet wide and a league long, was a favorite promenade. The quay on the Saône was alive with commerce and crowded with merchandise. One of Lyon's four bridges was a bridge of boats. Jefferson did not take time to study the way it functioned, as he did later in Italy and in the Rhineland.[16]

Ever since its construction by the architect Sufflot in 1756, the city's Comédie had been one of the principal sights of Lyon, even though it was architecturally inferior to the theaters at Nantes and Bordeaux. François de Liancourt wrote that its pit, balconies, and three tiers of loges presented a "refined and elegant" spectacle on Sundays and feast days. He was much impressed by the "magnificence" and "luxury" of Lyon's *beau monde*, remarking with aristocratic disbelief: "The wives of merchants and bankers surpass the most elegant ladies of Paris in conspicuous display." Since Jefferson, usually an inveterate theatergoer, left no record of attending Lyon's theater, it must have been closed when he was there. One wonders whether Jefferson understood about or condoned Lyon's "elderly wholesale merchants," who formed the governing class of officials called *échévins*. As an aristocrat, Liancourt was contemptuous of both the *échévins* and Lyon's partial autonomy, saying that its guards were too superannuated to prevent crime, and its judges too guilty of conflicts of interest and too fearful of the mercantile community to mete out justice, especially in enforcing laws against usury.[17]

Leaving Lyon on March 15, Jefferson passed through St. Fond and St. Syphorien before reaching Vienne, where he lodged at the Hôtel de la Poste. After "seeing things," he jotted down his anger at how "Barbarians" of the Middle Ages had "totally defaced" the so-called Praetorian Palace by transforming it into a church. Jefferson might have been less angry, if he had known, as do we, that the building had been built as the Temple of the God-Emperor Augustus and the Goddess-Empress Livia in 26 B.C. The city's Roman theater was hidden beneath the ruin and accumulation of centuries, but Jefferson did see "the sepulchral pyramid," south of the town, which once had been the *spina*, or turning point, for its circus in Roman days.[18] Traveling by way of Villalivre and the locks around the rapids of the Rhône, he observed that that river usually makes two terraces, which he explored happily, discovering in the neighborhood of Lyon more wheat than wine but toward the village of Tain more wine than wheat. Comparing the Rhône, with its "romantic, picturesque and pleasing air," with the larger Susquehanna River of Pennsylvania and Maryland, he remarked on how the former was sometimes a "huge torrent, rushing like an arrow between two high precipices often of massive rock," and at other times "subdued." Although the distant mountains were still covered with snow, he found the almond in bloom and the willow "putting out its leaf."

The intricacies of viticulture fascinated Jefferson. Near Tain he found that the eastern slopes of the Côte Rotie produced wine "of the first quality" called Hérmitage. It was a blend of grapes in a ratio of eight red for one white, which he noted "cannot be drunk under four years." Here in the Côte Rotie, day laborers fed themselves, and yearly workers received in addition to the same wages and food allowances as in Burgundy "plenty of cheese, eggs, potatoes, and other vegetables, and walnut oil with their salad." Although wheat fields and wheat laborers were engaged by the year, vineyards and their laborers were engaged for longer periods. The vineyard laborers planted vines between six and eight feet apart, sometimes in double rows two feet apart. Jefferson sketched the region's primitive three-piece, ox-, ass-, or mule-drawn plow, made of two crooked pieces of wood attached to either end of a beam bearing the plowshare. Because the roads between Lyon and St. Rambert were neither paved nor graveled, he was not able to travel as quickly as he had expected. He spent the night of the seventeenth at the Hôtel de la Poste at the village of Chez Revel before being ferried over the Rhône and the Isère to Valence, on the west bank, in order to spend the night at Montilimar in the Hôtel Royal. He hired a guide and made notes about the cultivation of almonds, which had been introduced in the sixteenth century from the Middle East, but he said nothing about Montilimar's famous nougat, made of almond paste and honey, since it was not the season for this specialty of the inhabitants of the Vivarais.[19] Pierrelattre was only a small walled village of about fifty souls when Jefferson changed horses at its *relais des chevaux*. Its environs today are dominated by a large atomic power plant.[20]

Recrossing the Rhône, Jefferson entered Orange. "Here begins the

The Theatre at Orange, from an old
French print.

country of olives!" he exclaimed. Although there was snow on the high hills, Jefferson did not encounter the chill wind known as the *vent de bize*. He found that although Orange had been incorporated into the kingdom of France for a century and a half, he had to pay customs duties upon entering and leaving its precincts. He grumbled over this internal customs duty, which was one of the things he and all good men of the Enlightenment placed high among what they saw as abuses that plagued France during the ancien régime. Although he paid without complaint more than he usually did to dine and see the sights, he was indignant that the city of Orange was using stones from its great second-century amphitheater—which, along with its Augustan triumphal Arch of Marius, was still emerging from its medieval cocoon—to pave a road. Liancourt said that even though Roman Orange had been only a military outpost, its thirty-six-meter-high theater was ten times larger than any in eighteenth-century Paris. Henry James later remarked that not only was the theater the biggest thing in Orange, it was "bigger than all of Orange put together."[21]

Of all the places that Jefferson visited in Europe, the one about which he is most frequently quoted is Nîmes. Actually, he made two visits there, between which he went to Italy and elsewhere in Provence. (Because Nîmes was especially significant to Jefferson, both his visits there are dealt with in chapter 9.)

Zig-zagging through the delta of the Rhône in order to cross its mouths most expeditiously, Jefferson passed through Tarascon, whose fifteenth-century, Bastille-like château guarded a bridge. Because of the season, he did not encounter the profusion of carts and wagons that Arthur Young did at the time of the great autumnal fair in nearby Beaucaire. Jefferson went on the great road between Provence and Languedoc to the town of St. Rémy-en-Provence so that he could inspect the nearby site of Roman Glanum. He lodged at the tavern Cheval Blanc and bought books about the local antiquities. Most of the ruined town was excavated later, but in the 1780s its two greatest monuments were visible and already known to Jefferson from pictures by Clérisseau and Robert: the A.D. 40 Municipal Arch and the Tomb of the Julii, with their garlands and almost life-size figures of warriors.[22]

On March 25 he recrossed the Rhône at Pont Royal to the east bank and drove through Orgon and St. Cannat to Aix. Writing to William Short, who forwarded mail there from Paris, he exclaimed: "I am now in the land of [wheat], wine, oil, and sunshine. What more can man ask of Heaven? If I should happen to die at Paris, I will beg of you to send me here, and have me exposed to the sun. I am sure it will bring me to life again." Because Aix had been since Roman times a thermal spa, Jefferson had made it one of his principal destinations, in hope that its mineral waters might restore strength to his injured wrist. Alas! In four days' time he took forty douches, "without any sensible benefit." Satisfied with his lodgings at the Hôtel St. Jacques, he praised the city as the "cleanest and neatest I have ever seen in any country."[23] People must have pointed out to him the house of Victor Riqueti, Marquis de Mirabeau, whose dissolute but eloquent son Honoré Gabriel Riqueti, Comte de Mirabeau, had been a political prisoner between 1775 and 1781 in the Château d'If at Marseilles and in the Château de Vincennes outside Paris. The father had been a physiocratic writer, and the son was soon to win enduring fame as the voice of the Revolution.[24] Jefferson delighted in the high-toned simplicity of Aix, where there were straight streets, fine town houses, and elm-shaded

83

Vue de la Ville de Beaucaire, engraving of a painting by Joseph Vernet (1714–89). Although the annual fair here attracted great crowds, the good roads and bridges were not crowded at other times.

Vue de Deux Monuments Antiques près de St. Rémy en Provence, 1777, painting by C. Lamy, engraved for sale at Paris and St. Rémy. This print was owned by Jefferson. The remains of Roman Glanum excited Jefferson.

promenades but "few assemblies, routs, and other occasions for the display of dress." He undoubtedly saw the various schools that now form the university. He went twice to the Comédie, where Madame de Pontheuil, "the most celebrated actress of Marseilles," tried to show in two minor dramas her superiority to "Madame Dugazon and some other of the celebrated ones of Paris" in action, beauty, ear, taste, voice, and youth.

Although Jefferson was in many ways a most practical man, looking to the utility of things, he was interested in the study of foreign languages more for their own sake and as a diversion than for practical use. He had studied Latin, Classical Greek, and Italian in Virginia, and John Paradise had taught him a little Modern Greek. He had picked up a smattering of German, although his 1788 journey to the Rhineland would show him how insufficient it was for his needs as a tourist. Jefferson's brief sojourn in Provence and Languedoc was a delight to him as a linguist and etymologist because it gave him an appreciation of Provençal not as a dialect of the French but as its parent. He perceived that if Latin was the original language, Tuscan was a degeneration in the first degree, Piedmontese in the second, Provençal in the third, and Parisian French in the fourth. Claiming that an understanding of Italian enabled him to understand Provençal, Jefferson remarked on the latter's "beauty," in which the ballads of the troubadours had delighted cultivated Europeans for centuries.[25]

Beginning on March 29, Jefferson spent a week in the Hôtel des Princes at Marseilles, where his health and sightseeing were subordinate to making a semiofficial investigation of trade in general and of the Italian rice trade in particular. Not satisfied by what he could learn about rice at Marseilles, he determined to press on through Piedmont-Sardinia to the banks of the Po River. He drew a sum of money from Monsieur Bréthous against Ferdinand Grand's letter of credit but did not record much about his stay, although he employed several local valets to guide him in an inspection of the port facilities and the commercial section of the metropolis. He called on two friends of the scholarly abbés: the merchant André Sasserno and Monsieur Bernard, the co-director of the Royal Observatory and a member of the

Academy of Marseilles. The latter was out of town, but Sasserno proved to be very helpful both by giving him a letter of credit more apt to be accepted by Italians than one on a Paris bank and by helping him make plans to smuggle unmilled rice out of Piedmont, where state policy concerning the method of cultivating and processing this staple was so carefully guarded that the penalty for its unauthorized exportation was death. The American also visited Philip Mazzei's friend Antonio Soria, "one of the most considerable merchants" of the city, and he saw Chastellux's friends Audibert and Bergasse, the latter of whom was an expert on shells. Jefferson was punctilious in acknowledging such introductions, which he said resulted in "good dinners and good company."[26]

Doubtless he would have agreed with the young Comte de Liancourt's praise of the newer part of Marseilles, compared with the city's older, "very dirty and very villainous" part, which was characterized by steep hills, narrow streets, and ill-built houses. Delighting in the eighteenth-century squares and fountains of Marseilles, Liancourt found the Cours a lovely, sanded promenade separated from the carriageway by an *allée* of elm trees and adorned at its center by the architect-sculptor Puget's Medusa Fountain. Undoubtedly Jefferson visited the Hôtel de Ville, on whose ground floor was located the Bourse, as the combined stock exchange and chamber of commerce was called. Puget had designed the Hôtel de Ville

L'Entrée du Port de Marseilles, ca. 1765, painting by Joseph Vernet (1714–89). Jefferson visited here twice and inspected the Château d'If, which guarded its outer harbor.

Façade of the Château Borély, drawing by
Charles Louis Clérisseau (1721–1820).
Located on the eastern periphery of
Marseilles, this was the residence designed
by Clérisseau that Jefferson knew best.

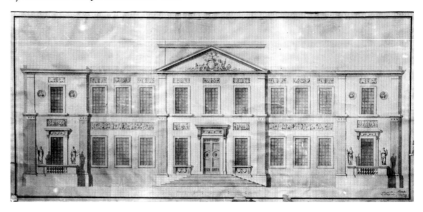

in 1673 and had himself executed the caryatides supporting a grand balcony that commanded a view so panoramic that Liancourt exclaimed: "All Marseilles is on its doorstep." Besides the port, one could see the Royal Marine Observatory, which also housed the Academy of Sciences, Belles-Lettres and Arts. Although Liancourt considered Marseilles less important and picturesque than Bordeaux, his description of it fills a lacuna in Jefferson's writings. The tortuous channel to the port of Marseilles rendered it safe from the greatest storms. About six hundred merchant vessels could use the harbor at the same time. Of its two quays, the one facing north was for unloading cargoes directly onto carts. At its western end was the square hulk of Fort Saint Nicholas, a citadel rebuilt in 1660 based on plans by Vauban. The rectangular quay facing to the east possessed double-purchase cranes to unload goods from ships to the ground. Because Marseilles's foreign trade was principally with the Levant, northern Africa, Spain, and the West Indies, its quayside was filled with heterogeneous throngs in exotic garb.[27]

Jefferson visited the Château d'If, that grim harbor fortress used as a political prison. En route he passed the Lazaret, or infirmary, where merchant mariners suspected of bearing contagious diseases were isolated while their vessels were inspected in the Quarantine, or outer harbor.[28] Jefferson was happy to escape from such uncongenial scenes to the nearby estate of Comte Borély, to which his friend Clérisseau probably had directed him, even though another architect had completed its neoclassical château utilizing some of Clérisseau's 1767 design. Borély's was the grandest of Marseilles's *bastides*, or summer homes. The younger Borély, although he was the son of an import-export merchant who had become an *échévin* at the age of fifty and a comte three years later, had left trade to become a collector of Italian pictures and Greek and Roman statuary. Then, as now, his château possessed magnificent vistas of land, sea, and all the ships entering or leaving the port of Marseilles. Perhaps thinking of Monticello's meager supply of water, Jefferson made a sketch of the windmill that worked the château's water pumps.[29]

Departing Marseilles, Jefferson traveled on powdery white roads and enjoyed the vineyards and groves of olives, oranges, and pomegranates of Provence on the way to the great naval base of Toulon. He spent two nights there, perhaps at the Croix de Malte, where young Liancourt and his tutor lodged in 1783. Liancourt had called on the commandant, who arranged for him a tour of armories, bakeries, barracks, basins, drydocks, forges, foundries, magazines and ropewalks. The young chevalier was spellbound by the *galériens*, as the French called the fettered, life convicts, some of whom were chained to their benches of galleys, while others worked as artificers on shore by day but were chained to their bunks at night. Although Jefferson was a diplomat of an allied country, he did not inspect the great, closely guarded dockyard or what Arthur Young termed a "completely secure and land-locked harbour."[30]

Following second-rate roads along the coast, Jefferson went to Hyères. Although it was to become the westernmost resort of the Riviera two centuries later, Hyères was then noted for growing oranges and refining salt from sea water caught in shallow ponds. Its wetlands supported an infinite variety of wild fowl. Jefferson breakfasted at the Hôtel St. Pierre before inspecting the king's and other orange groves. Although Hyères's location

Port d'Antibes, engraving of a painting by Joseph Vernet (1714–89). Jefferson paused at Antibes, the easternmost city on the French Riviera, after visits to Toulon and Hyères and before crossing into Sardinia-Piedmont.

at the foot of a high mountain usually assured protection from freezing north winds, the unusually severe winter storms of 1786 had nearly destroyed the trees. It was not the harvesting season for the fruit, so Jefferson neither agreed nor disagreed with Arthur Young's conclusion that Hyères was "praised much beyond its merit."

At Fréjus, Jefferson saw vestiges of another Roman city: an aqueduct, an amphitheater, an arena, a theater, and the so-called Lantern of Augustus. The lantern once had been a harbor beacon, but much to Jefferson's curiosity, centuries of erosion and silting had put several miles of grit between the town and the sea, thus isolating the stone pinnacle. Liancourt sourly reported that although the Romans had been able to bring a profusion of fresh water to Fréjus by aqueduct, in the 1780s the town possessed only one small fountain of sometimes salty water.[31] The next leg of Jefferson's journey took him inland by way of Cuers and Pignon to St. Luc, where the need for carriage repair required him to spend the night at the Hôtel de Sainte Anne. The following day he made good time through five villages before again reaching the coast, at Antibes, where he spent the night of April 10. Antibes was then a fortified frontier town whose small port was protected from storms by a mole. Jefferson's expenditure for "seeing" could not have been for a tour of the menacing Fort Carrée; it could only have been for a guide to vantage points from which to enjoy the glorious seascape of Cap d'Antibes and the tender night luminescence of the Côte d'Azur. From Antibes Jefferson crossed the Var River, France's border with the king of Sardinia's province of Piedmont, on April 10, 1787, and proceeded to Nice and northern Italy.[32]

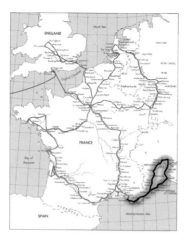

7 Northern Italy

THOMAS JEFFERSON'S HURRIED JOURNEY ALONG THE FRENCH AND Italian Riviera and through northern Italy between April 10 and May 2, 1787, so strained his constitution that after his official correspondence was done, he was able to write few detailed letters or notes in his account book about what he had seen. He wrote Maria Cosway that his had been only "a peep . . . into Elysium."[1] Of no place that he visited in Europe was it more true than of Italy that he relied on printed books to remind him of the country's buildings and works of art. He was already familiar with Joseph Addison's *Remarks on Several Parts of Italy*; and his newly purchased copies of the *Guide pour le voyage d'Italie en poste*, Bianconi's *Nouva guida di Milano*, and Brusco's *Beautés de Gènes*, would refresh him later concerning Italy's monuments, paintings, and sculpture, as well as agricultural and utilitarian matters.[2]

Emphasizing his private, unofficial status, Jefferson admitted his rank in Italy.[3] Although he was predisposed in favor of an excursion thither, his decision to go came only after he was sure that he could not obtain at Marseilles as much information as he desired about Italian rice,[4] and even then he went for the briefest period possible. Jefferson left Marseilles and proceeded overland to the Piedmontese port of Nice, where he made plans to cross the Maritime Alps through the Tende Pass to Cuneo and descend the plain of the Po as far as the rice fields in the great triangle between Vercelli, Milan, and Pavia.[5] At Nice, Baron Le Clerc, the banker to whom Ferdinand Grand had referred Jefferson, gave him a letter of reference to the banking firm of Ricard Bramerel at Genoa to help in case of an emergency.[6] Jefferson had not sought letters of introduction from the Sardinian ambassador to the court of Versailles, the Conte de Scarnafis, an unrelenting advocate of absolutism who had been haughty in transmitting his government's refusal to enter into a commercial treaty,[7] but the philosophical abbés Arnoux and Chalut and his one-time Albemarle neighbor Philip Mazzei had provided letters of introduction to some Italian scholars.[8] Still another well-wisher who provided entrée was a Milanese gentleman named Gaudenzio Clerici, who urged the American minister leisurely to enjoy "the serenity and mildness" of climate that made Italy the "Garden of Europe." It is not clear whether the two men had first met in America, where the Italian claimed friendship with David Ramsay, the South Carolina botanist and historian. Jefferson probably visited Clerici at Milan and certainly sent to his door a number of Americans on their grand tour.[9]

When Jefferson crossed the Var River from France into the kingdom of Sardinia on April 10, 1787, he had been absent from Paris for six weeks.[10] Refreshing himself at Nice, he lodged at the Hôtel de York, employed a man named Dominique as *valet de place*, visited the royal botanical garden, and called upon some of those to whom he carried letters of introduction. The rather strait-laced Virginian lamented that Nicoise society was "gay and dissipated," but he may have told himself that such was the natural consequence of absolutism in the kingdom of Sardinia. Perhaps he recalled Addison's verse contrasting the "smiles of nature and the charms of art" with Sardinia's oppressive and tyrannical rule, which beggared its subjects.[11]

When he learned that the snow in the Maritime Alps was too deep to allow the transit of vehicles, Jefferson left his own carriage at Nice. He bought some oranges and a portmanteau before engaging mules and muleteers to convey him and his valet ninety-three miles through the Tende Pass. The road through the pass was considered an engineering marvel; by its *lacets*, or hairpin curves, one ascended the 4,230-foot-high Col de Braus.[12] Jefferson told Maria Cosway that in good weather "you may go in your chariot in full trot from Nice to Turin, as if there were no mountain." Just as in France, there was a royal system of relays whose postilions drove teams of horses from one way station, or post, to the next, about twelve miles distant. He noted, and probably ate as a local delicacy, the speckled trout of the Roya River below the great Gorge of Saorgo. There he described to Mrs. Cosway what he declared was the "most singular and picturesque" sight he had ever seen: "The castle and village seem hanging to a cloud. . . . On the right is a mountain cloven through to let pass a gurgling stream; on the left a river over which is thrown a magnificent bridge. The whole form a basin, the sides of which are shagged with rocks, olive trees, vines, herds, etc." He insisted that she should paint it.[13] Forty years later there was among Mrs. Cosway's art collection just such a painting.[14]

Once Jefferson crossed the pass to Limone di Piemonte he could see the plain of the Po. He exchanged his mules and muleteers for a two-horse carriage with a postilion and a cock, or extra, horse before spending the night and breakfasting in the Croce Bianca Inn at Cuneo. He remarked neither on the inn's lack of window shutters nor on its dreadful privy. During the four changes of post horses between Cuneo and Turin, he jotted down impressions of the rich agricultural lands through which he traveled. He

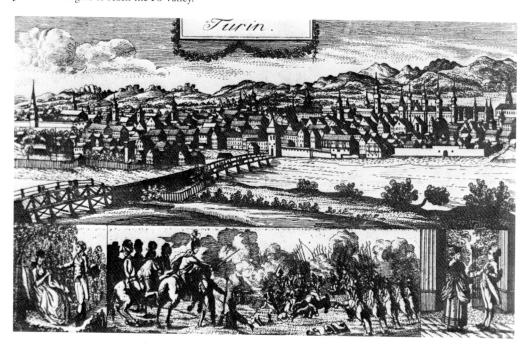

La Cittadelle di Torino nell' assiedo Austro-Russo del giunno 1799, ca. 1799, engraving by Antonio Maria Stagnon. After crossing the Maritime Alps amid melting snows, Jefferson was glad to reach the Po Valley.

lunched at Racconigi, the site of the palazzo of the Carignano branch of the House of Savoy, whose park and gardens have been attributed to Louis XIV's landscape architect, André Le Nôtre. Although the edifice is separated from the village by only a wrought-iron grille, Jefferson did not record entering either the grounds or the palazzo, famous for its soaring rococo hall. Nearby the Po was about fifty yards wide where he crossed it on a wooden roadway resting on "swinging batteaux" moored to the riverbank by cables and supported at their midsection by canoes. Although Jefferson was a collector of Indian artifacts and a recorder of Indian languages and customs, he did not remark that these canoes were dugouts like those of the North American Indians.[15]

Jefferson arrived at Turin in the late afternoon of April 16 and took lodgings at the Hôtel d'Angleterre for a four-night stay before getting money from Messieurs Tollot *et fils* on his letter of credit from Le Clerc's bank at Nice. He undoubtedly approved of Turin's straight, broad streets, inherited from Roman days and now lined by brick houses, but he did not comment on the Villa Madama, which some thought equal to the Hall of Mirrors at Versailles.[16] Jefferson followed the local custom in joining at common table about a dozen persons for a *table d'hôte* dinner. The American epicure commented that the local "red wine of Nebiule," similar to the present-day Fraisi, was "pleasing." He noted, "It is about as sweet as the silky Madeira, as astringent on the palate as Bordeaux, and as brisk as Champagne." He also noted favorably the "thick and strong" red wine of Monferrato, similar to today's Dolcetti.[17]

After Jefferson determined that he could not obtain at Turin detailed information about rice, he felt free to devote several days to the history and fine arts of Piedmont, which Maria Cosway, who was familiar with them from a brief residence there, probably had told him about. On the first and second nights of his visit he attended comedies, presumably at the theater of the Duca di Carignano. He bought some maps and the guidebooks *Italie en poste* and Carlo Bianconi's *Nuova guida di Milano.* In seeing the sights of Turin, it was conventional to devote a morning to the Palazzo Reale, the Duomo, the royal chapel of the Santissima Sindone, and the church of San Lorenzo.[18] The first of these may have pleased him because both its buildings and its pictures were relatively modest. Among the pictures were Van Dykes and at least one each by Carlo Cignani, Gerard Dow, Sassia Ferrata after Raphael, Guido Reni, and Lorenzo Sabbatini.[19] If he had been more interested in churches and palaces, he might have agreed with the New Englander Theodore Dwight that the city's early-eighteenth-century palazzi and churches were remarkable only for the "barbarisms of their cupolas,"[20] or even with the Irish Jesuit priest John Chetwoode Eustace, who condemned the architects, Guarino Guarini and Filippo Juvara, for preferring "twisted, tortured curves and angles" to the "unbroken lines and simple forms of antiquity." Even if he did not commend any of Turin's churches, hospitals, palaces, or theaters, Jefferson did not inveigh against them for "glare, glitter and confusion," as did at least one extreme neoclassicist.[21]

At Turin Jefferson probably presented his letter of introduction to the Abbé Deleuze, a member of Turin's academy and a professor at the university.[22] The academicians enjoyed good repute, and the students were "considered as part of the court and admitted to all its balls and amusements." The university was housed in a large structure of two stories built about an arcaded court. It boasted a library of more than fifty thousand volumes, a museum noted for its collection of statues and antiquities, a well-appointed hall of anatomy, and an astronomical observatory. Furthermore, the university was endowed for twenty-four professors, all of whom gave daily lectures.[23] Jefferson could not have failed to envy despot-ridden Piedmont's possession of cultural facilities that he had recommended for Virginia but that virtuous commonwealth refused to support. News of his presence made him a momentary object of curiosity. Among the savants, the word spread quickly that "Monsr. de Jefferson was . . . philosofizing" there.[24] From what these learned men had to say, Jefferson may have hoped to reconcile the condemnation of Piedmont by Louis XIV's minister d'Argenson as a state hopelessly "enmeshed in bureaucratic red tape" with the fact that it enjoyed a uniform system of taxation and abolition of manorial dues.[25] He found time to inspect the nearby sites of interest.

Jefferson engaged a carriage to visit the basilica church of Superga and the royal palazzi of Moncalieri and Stupinigi. The mountain of Superga is a more compelling sight from the banks of the Po than that of Monticello from the Rivanna, but the view from both summits reveals rolling plains to

the east and high mountains to the north and west. Since it was Jefferson who popularized the name Piedmont as an American geographic term, it is clear that he perceived the similarity of terrain. The basilica was built both to commemorate Piedmont's success in breaking the French siege of 1706 and to serve as a royal mausoleum. A monument best seen from afar, its scale, classical portico, curved surfaces, forest of pillars, and carved reredoses are very grand. It was not the season for the court to reside at Moncalieri when Jefferson visited its Palazzo Reale, located on the southern slope of the mountain. Its reddish, rectangular complex with round corner towers had been rebuilt often without altering its fortresslike character. Then mainly the residence of lesser members of the house of Savoy and retired courtiers, the palazzo was tangible evidence of how force and privilege undergirded monarchical institutions. Of the Superga, Jefferson recorded only his irritation that his postilions raced their six-horse carriages down the precipitous road "to prove the brilliance of themselves and of their steeds."[26]

Almost ten miles from Turin was the Palazzina di Caccia at Stupinigi. Its first and greatest architect was Filippo Juvara, whose initial concept of a hunting lodge, in which only the king, a few courtiers, and several servants would sleep, had been lost in thirty years of additions and rebuilding. When Jefferson visited Stupinigi, the palazzina had become a palazzo, swollen to accommodate the prolific royal family and its entourage. The *salone centrale*

Veduta di Stupinigi, ca. 1780, engraving by
Ignazio Scolpius del Borgo. By the time
Jefferson visited, this royal residence
outside Turin had grown from an intimate
hunting lodge to a sprawling palace.

was a stage for sumptuous entertainment located at the junction of four
wings, two of which were devoted to royal apartments and two to banqueting halls. This great room had been raised from two to three stories; on the
ceiling was a fresco of Diana departing at dawn for the chase, and on the roof
was a huge statue of a stag. Sacheverell Sitwell has said that this room is "one
of the most successful of baroque interiors," but Richard Pommer, in his
authoritative work on Piedmontese architecture, makes it clear that however fine Stupinigi was to begin with, this room and the building of which
it is a part have been grievously afflicted by giganticism.[27]

Jefferson left no memorandum of having inspected any of Turin's nine
"hospitals," which, under the auspices of church and state, provided "provisions and employment to the poor, education to the orphans, a dowry to
unmarried girls, and an asylum to the sick and decayed."[28] He did not repeat
Addison's description of how the Turinese diverted water from the Po to
flush out the gutters of major streets and to provide protection against fire.[29]

On April 19, Jefferson's postchaise brought him to the Albergo di Tre
Re at Vercelli, the rice-market town. There he made clandestine arrangements to see with his own eyes how rough rice was husked and to smuggle
some seed rice out of the country on his own person. This was a daring
exploit, since Sardinian law prescribed death as the penalty for the unauthorized export of seed rice. Ultimately, Jefferson deduced that because the
Italian milling process differed little from that employed in South Carolina,

there was a varietal difference in the rice of the two localities. Regardless of which was the better, the South Carolinians to whom he sent Italian seed rice preferred their own.

After passing through customs and crossing the Agogna River, Jefferson hastened through Novara to Milan, where he lodged at the Albergo Reale.[30] The Conte Francesco dal Verme proved to be a hospitable friend, directing him to whatever merited most attention in the Lombard capital during a visit of three nights and two days.[31] An acquaintance of Franklin and Adams who had visited the United States in 1783–84, Dal Verme was a good cicerone, to whom Jefferson subsequently sent a gift of books that included *Notes on the State of Virginia*. In the next several years Jefferson directed to him several Americans on their grand tour. Undoubtedly Jefferson and his new-found friend discussed the controversial reforms decreed by the Hapsburg Emperor Joseph II in the duchy of Milan. They shared scientific interests as well as a fondness for gadgets, such as a pendulum odometer for carriages. Remarking on his envy of the Marquis de Chastellux's visit to Monticello, the Italian exclaimed that he would like to be transported thither in a balloon.[32] Jefferson's visit to Milan was so brief that he could not accept, as William Short did eighteen months later, the invitation of Conte Luigi di Castiglioni to inspect his villa, about a dozen miles from the city on the way to the Italian lakes. From Short's account, his patron would have enjoyed such an excursion not only for the beauties of the landscape but also because the Castiglioni were "zealous botanist[s] . . . as much attached to American plants & trees as . . . to Americans."[33]

Years later, Stendhal observed that the Milanesi believed that the "true patent of nobility" was to build a fine palazzo. Certainly, Jefferson would have agreed with his observation that new "social requirements" so outmoded interior arrangements of palazzi built in the sixteenth century by Palladio and his school that the chief features of older Italian residences worth preserving was their "lofty" and "salubrious bedrooms."[34] Jefferson singled out two Milanese town houses as noteworthy: the Casa Candiani and the Casa Belgiojoso. Although he stated that he preferred the first of these, the recent work by the architect Appiani, it was the Casa Belgiojoso that he described. The architect Martin had built it in the mid-eighteenth century on the Via Moroni, a block north of the Piazza della Scala. Especially pleasing to Jefferson was its small cabinet, whose ceiling was painted *en grisaille* to represent hexagons and classic busts, and its salon, whose walls and floor were sheathed in scagliola. Jefferson was fascinated by scagliola, in which marble dust of various colors was reconstituted into a stonelike veneer that was "scarcely distinguishable from the finest marbles."[35] It is remarkable that Jefferson did not mention the splendid Palazzo Clerici, in the same neighborhood, which had been built in the first half of the eighteenth century. With fine furnishings, it possessed a large fresco by Giovanni Battista Tiepolo depicting how the chariot of the sun, driven by Mercury, illumines the world. Jefferson attended the comedy once, but he made no mention of going to Giuseppe Piermarini's 1778 La Scala opera house, one of the largest and handsomest in Europe, with six tiers of thirty-six boxes and sofas in the pit.[36]

Northern Italy

Almost surely Jefferson visited the Palazzo di Scienze, Lettere, e Arti. This was a former Jesuit college that the Emperor Joseph II had secularized and expanded to accommodate a student body of twelve hundred. Built by Francesco Maria Richini in the sixteenth century, it was a typical northern Italian collegiate complex built around a courtyard and enclosed by two stories of arcaded loggias. Its great picture gallery, the Brera, did not exist then, but its smaller and less notable collection of paintings and sculpture gave Jefferson "much amusement."[37] Alerted by Addison's *Remarks on Italy* that the Biblioteca Ambrosiana had spent "more money on pictures than on books,"[38] Jefferson may have seen its paintings as well as its collection of manuscripts and drawings by Leonardo da Vinci, whom he esteemed enough to purchase later a copy of his *St. John*. It is possible that Jefferson's admiration of Jesus Christ, as distinct from sectarian religion, might have led him to the refectory of the former Dominican convent attached to the suburban church of Santa Maria delle Grazie to see Leonardo's *Last Supper*,[39] but he never said so. Despite his anticlerical predilections, Jefferson could not ignore the Duomo of Milan. Addison had written that it was "not half-finished, and the inside is so smutted with dust and the smoke of lamps, that neither the marble, nor the silver, nor brass-work show themselves to advantage."[40] We can be sure that Jefferson climbed to its roof in order to perceive the cityscape. Jefferson was far from complaining that the enlightened despot Joseph II had curtailed construction of the Duomo. The author of the Virginia Statute for Religious Freedom left no doubt of his low opinion of the Duomo in particular and of Italian churches in general: "The Cathedral of Milan [is] a worthy object of philosophical contemplation, to be placed among the rarest instances of the misuse of money. On viewing the churches of Italy, it is evident without calculation that the same expense would have sufficed to throw the Apennines into the Adriatic and thereby render it terra firma from Leghorn to Constantinople."[41]

When the Ospedale Maggiore of Milan loomed before him, Jefferson presumably relied upon his guidebook to satisfy his longstanding interest in prisons and hospitals. Since the fifteenth century, the Ospedale's series of rectangular courts had housed the medical, nursing, and other social services of the duchy. Its buildings combined Gothic and Renaissance architectural features. Sometimes referred to as Milan's Ca' Grande, the complex had three hundred rooms for the ill in its lazaretto or wards, plus other rooms for twelve hundred working convalescents. Although its rooms were airy and clean, the huge structure was surrounded by a stream whose convenience for sewage purposes must also have induced fevers that periodically reduced the number of inmates. As a classicist, Jefferson probably visited the Basilica di San Lorenzo Maggiore, the site of the city's major classic remains, sixteen marble Corinthian columns that in the third century A.D. had led to the baths of Roman Mediolanum.[42]

Jefferson resisted the temptation to travel more widely in Italy before returning to France through Genoa. He wrote to Maria Cosway: "I took a peep only into Elysium. I entered it at one door, and came out at another. . . . I calculated the hours it would have taken to carry me on to Rome. But they were exactly so many more than I could spare. Was not this provoking? In thirty hours from Milan I could have been at [Venice]."[43] Nor did Jefferson go to Vicenza to observe firsthand any of the buildings of Palladio, whose published elevations, sections, and plans he had so admired before coming to Europe. Although he was truthful in saying that he did not have time enough to go to Vicenza, one cannot ignore that Clérisseau's low opinion of Palladio's work must have led Jefferson to consider it as a less than imperative object of sightseeing. Nor did he find encouragement in the example of Joseph Addison, who had gone to Verona, Padua, and Venice but not to Vicenza.

Jefferson turned south when he left Milan after breakfast on April 23. After leaving the city, he followed the usual tourist custom of observing the local manufacture of cheese.[44] He broke his journey to visit the former Carthusian monastery, the Certosa, about five miles north of Pavia. Although Pavia was not the "metropolis of a kingdom," it was no longer the "poor town" that Addison had visited some seventy years before. He had remarked on its seven "very large and neatly built" colleges, one of which was named for Borromeo, and on the fact that natives misidentified its statue of Marcus Antonius as being of either Constantine or Charles V. Jefferson made no comment on the Certosa's Lombard Romanesque architecture or on its recent disestablishment by Joseph II, who had diverted much of its former income to support expansion of the hospitals and educational institutions of Milan and Pavia. Jefferson lodged at the Albergo Croce Bianco, famous as Pavia's best hostelry for more than a century. He employed a local guide to show him the botanical gardens, the city, and the university. He may even have taken a turn about the university's "noble library, grand halls for lectures, anatomical galleries, . . . and several well-endowed colleges."[45] If he did not already know it, he must have learned that since the fourteenth century this university had produced great scholars, such as Pietro di Pavia, the early master of the University of Paris, and Jefferson's contemporary, the scientist Alessandro Volta.

From Pavia, Jefferson traveled south toward Genoa, spending the night of the twenty-fourth at Novi in the Hôtel de la Poste and dining at Campomorone in an inn whose doubled-up name, A La Rosa A Rosa, must have tickled his fancy. Discharging his old equipage and employing a new one, the weary traveler drove into Genoa, which was said to have been sited by Janus to face toward both Italy and France. Dissatisfied with his initial lodgings at the Sante Marthe Inn, he moved to the French-style Hôtel du Cerf, where he engaged a room overlooking the Mediterranean and feasted on a dozen tiny game birds called ortolans. During three days in Genoa he spent freely on sightseeing and transportation, undoubtedly using Addison's *Remarks on Italy* as a guidebook, because he recommended it to Americans traveling there.[46] Addison claimed that the only thing that Genoa had to show of antiquities was a bull-headed iron rostrum of a Roman ship at its arsenal. Declaring that the republic of Genoa was very poor, although some of its citizens were very rich, the Englishman had asserted that the city made "the noblest show" in the world, because of the "splendor and magnificence" of its great private palazzi. Most of the thickly clustered houses were painted on the outside and gave a "gay and lively" appearance, besides being considered "the highest in Europe." Everyone seems to have considered the Palaz-

Il palazzo del Principe [Doria Pamphili] at Fassolo. Jefferson admired the gardens of this palace outside the city of Genoa.

zo Durazzo the finest inside the city and the Palazzo Doria the best outside its walls. Neither was guilty of being so overdecorated, as some were, that their walls were "covered with painted columns of different orders" of architecture. Jefferson visited both of these famous palazzi and one other in Genoa's suburbs.[47]

The first of these "lofty palaces" was the Palazzo Marcello Durazzo, then owned by the Marchese Jean Luc Durazzo, to whom Jefferson carried a letter of introduction from Christoforo Vicenzo di Spinola, the minister of the republic of Genoa resident at the court of Versailles.[48] Located on the uphill side of the Via Balbi, this palazzo was mistakenly thought to have been built in the late sixteenth century by the architect Galeazzo Alessi, reputedly a student of Michelangelo's and a contemporary of Palladio. In fact it was mostly the work of Bartolomeo Bianci, and it was much improved by the addition of Andrea Taglifici's eighteenth-century façade, vestibule, and double stairway. Jefferson urged all Americans who visited Italy to go thither. He had no need to write memoranda of the Palazzo Durazzo, since his guidebook, Brusco's *Beautés de Gènes*, devoted five pages to its paintings and contained an illustration of its street façade. According to Brusco, its frescos were in the Bolognese style of Jacques Bena, Simone da Pesaro, and Domenico Piola. Of its collection of paintings, Brusco listed works by such famous artists as Caravaggio, Agostino and Annibale Carracci, Guido Reni, Rubens, Titian, Van Dyke, and Veronese. Remarkably for that day, this guidebook distinguished between originals and those that were copies or "of the school of" a famous artist. Among the family portraits were several by Hyacinthe Rigaud, who had painted Louis XIV and the young Louis XV. Jefferson may have visited the Marchese di Spinola's palazzo and possibly those of other members of his family, who had been patrons of Peter Paul Rubens. The Genoese diplomat's palace was called the Palazzo Alla Catena. Not so splendid as the Palazzo Marcello Durazzo, it nonetheless boasted three works by Guido Reni and one by Correggio among about a dozen important paintings.

As a man who not only provided his own house with many windows but amplified them by skylights, Jefferson may have passed quickly by the striped, Gothic cathedral church of San Lorenzo, which his guidebook told him was "badly lighted."[49] A resolute anticlerical, he probably thought that the churches of Genoa were guilty of too much ornament and glare and too little simplicity.[50] As Fiske Kimball put it, the "free and florid art" of Milan and Genoa awoke in Jefferson no "spiritual affinity."[51]

The Palazzo Doria Pamphili still glistens whitely on the western verge of Genoa. In Jefferson's day it was called the Palazzo Doria Principe. Whether or not Jefferson had met in Paris Monsignor Giuseppi Doria Pamphili, who had served as papal nuncio at Versailles since the early 1760s,[52] his failure to mention this "earliest" and "most familiar" of the "great" palazzi of the city fits his usual pattern of relying on guidebooks for information about well-known curiosities. In the 1530s Admiral Andrea Doria had employed the artist and architect Perino del Vaga to create this palace in Genoa's western seaside suburb of Fassolo. It had an impressive Renaissance portal on its north side and a capacious courtyard facing south before a long, arcaded façade. The one-time governor of the Commonwealth of Virginia must have smiled if he read the inscription "Deliverer of the Commonwealth" on Doria's statue.[53] The palazzo's five-bayed Doric loggia was decorated with heroic murals of Doria's ancestors, and its ceilings, with Roman gods and republican heroes. Nautical themes were invoked in the villa's great hall, courtyards, and gardens by Taddeo Carlone's Neptune, Marcello Sparzio's Jupiter, and statues of Tritons.

On the north side was a terraced hillside, on the south a courtyard and Renaissance gardens with geometric beds and clipped shrubbery. Although English travelers at the end of the seventeenth century had admired the villa's gardens, Jefferson in 1786 probably did not. Because he already had experienced a profusion of exotic plantings in a dramatic setting, he was not prepared to mistake these for "a second Paradise," in spite of its "cypress, myrtles, lentiscuses, . . . orange trees, citrons, and pomegranates, fountains, grots, and statues." Preferring romantic, English-style gardens, Jefferson undoubtedly considered the Palazzo Doria's parterres and geometric forms too old-fashioned. Furthermore, in Brusco's *Beautés de Gènes* a full-page illustration emphasized the palazzo's old-fashioned forecourt and crenelated, bastionlike walls along the sea.[54]

At Genoa the American minister took pleasure in consulting about mantlepieces for future delivery to Virginia with the marble cutter Antonio Capellano, whose establishment was situated on the waterfront near the Ponte della Legne. When William Short visited the city two years later, he got Capellano's prices for carving several different "chimney pieces" for which Jefferson supplied sketches.[55] Jefferson indulged his horticultural interests by visiting the excellent gardens of the Conte Durazzo at Nervi, to the east of Genoa, and of the Principe Lomellino at Sestri, to the west. Subsequently, he advised American travelers to visit the former because it possessed a vegetable garden surpassed only by Woburn Farm in Surrey, England. The flower gardens of the Principe Lomellino, he exclaimed, were the "finest I ever saw out of England."

How to return to Nice, where he had left his own carriage, presented a problem for Jefferson. Because there was no continuous road from Genoa to Nice, he embarked in a little ship on April 28, 1787, even though he was not a good sailor. Hardly out of the harbor, she was beset by the *libeccio*, a fierce southwesterly wind, of which he should have had ample warning from Addison's *Remarks on Italy* and Brusco's guidebook. The Gulf of Genoa was put into so nasty a chop that not only did he become "mortally sick"[56] but the captain thought that conditions were serious enough to put into the little fishing port of Noli, forty miles west of Genoa. Ironically, there was a good road from Genoa as far as, but no further than, Noli. With mixed emotions, Jefferson paid off the captain. Abandoning hope of a comfortable voyage on a placid sea, Jefferson decided to go on by land, "clambering [up] the cliffs of the Apennine[s], sometimes on foot, sometimes on a mule according as the path was more or less difficult." Two nights of miserable inns at Albenga and Oneglia and two days of alternating between narrow pockets of coastal plain and desolate mountains would have depressed even a traveler as determined as Jefferson. Finally, on April 30, Jefferson reached

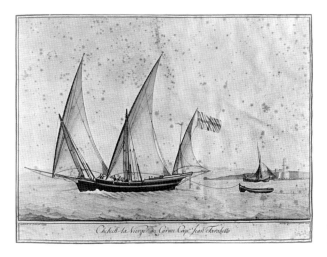

Chebek la Vierge da Carmine, Capn. Jean Tarabotto, ca. 1798, Civic Naval Museum at Pegli, Italy. The ship in which Jefferson sailed on the Gulf of Genoa may have resembled this one.

San Remo, where he lodged at the Auberge de la Poste. Although Addison had said it was "a very pretty town," Jefferson was too exhausted to comment. The next day, May 1, he breakfasted on oranges at Menton and reached Nice, and he crossed the Var River into France on May 2. The reason there were then no coastal roads on the Italian Riviera was because the kingdom of Sardinia believed that it enjoyed military security by not building roads that France could use as an invasion route. Consequently, there were only *corniches*, or mountain pathways capable of accommodating only mule and pedestrian traffic. Jefferson presciently opined that someday there would be a fine road "along the margin of the sea," creating "one continued village," by which "travelers would enter Italy without crossing the Alps."[57]

Jefferson, the lover of art and architecture, wrote little about what he saw in northern Italy. His guidebooks and pocket account book, more than correspondence or notes, were his chief resource about the "worthy" buildings and collections of paintings that, as he wrote La Fayette, he always visited.[58] Much of what he saw differed little from what he already had seen in France, what he had discussed with his intimates at Paris, or what he had learned from books. Except for the marble mantlepieces that he got for Monticello, what he saw in northern Italy merely reinforced his conclusion that it was not Palladio but modern architects like Clérisseau who should provide the inspiration and models for the future.

Central and southern Italy influenced Jefferson even less. He considered going thither with his friend Baron de Geismar,[59] and he advised young Americans, especially the three young men he called his triumvirate—John Rutledge, Jr., of South Carolina, Thomas Lee Shippen of Pennsylvania, and his adoptive son, William Short—to travel throughout Italy. When the three did go there, Jefferson gained instruction as well as pleasure from their letters. He commissioned Short to get marble for Monticello's fireplaces at Genoa,[60] to buy a pasta mold for making macaroni and spaghetti at Naples, and to save notations of travel accommodations for his own subsequent use.[61] Perhaps the most important contribution that any of this triumvirate made to Jefferson's understanding of the fine arts came from Short, who helped restore his belief that Americans could profit from the study and acquisition of works of art and who allayed his fear that "Painting [and] Statuary [might be] too expensive for the state of wealth among us." Jefferson and Short came to agree that their appreciation of architecture kept under control "what might otherwise become a passion. . . , a love of pictures and statues."[62]

Jefferson popularized for American usage the geographical term "piedmont." Despite his annotated derivation from Palladio of many details of Monticello,[63] Jefferson saw that residence not so much with his Italian eyes as with his French eyes. While Jefferson's neoclassical credo was based on an amalgam of all that he had read and seen, he had seen more of French models than of Italian models. While it is true that Jefferson gave the word *piazza* familiarity among Americans,[64] there are too many prototypes for the piazzas with which he terminated the wings of Monticello to claim special kinship for any Italian structure. That the palazzi of Genoa used hillside basements merely reenforced his existing plans to locate Monticello's housekeeping rooms there. He had commenced to build Monticello in an academic, scaled-down Palladian manner, but he ended up with an inventive, individualistic structure more in Clérisseau's modern, Louis XVI style. The kinship of the University of Virginia's Rotunda with the Pantheon at Rome and Palladio's church at Maser is a matter of familiar comment, but only the Rotunda possesses oval rooms, so characteristic of the Louis XVI style. If the universities of Turin, Milan, and Pavia had any architectural influence on Jefferson's plans for the University of Virginia, it was not lasting. His first design for the school did call for a large square *cortile*, or courtyard, surrounded by arches on piers and punctuated by pavilions, suggesting the courtyards of universities in northern Italy, France, and England. In any case, Jefferson's final plan for his university discarded the *cortile* for a more original, elongated U-shape, for which the plan of the French king's retreat of Marly may have been a model.[65]

Jefferson neither went to Rome to improve his concept of what was chaste and correct nor to Vicenza to see a building designed by Andrea Palladio. He gained his only firsthand knowledge of Italy in the Piedmontese provinces of the kingdom of Sardinia, the Austrian duchy of Milan, and the republic of Genoa. At his own mountaintop villa, Monticello, Jefferson planted a few of the Lombardy poplars that the Italians cherished as the tree of liberty, and at Washington he later caused double rows of them to be set between the president's house and the capitol.[66] From the *piano nobile* of a Franco-Italian Monticello, Jefferson could look past paintings and statuary through arcaded piazzas and columned porticoes upon scenes that, if they were not Elysian, were at least an arcadian Piedmont and recall that Piedmont was halfway between Venice and Paris.

8 Nîmes and Clérisseau

MOST ADMIRERS OF JEFFERSON KNOW THAT THE ROMAN TEMPLE at Nîmes called the Maison Carrée served as the prototype for Virginia's capitol, but many do not know that Jefferson and the French artist-architect Charles Louis Clérisseau chose this prototype and completed their plan for the capitol *before* Jefferson went to Nîmes or wrote that he gazed at the old temple in the moonlight, as a lover might gaze at his mistress.[1] Of all the buildings that Jefferson saw in Europe, the Maison Carrée evoked his highest praise for its "dignity" and "preservation," and it had the greatest influence on him. He went there twice during his journey through southern France in spring 1787.[2]

Jefferson first visited Nîmes between March 20 and 24, when he lodged at the Hôtel du Luxembourg. He made six entries in his journal of expenses for "seeing things." He was barbered, he had his clothes washed, and he bought two dozen white and one dozen black silk stockings with his initials on them. He was liberal in tipping both Petitjean and Blondin, his *valet de place*. Jefferson had a tailor make some small adjustments to his wardrobe, he drew on his bill of exchange, and he bought some books and "medals."[3] Although he had been "nourished with the remains of Roman grandeur" ever since leaving Lyon, it was Nîmes that he considered to be the greatest example in France of "Roman taste, genius, and magnificence [to] excite ideas."[4]

On his first trip to Nîmes Jefferson crossed the Rhône River at Pont

La Maison Carrée, les Arènes, et la Tour Magne de Nîmes, ca. 1786, painting by Hubert Robert (1733–1808). Jefferson wrote Madame de Tessé that he looked on the Maison Carrée as a lover would look on his mistress in the moonlight.

Saint-Esprit over a fourteenth-century bridge of twenty-four arches canted to meet floods at an angle. Unfortunately, the bridge was so narrow that two vehicles could hardly pass one another. After his hurried trip to northern Italy, he made his way back to the Rhône toward Nîmes again on May 10.[5] On his second, fleeting visit to Nîmes, Jefferson went by way of another favorite scene of Clérisseau's and Robert's, the Pont du Gard, part of an aqueduct built in 19 B.C. to conduct water fifty kilometers to Nîmes through rocky terrain planted in olive groves. This bridge over the River Gard is 275 meters long and 48 high. Its upper story of arches carried the aqueduct; not only did the two lower courses provide support but the lowest one carried two divided lanes of traffic. The survival of this structure is particularly remarkable, since, as Jefferson noted, its maintenance did not extend to the removal of wild fig bushes growing in the bridge's masonry joints.

In March 1787 Jefferson also visited Arles, once the third largest city of the Roman Empire and the capital of Gaul. Its principal "sight" was its great, oval arena, which, like that at Nîmes, he equated with amphitheaters. He concluded that the one at Arles was the more complete, even though the "whole of the entablature" was gone, "and of the attic, too, if there was one." He complained that "the whole of the inside, and nearly all of the outside" of the arena of Arles was "masked by buildings" said to house a thousand residents. Nearby, he misunderstood two fine Corinthian columns as having belonged to its ancient capitol instead of to its public baths. He did not understand that the city's Egyptian obelisk had been a memento of veterans of Julius Caesar's Egyptian campaign and once the *spina* of its circus, because it had been embellished with a cross and reerected in front of the cathedral. Near Arles Jefferson wrote in his account a rare expression of humor, reporting that a local roadway lined with hundreds of ancient stone coffins was called "les champs elysées."[6]

Jefferson had been encouraged to see the Maison Carrée early in 1786 by his new French friends, three of whom might have commended to him the artist-architect Charles Louis Clérisseau: the Abbé Arnoux, the Duc de La Rochefoucauld, and the Comte de Tessé, all of whom were patrons who had underwritten publication of Clérisseau's great book *Antiquités de la France* in the previous decade. Jefferson bought a copy from the author,[7] and he was desirous of seeing for himself the chiefmost of the classico-romantic scenes of Provence that had made Clérisseau's reputation. The Maison Carrée and other ancient monuments of the area also had been celebrated by the artist Hubert Robert in the four scenes of neoclassical Provence that he painted for Marie Antoinette's apartments at Fontainbleau, which were to be exhibited in the Salon of 1787.[8]

Although Jefferson's visits to Arles and the Pont du Gard were interesting, his two visits to Nîmes were highly significant because of his and Clérisseau's choice of the Maison Carrée as the model for the Virginia state capitol. After Jefferson had been in France for several months, he received a request from Virginia's legislative committee entrusted with contracting for the construction of the new building at Richmond.[9] For a long time he had wished for Virginia's new seat of government a newer and better structure than the old colonial capitol at Williamsburg.[10]

Charles Louis Clérisseau (1721–1820),
caricature, 1752, by Pier Leone Ghezzi
(1674–1755).

From the time that Louis XV had begun clearing the arena at Nîmes
of its medieval clutter, the city had become a favorite resort for French
antiquaries. Excavation of its Roman remains was not completed until
1809. The most famous of the city's ancient monuments was the celebrated Maison Carrée, built in the second century A.D. as a temple dedicated to two sons of the Roman emperor Augustus. It had been converted
to a church for centuries before the rage for Roman antiquities became so
great that the king had been able to clear out Catholic priests to make the
structure an archaeological museum. Jefferson wrote Madison that "we
took as our model the Maison Carrée of Nîmes, one of the most beautiful,
if not the most beautiful and precious morsel of architecture left us by
antiquity." By "we" he meant Charles Louis Clérisseau and himself.[11]

One of the great Paris salons of the 1780s, where Jefferson may first
have heard of Nîmes, the Maison, and Clérisseau, was that of Comtesse
Adrienne Cathérine de Noailles de Tessé. She and her husband, René
Mans, Comte de Tessé, were patrons of U.S. diplomats in their *hôtel particulier* at Paris and at their country estate at Chaville, on the road to Versailles. The comtesse was a childless aunt of the Marquise de La Fayette,
her namesake. She was a motherly Lady Bountiful, whom some Americans
called "aunt" in imitation of La Fayette. It is a little difficult to take seriously her reputation as an imposing hostess. She had small, piercing eyes
set in a pockmarked face. Often, a nervous tic twisted her mouth into a
grimace, but she was considered "infinitely witty" in conversation. She was
only two years older than Jefferson. Thanks in large part to him, she was
able to form at Chaville a notable collection of New World flowers, plants,
and trees. Although the Comte de Tessé was a rheumatic and "silent par-
ticipant" in his wife's salon, it was he who proposed giving the Virginian a
sculpture as a memento when he returned to America. Typically, it was
Madame's name that was inscribed as the donor of what Jefferson used as a
pedestal at Monticello.[12]

No biography of Jefferson omits his famous letter to Madame de Tessé concerning his first visit to Nîmes: "Here I am, Madame, gazing whole hours at the Maison Carrée, like a lover at his mistress. . . . Were I to attempt to give you news [from here], I should tell you stories a thousand years old." But few, if any, biographers of Jefferson take note of the fact that in some respects she may have topped him in her response. She was not accustomed to allowing another to be the only one to express exalted sentiments. In replying to Jefferson's letter, she professed that his account was so fresh and immediate that she felt herself transported to Roman times, just as when she read Homer and Cicero. When she shared Jefferson's epistle with Philip Mazzei, she said that he listened to it as if it were one of the letters of the Apostles to the early Christians.[13]

Although the Maison Carrée is said to have been built in the style of the Parthenon, it is convenient for an American to describe it by comparing its dimensions, form, and function with those of its goddaughter, the Virginia state capitol. The Maison Carrée measures forty feet, eight inches wide and seventy-eight feet, two inches long. Almost twice the size of the temple, the Virginia state capitol is eighty-three feet, eight inches wide and one hundred forty-six feet long. Compared with the Roman temple's one story, Virginia's capitol has three and one-half stories of usable space. The former is a small, windowless temple set on a platform. The latter is about eight times as large, punctuated with two floors of seven windows on each side of the structure, which is set on a high and usable basement and has a usable attic. The temple was never intended to serve a large concourse of priests and worshipers simultaneously. While the temple is on a flat site, the capitol is on a hill that falls off so sharply that there is at the basement level a difference of about fifteen feet between the front and the rear of the building. While the temple faces east, as if to reflect the light and might of Augustus's Rome, the Virginia capitol faces west, as if to the future of America. The only natural light for the temple comes from its eastern portal, and its gloom suited its magical purposes. On the other hand, Virginia's capitol had abundant light, symbolic of the virtuous Commonwealth and serving the needs of its executive and judicial branches of government, as well as its bicameral legislature.

Both structures have six columns across the front of their porticoes, but those of the Maison Carrée have Corinthian capitals over fluted columns, while those of the Virginia capitol have Ionic capitals over smooth shafts. The portico of the Roman temple is deeper and has two freestanding columns on each of its sides, while the Virginia structure has only one on each side. Consistent with Jefferson's religious and civic beliefs, there is no religious chapel in the capitol. Within its rectangular form there is, however, a rotunda thirty-five feet in diameter, which, although it was planned as a conference room, has had as its centerpiece almost from the beginning Houdon's full-size, standing statue of George Washington and thus has served as a kind of civic shrine. Anticipating his theme of simplicity, so widely commented upon after 1801, Jefferson eliminated one range of columns from the portico and substituted Ionic for Corinthian capitals, and smooth for fluted columns.[14]

Clérisseau played a pivotal role in the evolution from the Palladian to the Louis Seize neoclassicism in France and to the neoclassicism of Sir

Plaster Model of the Virginia State Capitol, 1786, by Bloquet (active in the late eighteenth century) after a design by Charles Louis Clérisseau (1721–1820).

William Chambers and Robert Adam in Great Britain. After winning the Prix de Rome in 1746, Clérisseau had become one of Gian Paolo Pannini's students and a friend of Giovanni Battista Piranesi's and Johann Joachim Winklemann's. To supplement his stipend from the Académie française, he sold sketches of Roman antiquities and tutored Britons on their grand tour. It was said that George III's architect, Sir William Chambers, learned all "his notions" of architecture and antiquities from Clérisseau. In the 1750s Clérisseau instructed in perspective drawing and things antique Robert Adam, who declared that his mentor possessed "the utmost knowledge of architecture, of perspective, of designing, of colouring I ever saw. . . . He raised my ideas. I wished above all things to learn his manner; to have him with me at Rome; to study close with him and to purchase his works."[15]

For the next eight years Clérisseau was employed first by Robert Adam and then by James Adam. With Robert Adam, he explored near Rome the ruins of Hadrian's Villa and the Baths of Caracalla and the Baths of Diocletian. He accompanied Robert to Vicenza, where in studying its great villas Clérisseau formed a very low opinion of Andrea Palladio. Robert Adam echoed his French teacher when he said that Palladio was a "fortunate genius who purchased a reputation at an easy rate" and whose plans and elevations were "ill-adjusted."[16] Clérisseau supervised at Venice the engraving by Bartolozzi and Zucchi of his own and Adam's drawings for *The Ruins of the Emperor Diocletian's Palace of Spalatro*, which Adam published at London in 1764 with scant credit to the guileless Frenchman for anything and with exclusive credit to himself. Some have said that Clérisseau was the first to depict archaeological findings and measured drawings in perspective views that included landscape and people. Clérisseau's next book, *Les Antiquités de la France*, included those of Nîmes. He was unlucky as an artist in that he did not receive the credit he was due. He was unlucky as an architect because, although his clients accepted his designs for structures, either they did not build them, as in the case of Catherine the Great's triumphal arch, or they employed other architects to execute and modify his work, as in the case of the Château Borély. He is most famous for having introduced others to his own post-Palladian, neoclassical style: James and Robert Adam, Sir William Chambers, and Thomas Jefferson.[17] Allegations that Clérisseau could not learn any other language than French and that he was a difficult person to get along with, prickly and resentful of authority, find no support in Jefferson's writings.

It remains a matter of discussion, if not dispute, whether Jefferson had arrived at the fundamental scheme of the capitol before he went to France or saw any of Clérisseau's works. Was the French architect merely one who helped him with the model or the expert whose part in designing that structure was at least equal to Jefferson's? Any answer to the question must remain speculative. However confident Jefferson was of his own talents as an amateur architect, in 1785 he adopted the practice of enlisting professional architects for important projects. In 1785–86 it was Clérisseau; in the first two decades of the nineteenth century he chose Benjamin H. Latrobe and Robert Mills. Wherever Jefferson went in Europe, he made a point of visiting buildings designed in whole or in part by Clérisseau and his students, notably the Château Borély near Marseilles and Moor Park and Osterly near London. Jefferson probably had studied the plans and pictures in Clérisseau's *Antiquités* before he engaged the architect's professional services to adapt plans of the temple for the Virginia state capitol and to provide a plaster model. Clérisseau was not a mere technician who "helped him with the model" but the expert whose part in designing the capitol was primary.

Jefferson was more generous in giving credit to professional architects than many of his admirers have been. One must honor him for his willingness (and ability) to learn from experience during his five-year stay in Europe, when he had the opportunity of improving his understanding of architecture by personal observation and by accepting advice from an outstanding professional architect like Clérisseau. Jefferson never called himself an architect. Between 1785 and 1789 he evolved from an old-fashioned follower of Palladio to a practitioner of Clérisseau's style of neoclassical architecture. Besides requiring a great reduction of scale, this had the effect of making Monticello after 1790 and Poplar Forest from the outset more comfortable and convenient houses.

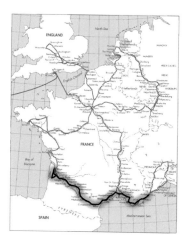

9 Through Languedoc and Gascony
to Toulouse and Bordeaux

AFTER HIS FATIGUING ITALIAN JOURNEY, THOMAS JEFFERSON DID
not immediately have the luxury of traversing in a leisurely fashion the
Canal Royal de Languedoc, now called the Canal du Midi, from the Mediterranean to Toulouse and thence to the Atlantic. Before doing so, he had
to retrace his steps through Provence and recross the Rhône at Avignon
and, at the same time, see the sights of the little papal enclave. At Antibes
on May 2 he was once more in his chariot, with Petitjean to cope with
postilions, hostlers, and servants of roadside taverns. Jefferson followed
the coastal road to Fréjus before turning inland to breakfast at Luc on May
3 en route to Aix, where he lodged again at the Hôtel St. Jacques. He was
happy to receive there letters that William Short had forwarded from
Paris. The next day Jefferson went again to Marseilles, where he lodged a
second time at the Hôtel des Princes. On this visit to France's southern
metropolis he had his carriage repaired and drew cash from Bréthous's
bank upon Grand's letter of credit.[1]

Retracing his course for twenty miles toward Aix, Jefferson spent a
night at Orgon. He ferried across the Durance River near Avignon, where
he visited the tomb of the poet Petrarch's beloved Laura before engaging
horses to take him to the celebrated Fountain of Vaucluse. A measure of how
important he considered this episode is that he wrote two letters about it to
his daughter Patsy, regaling her with the vernal beauties of the countryside,
watered by the numerous branches of the Sorgue River. At the base of a low
but precipitous mountain, water bursts to the surface of the earth to form
what is called the Fountain of Vaucluse. On a cliff is perched a ruin, described
by local folk in the 1780s as the "château of Mons[ieur] Petrarch and Madame Laura." Actually the poet had resided there as one of the entourage of

the bishop of Cavaillon. When Jefferson visited the fountain the stream was
a bubbling torrent. Although there was still snow on the mountains, farmers
were mowing hay in the valley, and the olive trees on the "impending" hills
had just put out new foliage. He described the Sorgue as being about twenty
yards wide and four or five feet deep, containing "fine" trout, and having
such rapidity "that it could not be stemmed by a canoe." The little valley's
romantic associations seemed to be confirmed by the presence of so many
nightingales that it seemed as though "every tree and bush was filled with
[them] in full song."[2]

Uplifted and refreshed, Jefferson returned to Avignon, where he lodged
the night of May 8 at the Hôtel de St. Omer. The little city-state levied such
low taxes that it had hardly enough to pay the wages of a papal vice-legate
and a handful of guards. Jefferson dutifully inspected the fourteenth-century Palais des Papes but left no description of the large complex. The
famous Pont d'Avignon was, of course, a picturesque ruin in the 1780s. To
cross the Rhône, Jefferson's little entourage was ferried across to Villeneuve-
les-Avignon, where he visited the Carthusian monastery. Whether he did so
in order to inquire about the monks' celebrated cordial or to facilitate getting a fresh team of horses is not clear, but he viewed the religious establishment and sat in the octagonal summerhouse within its cloister. He doubled
back to Nîmes for a long, last look at the Maison Carrée and to collect some

articles he had bespoke. Lodging again at the Hôtel du Luxembourg, he engaged a local valet and freshened himself. Since there was no theater there, he amused himself by attending a circus. He bought from a dealer a wooden model of a bronze *askos*, or antique vase, whose original was displayed at the local museum. At first, he intended to present it to Clérisseau, but he ended up keeping it for himself, and in 1801 he commissioned Thomas Claxton of Philadelphia to copy it in silver. Although it was used as a sauceboat at Monticello, Jefferson called it a "ewer," and family members called it "the duck."[3]

Leaving Nîmes on May 11, Jefferson and Petitjean proceeded into the province of Languedoc, the exploration of whose great canal was one of Jefferson's principal goals. His travel through Languedoc and Gascony took him through country reeking from a millennium of bloody events. For him, however, the wars of the Visigoths and Moors, the Albigensian crusade, the dynastic wars of the Plantagenets, the Angevins, and the Valois, the Black Prince and his transitory conquests, and the contests of Protestants and Roman Catholics held no interest; they were merely benighted episodes between the Age of Augustus and the Age of Enlightenment. On the way to Montpellier he breakfasted on May 11 at Lunel, where he ordered some white Muscat wine for himself and one hundred bottles as a gift to the new French minister to the United States, Comte Elénore François Elie de Moustier.

He did not comment on the charms of Montpellier. Because the hilltop city possessed fine promenades and parks, as well as crooked streets, Young thought that it had "more the aspect of a great capital than [of] a provincial city."[4] Besides being on the way to the great canal between the Atlantic and the Mediterranean, Montpellier had for Jefferson the added inducement of being the nameplace for the Virginia estate of his friends the Madisons. Never bothered by precision in spelling, Jefferson spelled the name of the French city "Montpelier." During the two and one-half days of his stay, he bought supplies for the next part of his journey, even though William Short had warned him that, according to Jean Jacques Rousseau, the people of Montpellier looked on strangers as animals to be preyed upon, robbed, and have their brains knocked out. Jefferson replied to his secretary that pillaging strangers was universal and that Rousseau should have limited his condemnation to postilions, *voituriers*, tavernkeepers, waiters, and workmen, because the majority of people in Montpellier were "as good as any people I have ever met with."[5]

A secret mission at Montpellier required Jefferson to abandon his usual custom of lodging at a hotel, inn, or tavern. Instead he engaged an apartment, in whose greater privacy he might conduct an interview scheduled months before with José da Maia, a Brazilian revolutionary whose descriptions of unrest and appeals for aid from the United States Jefferson attended with discreet politeness. In reporting this meeting to John Jay, he assured the secretary for foreign affairs that he had taken pains to ensure that Da Maia understood that he spoke only for himself; that the United States were "not in a condition . . . to meddle in any war"; and that "we wished particularly to cultivate the friendship of Portugal." In effect, Jefferson wrote Da

Maia off as calmly as he wrote off what he spent on the revolutionary's entertainment.[6]

Jefferson paid attention neither to Montpellier's history of political and religious wars with disputatious neighbors nor to its Romanesque buildings. For diversion he attended the theater. To relieve physical discomfort he bought "bougies" to use as suppositories for hemorrhoids. For use some time in the future, he bought a packet of seed of a special variety of St. Foin hay that perpetuates itself for five years despite two cuttings a year. For the next fortnight he bought necessities such as maps, a tin box, bread, wine, and oranges.[7] Jefferson may have visited the Université de Montpellier, which was a typical result of eighteenth-century consolidation, in this case of an old abbey, a Jesuit college, and a school of medicine founded by the Moors in the twelfth century that later had counted Rabelais among its students. Perhaps he visited the school's anatomical laboratory, where the air was circulated, so that a cadaver could be used "for a month without smelling bad." As a man of the Enlightenment, Jefferson favored secularizing abbeys and Jesuit colleges. He could not have anticipated that the university would become the scene of atrocities during the Reign of Terror.[8]

Montpellier had both expanded and been partly rebuilt in white stone since the American War of Independence. Its prosperity seemed to be enjoyed mainly by small tradesmen, who complained of the 30 percent escalation in the price of everything. Impatient to begin his travel on the Canal de Languedoc, Jefferson did not ponder, as did Arthur Young, on the enigma of throngs "alive with business" and the absence of any "considerable manufacture."[9] Jefferson did not say anything about Montpellier's distant views of the Alps, the Mediterranean, and the Pyrenees. Nor did he remark on its many fountains, fed by a league-long aqueduct, or on its parks, the Place Royal, commonly called the Pérou, and the esplanade. In the Pérou were an equestrian statue of Louis XIV and an *arc de triomphe* decorated by Bertrand de Montpellier with allegorical medallions celebrating the triumph of France over her enemies and the completion of the Canal Royal.[10] On May 12 Jefferson and Petitjean left Montpellier for Sète. Along the road Jefferson noted that Indian maize was the staple for the poor, and he pondered the merits of the muscat wine of Frontignan on his way to the eastern terminus of the canal.

After crossing a long arched causeway over tidal flats, Jefferson reached the city of Sète. Located on a spit between the sea and a lagoon and laced by canals, the city replicates the aqueous character of Venice. To provide an eastern terminus for the canal, the province of Languedoc had created this planned city between 1666 and 1678. During the reign of Louis XIV, Sète was as transcendent an example of urban planning as the canal was of civil engineering. Sited in the lee of a tufa peak on the periphery of the Etang de Thau, the city's citadel and outlying forts provided light fortification. Long jetties and dredged channels served a commodious port, whose chief trade was in wine and brandy. Sète was, and is, a good refuge from Mediterranean storms.[11]

At Marseilles, Jefferson had bought a map of the Canal Royal de Languedoc, or simply the Canal de Languedoc, as he and most people

Port de Cette, engraving of a painting by Joseph Vernet (1714–89). In some ways akin to Venice, this new city was built to be the eastern terminus of the Canal Royale de Languedoc.

called what is now the Canal du Midi. It had been the inspiration and accomplishment, between 1666 and 1681, of Pierre Paul Riquet, whom Louis XIV commissioned to build the canal at Riquet's expense, with the right to retain all its profits. The project absorbed Riquet's fortune and left him and his heirs deeply in debt. Forgoing tolls until 1724, as the price of gaining construction subsidies from the crown and from localities along the route, neither Riquet nor his heirs profited from the canal until 1768. In 1787 Riquet's great-grandson, Victor Maurice, Comte de Caraman, managed the family's canal. Their company charged reasonable tolls, operated mail packet boats, leased mill sites, and cultivated land along the right-of-way. But the cost of maintaining the waterway was so great that between 1776 and 1786 it generated less than modest profits.

The Canal de Languedoc was the world's first summit canal. Closed every August for cleaning and occasionally during icy months, its supply of water was great enough to keep it full, despite evaporation, theft, waste, and discharge at its terminuses. Its highest point is 189 meters above sea level near Lampy and St. Ferréol, where there are great impoundments. Between Sète on the Mediterranean and Toulouse on the Garonne River in the Atlantic watershed, it is 130 miles long with ninety-nine locks averaging eight feet in depth.[12] Travelers on mail packets enjoyed large, clean boats that differed little from cargo *péniches* but did not have provision for overnight accommodation or meals. For the eight-day transit of the canal, passengers had to bring on board whatever wine and food they intended to consume. The boat's skipper, called a *patron*, supervised a one-horse team, worked by a man and a woman from six o'clock in the morning until seven o'clock at night.

Even though Jefferson wrote in his notes about a forty-foot tow made up of fourteen rafts, he was more interested in the machinery for opening and closing the locks than in its traffic. He did not approve of the fact that women tended the locks, saying that they were not physically able to perform such work. He estimated that the system of operating the lock gates was so inefficient that it added a day to the transit. With plenty of time to make calculations, he suggested to officials that the canal company should install gates "turning on a pivot lifted by a lever like a pump handle, aided by a windlass and a cord." The officials promised to consider his plan.[13] A manual system somewhat similar to the one Jefferson proposed operates the locks today.

Leaving Sète and crossing the Etang de Thau, a brackish lagoon famous for its oysters, in a sailboat, Jefferson hired at Agde a small *péniche* to traverse the canal in eight days at a speed of between two and three miles an hour. Taking the wheels off his carriage, he set it on the boat to form a cabin in which to rest after pleasurable strolls on the towpath, but he spent every night on shore at one of the canal company's hotels. Jefferson declared to his feminine correspondents that the plane trees on the canal's banks were filled with nightingales in song. Contemplating improvement of such rivers of Virginia as the James and Rivanna, he carefully examined the canal's locks, mitered gates, tunnels, and bridges over ravines and streams. In the canal he saw an "abundance" of carp, chub, perch, and eels; on its banks he admired the profusion of yellow iris.

The first town he came to that was of any consequence was Béziers, whose fortress-cathedral, St. Nazaire, frowns from its eminence above the Aude River valley. Jefferson must have liked Béziers's combination of promenade and flower market, the Allée de Poètes. He inspected the canal's staircase of nine locks, the Neuf Ecluses, which raised floating boats sixty-six feet from the coastal plain to rolling country in an hour and thirty-three minutes. He may have watched impassive-faced men play at boule outside the grim cathedral. Although he surely studied the canal as a feat of engineering, he was also interested in how the canal had transformed such an isolated market town into an inland port big enough to accommodate abreast four vessels of a hundred tons apiece.[14]

Beyond Béziers the canal passes through a small tunnel, whose tufa hill Jefferson may have climbed to view a particularly fertile area made from a drained lake. A little farther was the Abbey of Argens-Minèrve, whose friars produced much the same *vin de la region*, Minèrve, as does the growers' syndicate today. Always interested in hospitals, Jefferson must have been pleased to find that the Knights of Malta maintained a hospice at Homps. Frequently the tall Virginian saw women laundering clothes beside streams and encountered on the towpath flocks of sheep being led by their shepherd and billy-goat custodians.[15]

In Jefferson's day the canal did not extend to Carcassonne because of the opposition of local grain and fabric millers, who feared losing some of their waterpower. He hired a horse to carry him several miles from the canal to Carcassonne, but he did not linger there. Instead of commenting on the antiquities or even the manufactures of the place, he remarked on flax "in blossom," Windsor beans "just come to table," strawberries and peas not yet mature, and the geographic limits of olive cultivation. In 1787 Carcassonne was composed of an old town, called La Cité, and a modern, new town. Restoration of the former lay sixty years in the future. It was still a romantic, walled Romanesque ruin that the natives considered a source of free building stone. The walls of its acropolis were "high, crenelated and flanked by a great number of towers, both square and round," enclosing an oval precinct guarded by a royal company of invalided soldiers so infirm that it was called "the Death Watch." Carcassonne had an "unhappy" legacy from the religious wars, in which the local Protestants had been almost completely eliminated. Elsewhere in Languedoc, Protestantism had enjoyed a revival since the mid-eighteenth century, but Carcassonne remained a center of orthodoxy. Jefferson must have been aware of the city's sad religious history, because he made an unusual, special entry in his accounts of making a modest and discreet contribution to its Protestant temple. The city's turbulent Visigothic, Saracenic, and Albigensian past; its pregunpowder crenelation, machicolation, curtain walls, turrets, moats, and drawbridges; its prenational economic and political status—everything about Old Carcassonne so perfectly represented what Jefferson most disliked that he did not bemoan the brevity of his visit to this relic of the Dark Ages.[16] New Carcassonne, on the banks of the River Aude, was an up-to-date but undistinguished town of good houses, straight streets, and numerous fountains. Today its Grande Place is adorned with a handsome pebble fountain surmounted by Neptune and with dolphins spouting jets of water.[17]

Between Castelnaudary and Toulouse the canal's banks are still lined with yellow iris and fine avenues of Lombardy poplars. In the distance loom the Pyrenees, and nearby are châteaux on wooded slopes.[18] As the owner of a grist mill in Albemarle County, Jefferson observed with interest the windmills outside the large town of Castelnaudary and the grain mills that utilized surplus canal water. He queried the millers about the kinds and cut of their grinding stones. Undoubtedly, Jefferson followed his own and La Fayette's advice to learn about a country by eating its peasants' fare, in this case Castelnaudary's highly seasoned *cassolet* of beans and mutton. Because it was the planting season, instead of the harvesting season, Jefferson misunderstood the countrymen when they said they grew "millet" to mean that they cultivated "Indian corn," when they meant milo, which is a kind of sorghum. That Castelnaudary was an advanced provincial town was demonstrated by its street lamps.[19] Here Jefferson hired a riding horse in order to visit the great reservoirs in the Black Mountains at Saint Ferréol and Lampy, thirty miles distant.

In these mountains on the northern border of Languedoc are many streams and waterfalls. Riquet had tapped their water rather than the water of rivers in order to avoid both the accumulation of sand and the litigation by riverine mill owners. He brought water from mountain streams to an upper reservoir at Lampy by stone-lined contour ditches called *rivolets* through heather-strewn, narrow, precipitous ledges. From the shallow upper basin the water tumbles into the deep main reservoir of Saint Ferréol. The 6.3 million cubic meters of water thus impounded amounts to more water than there is in all the rest of the canal system, so that in the summer, when the mountain streams dry up, the impoundment can feed the canal. The masonry dam of the lower reservoir is about ninety-five feet high. Tamed by the time it reaches a continental divide at Narouse, the water divides, part going to the Mediterranean and part to the Atlantic. Because Riquet had planned from the outset to make St. Ferréol a kind of park, he contrived there a spectacular *gerbe*, or geyser, with a sixty-foot jet. When the great, leathered valves controlling it were opened, the force and sound of the water were so great that eighteenth-century ladies pretended to faint.

The western terminus of the Canal de Languedoc, Toulouse, is located near the headwaters of the Garonne River. Here Jefferson lodged for two nights at the Hôtel du Griffon d'Or. He employed a local valet to help him see the sights of the city, while his regular *factotum*, Petitjean, oversaw the reassembly of his carriage. Unlike many eighteenth-century visitors, Jefferson neither praised nor condemned the architectural and political character of Toulouse. Some thought the newer promenades were "very pretty" and approved of the few long, straight, broad streets that traversed the city. To extreme neoclassicists, however, good construction in pink Gascon brick was inferior to almost anything in stone, and the Romanesque style of most of Toulouse's buildings was as loathsome to them as the Gothic. To enlightened centralizers, whether of monarchal or republican viewpoint, the survival from the medieval period of vestigial provincial autonomy in tax apportionment, appraisal, and expenditure was considered backward. Arthur Young thought the city had a "melancholy" aura; young Liancourt thought the people were "lazy"; and the historian Guibert said that they were more interested in splitting legal hairs than in making money.

As the capital of Languedoc, Toulouse retained a larger degree of autonomy than was approved by either a monarchist like Liancourt or a republican like Jefferson. The Grand Cadastre, or court, was the custodian of a kind of Doomsday Book called *Le Livre Cadastral*. This court apportioned the province's taxes among its parts. A second court, the Petit Cadastre, was a court of appraisal and appeals for individuals whose judges the provincial Estates elected every five or six years. This parliament held annual sessions in both Toulouse and Montpellier and was made up of the bishops, nobles, *capiteaux*, and the Intendant, or provincial administrator. At Toulouse it met in the fine Louis XIV complex of governmental buildings called the Capital. Jefferson probably gave no thought to visiting the medieval *donjon* behind the Capital, but the persistence of his local guide and his own passion for religious and political freedom may have led him to its adjacent courtyard, where Cardinal Richelieu's foe, the Duc de Montmorency, had been executed. Undoubtedly Jefferson visited the University of Toulouse and observed the adjacent sixteenth-century residences of local magnates. He probably paid little attention to the city's great Romanesque Abbey and

Church of St. Servan. It is unlikely that later, during the French Revolution, he recalled that there was at Toulouse, as well as at Paris, a church of the Jacobins. Since they were a reform group within the Benedictine order that emphasized preaching and Bible study, they needed churches whose width would accommodate a nonliturgical congregation better than conventional Romanesque or Gothic structures did.[20] Both at Paris and at Toulouse, the Jacobins' buildings were so functionally ideal for political debate and/or instruction that they became the sites of the revolutionary political assemblages popularly known as Jacobin clubs.[21]

Without improvement, the Garonne was not navigable between Toulouse and Bordeaux. When the archbishop of Toulouse, Loménie de Brienne, became Louis XVI's principal minister, he tried to improve the river by construction of a branch canal as a link to the Canal de Languedoc. It was not a success because of an insufficient supply of water, heavy deposits of sand, and the impermanence of berms and cofferdams.

On May 22, 1787, Jefferson resumed traveling in his carriage *en poste*. With Petitjean and postilions driving teams of horses from the *relais des chevaux*, he threaded his way down the rich valley of the Garonne by way of Montauban through fields that were planted in maize, wheat, and rye. With satisfaction he observed that farmers lived on farms rather than in villages; he spied many of their large cream-colored oxen, a few horses and asses, but no mules; and he noted with satisfaction that strawberries and peas had "come to table." He left no notes concerning the market town and great medieval abbey of Moissac, where he changed horses after a ferry trip across the Garonne. At Agen he lodged at the Hôtel Petit St. Jean, but he commented neither on the fine loggias of the marketplace of this episcopal town nor on the region's celebrated plums and prunes. He dined on a dish of ortolans at Agen—a rare treat.[22]

Jefferson had to cross the Garonne twice more before reaching Bordeaux late the evening of May 24, 1787. He and Petitjean lodged four nights there at the Hôtel Richelieu and feasted on fresh cherries, peas, and strawberries. We do not know whether its service was like that of Arthur Young's hotel, where, although meals were served on silver-plated dishes, the privy was a "temple of abomination." As usual, Jefferson engaged a *valet de place*, called in barbers, had his clothes washed, arranged for repairs to his carriage, and hired coaches to see the sights. He bought some maps and still another pocketknife for slicing fruit and cheese while traveling. He drew cash from the Grammont Féger Bank on Ferdinand Grand's letter of credit. He consulted with Thomas Barclay, the U.S. consul, about commercial affairs involving Bordeaux, the French Antilles, and U.S. ports. Ever generous and trusting, he advanced Barclay money from his own pocket until the young man could receive funds either from home or from Secretary for Foreign Affairs John Jay.[23]

So frequently has Jefferson been depicted as an agrarian that few realize how much he valued cities, their cultural advantages, and their commerce. Jefferson the city planner was delighted to see for himself the port of Bordeaux and its Place Louis XV, both of which so favorably impressed his contemporaries. The breadth and depth of the Garonne estuary at Bor-

Deuxieme Vue de Bordeaux, engraving of a
painting (ca. 1765) by Joseph Vernet
(1714–89). Jefferson visited the Graves and
Médoc vineyards from here and also
gathered data on Franco-American trade.

deaux afforded a superb anchorage for many large ships. Arthur Young
attributed the city's commerce and wealth to her enterprising merchants,
who were enthused by the new, low-tariff trade treaty between France and
Great Britain.

Along the river the city spread out in a great semicircle, cut by some
large, long, straight streets and interspersed with numerous squares faced
with good, modern houses. Its pride and showpiece was the half-ellipse of
the Place Louis XV. On its river side was a park at whose center stood Jean
Baptiste Le Moyne's bronze equestrian statue of Louis-Le-Bien-Aimé. On
its city side were Jacques Ange Gabriel's two neoclassical buildings in the
form of quarter-arcs, which housed the Bourse and the most important
branch of the Farmers General outside of Paris. Because the latter held a
monopoly on both the importation and the domestic sale of tobacco, Jefferson, being a Virginia tobacco planter, surely visited it. Besides functioning
as a chamber of commerce and an exchange, the Bourse afforded four galleries on which visitors could promenade while watching merchants below
contract for the sale of commodities in bulk.

The Place Louis XV provided an architectural and functional transition from the hurly-burly of the port to the residential and cultural parts of
the city. The fifteenth-century Château Trompette was a citadel that had
been improved by Vauban at the end of the seventeenth century, but all
agreed that it was no longer of any military use and should be demolished

and sold. Most houses facing Bordeaux's quay were of handsomely cut stone, and they matched the great houses of Paris in their luxury. Between 1775 and 1778 the architects Etienne and Bonfin had designed a three-story episcopal palace of such "great beauty," almost everyone in Bordeaux agreed, that no building in Paris could rival it. A handsome peristyle separated its ballustraded terraces from the public square. Of the city's promenades the most popular were the Cours and the Jardin Royal. Jefferson admired how the Bordelais trained elm trees to form arbors near the Riding School, designed by Jacques-Ange Gabriel and built by Claude Francin in 1754.[24] He also visited its ancient "circus, considerable portions of which [were] still standing," where he measured Roman brick and declared that their texture was "as fine, compact and sound as that of porcelaine."[25]

As a devotee of both architecture and the theater, Jefferson made haste to attend Bordeaux's famous Comédie, designed by Louis Victor. From the time of its completion in 1780, everybody agreed that it was the greatest such building in France. Occupying a city block, the Comédie has a portico of twelve large Corinthian columns. Besides the auditorium, it contains an elegant oval concert room and salons. Some noted that its gallery provided refreshment and an all-weather promenade, where one found "vendors of all sorts of merchandise." A few described the interior as "grandiose" and "rather heavy," but most Frenchmen thought it was "tastefully decorated in gold" and provided a "brilliant setting" for the beau monde. While an Englishwoman complained that the orchestra was "too small for so vast a hall," Frenchmen bragged that the elliptical amphitheater could hold two thousand persons and emphasized the grandeur of its peristyle of fluted columns, its two banks of columned loges, and a ceiling whose proscenium arch bore a scene painted by Robin to represent the rising sun and glory of Bordeaux. An Englishwoman complained that "the ladies of a certain world . . . are completely free to and do make remarks about the show while in progress," but Frenchmen saw things differently. Posterity has been the beneficiary of the extravagance of the ancien régime in spending so much in building and equipping the Comédie of Bordeaux. Unlike Young, Jefferson did not pontificate on the depravity of the French in performing theatrical pieces on Sundays. Nor did he seem to care whether wealthy merchants of the city kept dancing and singing girls of the Comédie as mistresses. On the other hand, he almost surely would have joined Young in deprecating the high play at the city's gambling tables.[26]

Bordeaux's greatest commodity was wine. It was the general belief that two-thirds of her inhabitants were engaged in producing, packaging, or shipping it. The second most important element of the city's trade was trade with Saint Domingue and the other French West Indian islands in flour, iron goods, glassware, and cloth. In the mid-1780s, Bordeaux accounted for 55 percent of the tonnage and 45 percent of the number of ships engaged in trade with the Antilles. In season, six of the largest transatlantic vessels were usually in the Garonne unloading their cargoes of West Indian sugar and coffee. In exporting wheat flour to the Antilles, the French sent only their highest quality, because it was least apt to mold or spoil.

Jefferson visited Bordeaux's most noted vineyards, which generally re-

Vue des Ruines de l'Amphithéatre de Bordeaux,
engraved by Allix after a painting by
Daubigny. Jefferson visited Roman remains
whenever he could.

*Through
Languedoc and
Gascony
to Toulouse and
Bordeaux*

120

main the best today. Of the white Bordeaux, he preferred the wine from three vineyards in the district of Graves, one of which still flourishes under the same name, Château Carbonnieux, which then belonged to the Benedictine monks of Saint Croix. Of the reds, he preferred two clarets that still go by the same name, although under different ownership: the Marquis d'Agicourt's Château Margaux, the Château Latour de Ségur owned by Monsieur Miromesnil, and the Hautbrion vineyard leased to a merchant named Barton.[27]

Accompanied by Petitjean, Jefferson quit Bordeaux on May 28, 1787. Because he lived in the Piedmont section of Virginia, he seems to have concluded that the best vines for Monticello would not be found in the flat, sandy lands in the vicinity of Bordeaux. While he was there, however, he made notes on how the vineyards were planted; he recorded how the grapes were pressed; and he bought wine. But he did not buy the slips, cuttings, or roots from whose grapes came Bordeaux's famous claret and Graves.

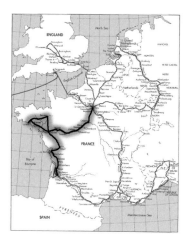

10 *From Blaye to Paris via Brittany and the Loire Valley*

ON MAY 28 JEFFERSON AND PETITJEAN FERRIED ACROSS THE Garonne near its junction with the Dordogne to land at the old town of Blaye. They lodged that night at the Hôtel de la Poste. The next day they did not follow the easterly route between Blaye and the Loire River valley by way of Angoulême and Poitiers in order to visit briefly the La Rochefoucauld estates at Rochefoucauld and Verteuil.[1] Instead they traveled northwest toward La Rochelle by roads close to and parallel to the Bay of Biscay. Thanks to long days and good weather, they were able to take the ferry across the Charente River to Rochefort before spending the night of the twenty-ninth at the ferry house tavern, the Grand Bacha, whose sleeping facilities consisted of four beds in a large room.[2] Rochefort had been founded by Louis XIV as a naval base to match the one at Toulon. Besides possessing the largest naval arsenal in France, it had a camp for three hundred convicts, who rowed galleys.[3] Before departing the next morning, Jefferson took coffee and called in a local barber.

Jefferson wished to visit La Rochelle in order to explore commercial opportunities for his countrymen. With a population of about twenty-one thousand and a lucrative commerce, La Rochelle was the sixth most important French port facing the Atlantic, even though it could accommodate only a couple of ships at a time and there was no drydock for repair or maintenance. Because he recently had obtained from the French government its *arrêt* permitting U.S. ships, sailors, and cargoes to take part in trade between French home and colonial ports on equal terms with their French equivalents, his visit was timely. Not only was La Rochelle's commerce then principally with Saint Domingue and Louisiana but it was one of the four French ports authorized to participate in the slave trade. In addition, La

Vue du Port de la Rochelle, ca. 1765, painting by Joseph Vernet (1714–89). Jefferson was interested in La Rochelle's trade with America, as well as its Protestant past.

Rochelle had a valuable commerce with northern Europe. Although the general cargo of Bordeaux and Nantes was greater than La Rochelle's, the latter devoted a greater proportion of its resources to the slave trade, used smaller ships than its competitors, and made disproportionally larger profits.[4]

Jefferson probably lodged at the Comte d'Artois Inn. In "seeing things" at La Rochelle, he undoubtedly walked out on the great dyke that Cardinal Richelieu had caused to be built in order to isolate the city from the English during the siege of 1628. The city's unfinished cathedral, designed by Jacques Gabriel, had little appeal for Jefferson. We do not know what he thought of La Rochelle's large, squarish *place d'armes* with its handsome fountain, *allées* of trees, or view of the port and harbor. A half-century after the end of the slave trade marked La Rochelle's withering, Henry James wrote that this square resembled "the piazza of some dead Italian town, empty, sunny, grass-grown, with a row of yellow houses overhanging it." Three great medieval towers frowned over the channel to the port, one cylindrical and the other polygonal, but each "battered, . . . infinitely weather-washed and sea-silvered." In Jefferson's day a great chain could be stretched between them in order to block entrance to the harbor, reenforced by a system of seventeen bastions and forts in the manner of Vauban. Visitors usually found La Rochelle to be a happy city whose streets were lined by stone arcades that "befit a land of hot summers." It was a bundle of contradictions, too. It was a French city with a Dutch air. Although most of its inhabitants were Roman Catholics, some thought them possessed of "Protestant vigor and cleanliness." Jefferson may have set his watch by the Great Horloge in its fourteenth-century square tower and admired the efficacy of the fifteenth-century Tour de La Lanterne as a lighthouse, but if he saw at La Rochelle any souvenirs of the persecution of the Huguenots, he did not remark upon them. His taste did not include appreciation of the city's French Renaissance Hôtel de Ville, whose curtain wall and arcade studded with statues gave privacy to a court before the building.[5] He probably entered its *grande salle*, where the Rochelais in 1628 had debated and decided whether to give in to the English and to undergo siege by the French.

Jefferson was able to depart from La Rochelle early and to drive through six villages of the Vendée before reaching Nantes two days later. This countryside was filled with orchards and great spreading trees. On reaching Nantes in the early afternoon, he bought a cane and a hat, posted letters, and made an unusual eighteen-franc contribution to "Le Temple," a Protestant congregation. When he reached the mouth of the Loire, he neither disparaged its beauty nor complained, as did many, that its shallowness made navigation difficult.[6] Fatigued from more than two months of travel, Jefferson lodged at the new Hôtel Henri IV, which some thought "the finest inn" in France and perhaps in all of Europe. Located in a small square close to the theater and as convenient for pleasure as for trade, it possessed the additional distinction of being "very cheap." The city's principal commerce was in selling to Saint Domingue and Martinique about ten thousand slaves taken every year from the Gold Coast of Africa. Nantes also traded in Belgian guns and cloth, as well as in coffee, coral, and sugar. Most of the city's "superb" public buildings, such as the Chambre des Comptes, were only ten years old. There were two semipublic parks, one the Launay and the other the garden of the Petit Capuchin monastery. The theater, built between 1783 and 1788, was of white stone with "a magnificent portico front of eight elegant Corinthian pillars and four others within." Its interior was all "gold and painting." Its presentations sometimes were by Parisian stars such as Madame St. Huberti. Jefferson left no record of having observed there, as Arthur Young did three months later, any hint of the revolutionary storm that was to engulf France.[7]

On June 1, 1787, Jefferson left Nantes. The countryside's crops of wheat, rye, and oats were green in the fields as he passed through the villages of Roche Bérnard, Moère, and Pont Château before taking the ferry to the north shore of the Loire in order to make a brief inspection of the southeastern part of Brittany. He did not consult Comte de la Bourdonaye, whom Madame d'Enville usually recommended as expert about everything Breton because he had been its "first syndic of the noblesse" for twenty-five years.[8] Jefferson was silent about how backward this province was in comparison with the rest of France, while Arthur Young wrote that one-third of its land was uncultivated, that "nearly all of it [was] in misery," and that the "savage" natives of Brittany had little more skill in husbandry than the "Huron Indians." According to Young, Brittany's roads were dreadful, its towns were filthy, its inns were abominable holes, and the houses were windowless "heaps of dirt." If Jefferson had not been exhausted, he too might have said that Breton women were "furrowed," not by age, but by labor, "to the utter extinction of all softness of sex." Although usually a prophet of progress and perfectibility, Young despaired of Brittany, concluding that it had nothing in it but privileges for the nobles and poverty for the rest of the people.[9]

Jefferson spent the night of June 1 at Muzillac. He made a quick getaway the next morning and ate his breakfast at Vannes, where the industrious made cloth and had dug a canal to get their goods to the ocean. He proceeded through the little fishing port of Sainte Anne d'Auray, where Benjamin Franklin had landed in France a decade earlier. In order to cross a deep arm of the sea, he took the ferry at Hénnébont for L'Orient, where he put up at the Hôtel de l'Epée Royale. For a while, the American War of Independence had transformed L'Orient from a village into a sizable port. Although there were two American ships there in June 1787, the city's peacetime trade had never recovered from losing its preferred status as the headquarters of the Compagnie des Indes in 1769. By 1787 some of the great brick and stone warehouses were ruinous.[10] Both because Jefferson needed to have his carriage repaired and because of his interest in maritime trade, he hired a local guide for "seeing." He returned to Hénnébont in order to take the road for central Brittany, where he spent the night of June 3 in the towered town of Josselin. The next day he reached Rennes, where he lodged at the Mouton Inn. He called for a barber and toured the principal sights. Since almost all of Rennes had burned in 1720, its Place, Parlement House, and promenades were modern. There were bronze statues of Louis XIV, Louis XV, and a symbolic Brittany, invoking the Goddess of Health.[11] Unlike Young three months later, Jefferson did not record evidences of local discontent arising from the high price of bread, the banishment of the Parlement of Rennes, a mysterious distribution of money for the rumored purpose of agitating the people, or the presence of six regiments encamped nearby.

Jefferson left Rennes early on June 5 and recrossed the Loire. He passed through six villages before he dined and lodged at Nantes, whither he had instructed William Short to send mail *poste restante*.[12] The following morning he called in a barber, engaged a *valet de place*, and sent out for a *traiteur* to bring him food. Certainly Jefferson was fatigued, if not half-sick. Late in the day of June 6 he traveled to Aucenis, where he lodged at the Hôtel de la Bretagne. He stopped to change horses at Le Plessis de Tours, but he was in too great a hurry to visit the old palace that Louis XIV had given to Cardinal Richelieu. Jefferson did observe from his carriage window the nearby chalk hills where the troglodytes live in houses that have fronts of masonry, cut from the soft white rock forming their backs.[13] It was too early for him to observe the local vendage, but he must have admired fine views of the Loire, woods, steeples, windmills, and nearby towns. A confirmed physiocrat in his dislike of customs duties, Jefferson must have grumbled when he came to the barrier across the road where customs officers searched the luggage of travelers passing from Bretagne to France proper.[14]

On the morning of June 7, 1787, three relays of horses took Jefferson's carriage through meadows to the bluffs of Angers, where the Maine River meets the Loire. The city's château stands on a peninsulalike promontory, encircled by seventeen tall, round towers and a wall at whose feet there was a great moat on the land side. Guides told visitors myths about "Queen Cécile," an iron maiden in which Louis XI was said to have tortured his prisoners. One may suppose that the reason why Jefferson did not linger at Angers longer than to take breakfast was because he was half-sick and strongly desired to get back to Paris.[15] After changing horses and postilion, Jefferson and Petitjean resumed their places, in the carriage and on one of the hired horses, respectively, for the next three stages of their journey. After dining at Roziers at La Croix Rouge in the late afternoon, they resumed their way and lodged at a roadside tavern called Les Trois Volées.

The next day Jefferson went along the north bank of the Loire, passing by the tall, beetling towers of the château at Langéais without even perfunctory comment. Perhaps he, like some English travelers, was struck by the contrast between the refined elegance of the château and the misery of the peasants. He reached his second stage, the city of Tours, in time for breakfast. He engaged there neither a guide nor a *valet de place* to point out the local curiosities before dining at La Galère. He crossed Tours's stone bridge of fifteen arches over the Loire, completed in 1779. Since the city had demolished its old Gothic bridge in 1784, this was now the only bridge across the Loire for miles. At its northern end was Tours's Place Royale, with the new Hôtel de Ville and museum. Unusual in France, the broad, paved rue de Choiseul had sidewalks, as well as a promenade built and planted by Henry IV.[16]

After two more relays of horses, Jefferson's carriage reached Amboise, a smallish and villainous town located in the shadow of the famous Valois château. There he left his chariot for minor repairs and hired a hack to go to Chanteloup, half a league distant, in order to inspect the celebrated estate of the late Duc de Choiseul, once Louis XV's principal minister. Characteristically, he recorded few of his impressions of the château's exterior or its capacious salon, dining room, and library, even though there were here four great paintings of ancient and modern Rome, painted by Clérisseau's teacher, Giovanni Paolo Pannini. Instead, Jefferson ruminated on whether the Duc de Choiseul merited his fame. When in the 1750s Louis XV had dismissed the duke and banished him from court, he had sent Choiseul as his ambassador to the Holy See at Rome between 1753 and 1757. On his return to France, the duke had built this château and a 120-foot-high Chinese pagoda. In the latter, he commemorated those who visited him in his exile by placing on its six stories marble tablets bearing their names. Beyond the pagoda was an artificial lake and a great forest. To facilitate stag hunting, ridings were cut through the forest on radii extending from the pagoda. Because Jefferson had been accustomed as a youth to hunting in Virginia across meadows and through woods and forests, he disapproved of the European practice of employing beaters to flush game from the forest into the *allées*, where nobles could gun down their beasts and fowl, as much for the purposes of parade as for sport. As a farmer, he may have admired the duke's dairy and herd of 120 Swiss cows, but what Jefferson found most interesting about Choiseul or Chanteloup was the fact that a king could dismiss an able minister for no good reason.[17]

From Amboise Jefferson proceeded to Veuve, where he spent the night of June 8, 1787. He set off the next morning and did not linger longer than to change horses at the insignificant *relais de la poste*, Chousy, and at the celebrated town of Blois. At the latter he made no record of his impressions of the ivied exterior of its famous château, which was tending toward decay. On the interior Jefferson must have been offended by the greed of the guides and the gullibility of the tourists. The tourists were so eager to show mementos of the assassination of Duc Henri de Guise two centuries before that they had almost scraped away the floor of the room where it happened in order to provide bloodstained chips of stone. In spite of decay, the city of Blois enjoys such a charming situation that it has an air of gaiety. Jefferson left no chronicle of which king had built which parts of the royal château. He did not comment on the sculpture of Louis XII astride his caparisoned warhorse, the celebrated staircase, or the Great Hall in which the French Estates General had met in 1576 and 1588, but he did look with favor on Jacques Gabriel's eleven-arched bridge over the Loire at Blois, completed sixty years before.[18]

On June 9, 1787, Jefferson left Blois and breakfasted at Menars, where he visited the modern château and famous garden of Madame de Pompadour's brother, the Marquis de Menars. He must have been too worn out to comment. Jefferson and Petitjean rolled on to the city of Orléans, where they lodged at the relay station inn. Jefferson bought some maps and was attended by the barber. Probably because he was suffering from headaches and because he was in a hurry to return home, he did not comment on the city. He did not even follow his custom of climbing the clock tower of the cathedral to admire the extensive plain of the Loire beyond *allées* of trees on the city's former ramparts, even though the modern improvements at Orléans—its nine-arched bridge, its monument to Jeanne d'Arc, and its sugar refinery—would ordinarily have pleased him. Certainly Jefferson had cause to say that having seen so much, he could see no more.

It is a pity that Jefferson did not delay his return to Paris for less than a day in order to visit the estate of the late Henri Louis Duhamel du Monceau at Denainville, between Orléans and Paris.[19] Indeed, it is almost inexplicable that he never found occasion to go there. The Frenchman's improved plow antedated by half a century the one Jefferson designed in 1789. It had been the main cause for the king's rewarding Duhamel with riches and honors, and his plow was well described in published works that Jefferson had recommended to his brother-in-law, Robert Skipwith, more than a decade before.[20] At Denainville Jefferson could have seen, besides plows, a device for drying wheat and fine plantations of cedars of Lebanon and Russian oak, both of which Duhamel had introduced to France. Whether Jefferson could have ferreted out at Paris or Versailles a model of Duhamel's plow is moot. It may be that he was more conscious of Duhamel's plow in Virginia than he was in France, because Condorcet's recent elegy on Duhamel's life emphasized his other accomplishments, reforestation and ef-

Pagode Quiosque de Chanteloup à M. le Duc de Choiseuil, ca. 1776, drawing by George Louis Le Rouge. Although weary of traveling, Jefferson made a detour to see the statesman's château, where he lived after his banishment from Versailles.

forts to free the grain trade.[21] Nor did the weary Jefferson stop to inspect Malsherbes's nearby estate, where among other plantations of trees there was one of mulberries more than two miles in length, even though he had given the Frenchman seeds of magnolia and of the Venus flytrap.[22]

By the morning of June 10, Jefferson's chariot wheels were aligned for the last time on his longest journey. He was able to go through three villages before breakfasting and seven more before reentering Paris after an absence of a little more than three months.[23]

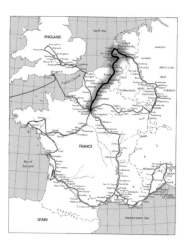

11 *The Netherlands*

IN HIS AUTOBIOGRAPHY THOMAS JEFFERSON DESCRIBED AS AL-
most happenstance his and John Adams's decision in March 1788 to borrow
for the United States almost half a million florins from Dutch bankers.[1] It
really was not that simple. Although the denomination of the loan was small,
the consequences of their success or failure in obtaining it were immense for
the infant, emerging United States of America.

Before the French Revolution, Amsterdam was the money capital of the
world, where France, Russia, the Holy Roman Empire, and the German and
Scandinavian states floated their "stock," as everyone then called bonds.
When the burghers of Amsterdam championed the cause of American independence, the United Netherlands had been a republic. The Dutch burghers, in addition to agreeing with America's liberal principles of trading
rights, had been so impressed by France's contribution of goods, men, and
specie in the war against Great Britain that even though the Netherlands
was not an ally of the United States as France was, it too drifted into the war.
In 1782, when the end of hostilities, the impending independence of the
United States, and a prosperous postwar trade seemed in sight, some Amsterdam bankers lent the United States about $2 million. These men were
at the same time capitalists, friends of U.S. independence, and advocates of
preserving for the Dutch people their individual and state liberties in the
confederated Dutch Republic. To float the first U.S. loan, Nicholas and
Jacob Van Staphorst, Nicholas Hubbard, and Wilhelm and Jan Willink had
formed a syndicate. They had contracted for the whole of a U.S. Five Million
Florin Loan to resell to their clients. Although at this time there was little
difference between bankers and brokers, the Van Staphorsts were primarily
bankers; the Willinks, large-scale brokers; and Hubbard, a private investor.

Simultaneously, the U.S. Congress had designated the syndicate of Van Staphorsts, Willinks the official European bankers of the United States.

The terms and conditions of the U.S. Five Million Florin Loan were conventional for the Amsterdam Exchange's practice concerning a country whose regular payment of interest might be risky. The bonds had been issued in 1,000-florin denominations, bore a 5 percent annual interest, and were redeemable in annual lotteries over a twenty-year period, with right of anticipation by the borrower. The syndicate contracted to float the issue on customary terms, receiving in advance a commission said to be 8 percent but in actuality a delivery of 1,000-florin bonds for 900 florins in cash. Until the 1790s, America had to send to Amsterdam annually about $300,000, or 1.2 million florins, to pay interest and redemptions. The syndicate maintained a market in both U.S. foreign bonds and also other U.S. certificates. At this time, America's depressed postwar economy and the poverty of the U.S. Congress prevented payment of 8 million livres to the French government and 1 million livres to foreign veterans. This was not merely embarrassing: it and the fact that Van Staphorsts, Willinks still had about two hundred unsold bonds of the U.S. Five Million Florin issue in their vaults discouraged any new American loan at Amsterdam or Paris. Nevertheless, speculators scented that there might be bargains in existing U.S. securities. Even Van Staphorsts, Willinks, and Hubbard were among those who sought to reap profits at the expense of a weak America and of a momentarily desperate kingdom of France.[2] John Adams remarked that one of the chief national characteristics of the Dutch was their "immeasurable avarice."[3]

Even while the government of France was trying to stave off bankruptcy between 1786 and 1790, she paid on behalf of the United States the interest due foreign veterans of the American War of Independence and the few Frenchmen who had joined the government in lending to the United States. As minister to France, Jefferson in 1788 was hard pressed to deny the accusations of America's bad faith that had been made in the French Assembly of Notables in 1786. Incessantly, insistently, and persistently speculators importuned him and the French government with schemes to buy cheaply America's debts to France and to exchange them dearly for titles to western lands in the United States. Jefferson feared that French officials might become so desperate that they might accept such a scheme. Partly because speculators depressed the market value of U.S. bonds, European creditors in the spring of 1788 became insistent in dunning Jefferson for sums owed to them. To cap the climax, Ferdinand Grand's bank at Paris declined to advance to Jefferson for ordinary diplomatic expenses a sum as small as a thousand guineas. It is true that Grand's bank was only a U.S. depository, but never before had it declined to advance funds when remittances from America to Van Staphorsts, Willinks were tardy. In March 1788 Jefferson had to turn to Van Staphorsts, Willinks, with whom he previously had had little business. He sensed both that they would resist making a new loan and that they would not advance him funds informally. In such a crisis, Jefferson determined that he must seek the "counsel" of his friend and fellow treaty commissioner John Adams.[4]

By 1786 Adams was the only American in Europe specifically authorized by the U.S. Congress to borrow money on its behalf. He had first visited the Netherlands in July 1780 to explore "whether something might not be done to render [the United States] less dependent on France."[5] Before going to London in 1785 as the first U.S. minister to Great Britain, Adams had gone to the Netherlands in his capacity as treaty commissioner in order to open formal diplomatic relations between the two republics and to negotiate a new loan with Van Staphorsts, Willinks, and Hubbard.[6] The bankers' response was to lend to the United States $185,000, a sum barely sufficient to finance for the next two years scheduled payments of interest, redemptions of bonds, and payment of U.S. diplomatic expenses. In actuality, this loan had been only a reloan of old money, on which the bankers enjoyed a *douceur* by charging a second commission on the new bonds.

At the same time that Jefferson was trying to fend off speculative scavengers, he learned on March 2, 1788, that John Adams would accede to the U.S. Congress's instruction to take formal leave of the Dutch authorities at The Hague before crossing the Atlantic. Adams sent Jefferson word that he would be "delighted to meet" him in the Netherlands.[7] Jefferson decided to hasten there in hope of their jointly persuading the bankers to make a loan similar to that of 1786 in order to avert what he described to George Washington as "something like bankruptcy."[8] Accompanied by his servant Espagnol, on March 4, 1788, Jefferson left Paris for the Netherlands on official business. Just as on most of his journeys, he and his valet traveled in his own cabriolet, employing the services of relays of horses and postilions from the *relais de poste*. His route took him due north from Paris to the border of the Austrian Netherlands. In his hurry, he did not take time to explore the countryside or the towns through which he passed other than to gaze from his carriage window or to stretch his legs while changing horses. He passed through a countryside mainly of forests and wastelands before coming to the first town of any consequence, Senlis.[9] From there to Brussels, he might have agreed with John Adams that the gentle plain was some of "the finest country I have any where seen." Unlike those travelers who show impatience when they have been delayed by breakdowns of transportation, Jefferson was accustomed to the necessity of frequent carriage repair. Even though he was hastening to catch up with John Adams, he remained patient when his cabriolet needed fixing at the way station of Pont St. Maxime. Since intermittent fitting of new packing and grease between the wheels and axle was standard procedure, the repair probably involved either realigning wheels or replacing broken harness. He did not stop to inspect the royal palace at Compiègne. Three posts later he alighted briefly at Coucy, whose name he rendered in his own fashion as "Couchy." Surrounded by a hilltop town, the medieval Château de Coucy was "formidable and grand," its five towers dominating the route between Paris and the Netherlands. Its great central tower was one of the largest of its kind: 90 feet in diameter and 180 feet high. Its corner towers measured 65 feet in diameter and 90 feet high. A moat and wall enclosed almost six acres. Jefferson was quite uninterested in its importance in either medieval or early modern times, when, at the time of the Fronde, Cardinal Mazarin had blown up parts of the castle to render it uninhabitable. It had been absorbed into the royal domain under Louis XII but had passed into the possession of the Duc d'Orléans, one of whose titles was Sire de Coucy.[10]

Jefferson traveled on the great north road with only brief pauses. He dined and spent the night at Peronne at the Grand Cerf Tavern. On April 5 he breakfasted at Cambrai, probably at the Hôtel de Bourbon. He did not linger to view the old-fashioned fortified Flemish frontier town, whose manufactures had made possible its "broad, handsome, well paved, and lighted" streets; nor did he need to be reminded that this country had been the site of "the bloodiest wars that have disgraced and exhausted Christendom." He crossed from France into the Austrian Netherlands at Valenciennes.[11] Jefferson continued his journey northward, supping and spending the night at a roadside inn before rising early, traveling about twenty-five miles, and taking breakfast at Brussels, the capital of the Austrian Netherlands, where he lodged at the Hôtel d'Hollande. He had no time to enjoy there what John Adams had thought "well worth seeing" in spite of the ignorance and superstitious bigotry of the people and "the knavery" of the priests. After seeing the places for the execution of criminals, young John Quincy Adams had declared that the city's statue of St. Michael trampling the devil was magnificent.[12] Heading northwestward, Jefferson changed horses at Malines and entered the great city of Antwerp before its gates closed at nine o'clock. He lodged and supped. On the seventh, he exchanged French livres for Dutch florins and observed, if only briefly, how the Flemish financiers did business. At this time he did not have an opportunity to view any of Antwerp's great paintings by Rembrandt and Rubens at the cathedral and in private collections. Because of loose sand in the road, Jefferson engaged a team of six horses, instead of his customary four, before going on to Agtenbroeck, where he crossed the Scheldt River into the United Netherlands.

It was a short distance further to Rotterdam, where he spent the night of March 8 and observed how the Prince of Orange's birthday was celebrated with the "most splendid" illuminations he had ever seen and a "roar of joy." All travelers to Rotterdam at that time saw in its Grande Place the statue of Erasmus holding a book in his hand.[13] On his arrival at The Hague, five miles distant, Jefferson was delighted to find John Adams still there because of the complications of his taking formal leave of the numerous Dutch officials to whom he was accredited. Quickly the two agreed that they must satisfy America's most urgent European expenses and also anticipate her needs for the next several years. In order to raise a total of about half a million florins, they determined to ask the Amsterdam bankers to relend money scheduled for redemption during the next two years and to sell all unissued bonds. This amount, they calculated, was enough to meet the scheduled bond redemption, to settle urgent bills, and to provide for diplomatic expenses until 1790, by which time, they expected, the new federal government would have reordered the financial woes it had inherited.

Although Jefferson never denigrated The Hague, he never lauded, as did the Adamses, its unspoiled character amid the beauties of the Flemish landscape, its lack of walls, its profusion of tree-lined promenades, and its central location, which permitted easy communication with the great cit-

The Courtyard of the Amsterdam
Exchange. Jefferson did not care for
bankers, but he and John Adams succeeded
in borrowing money from them here.

ies of the Low Countries by either road or canal.[14] Perhaps the Virginia
planter, well acquainted with paying interest on inherited debts, was more
skeptical of a nation of moneylenders than were the Adamses. Abigail
Adams implied that there was a relation between the cleanliness and industriousness of the Dutch and their aid to the virtuous United States. She
was impressed by Dutch law, order, prosperity, and charities, as well as by
the absence of "wretchedness, even amidst the immense concourse of Amsterdam." To her, the Netherlands seemed to be one great meadow between towns, whose houses and streets were all of brick, whose windows
had no broken or cracked panes, and whose woodwork was all freshly
painted. Except for the general profusion in Holland of gold earrings for
everyday dress and bracelets for holidays, she admired the country folk's
simplicity of dress, which she compared to that of immigrants to America.
Furthermore, she noted that "genteel people usually spoke French and
English."[15]

Several months before Jefferson's trip to the Netherlands, its stadt-
holder, the Prince of Orange, had succeeded in a coup d'état that transformed his elective office as the confederated republic's military commander into a hereditary kingship. He was able to accomplish this irrespective
of domestic opinion because of an unusual combination of factors. The king
of France had pledged military as well as diplomatic aid to maintain the
republic, but he had reneged because of his near bankruptcy. The king of

Prussia sent into the Netherlands troops to help the Prince of Orange, who was his brother-in-law. Great Britain by professing neutrality assured the pro-British prince's success. Needless to say, there were some harsh economic reprisals against the Dutch Republicans, who called themselves the Patriots. Most of the victims were Amsterdammers. Prussia's help was rewarded with ten wagonloads of gold from Amsterdam in 1788. Within two years the Patriots' defeat persuaded some Dutchmen to buy U.S. bonds as a safe haven. Since Jefferson was not at The Hague in an official diplomatic capacity, he did not have to visit government officials, and it was of little or no consequence to him that there were in 1788 no presentations at the prince's court. Because during the crisis France had withdrawn her ambassador, Adams and Jefferson were relieved of any obligation to pay him a ceremonial visit.[16]

On March 10, 1788, Jefferson and Adams drove in Jefferson's coach to Amsterdam, where they lodged at the Wapping Van Amsterdam, located at the corner of Russland and Klovenier Streets.[17] With the help of a *valet de place* named William, Jefferson was able to see the bustling commerce in Amsterdam's harbor, the industry of her citizens, the restrained splendor of her wealthy burghers, and the hard bargaining of her financiers. Like most observers, he was enchanted by the countryside's pleasant combination of activity and repose. He saw more practical details of how the Dutch managed their canals than he recorded, partly because he was busy and partly because he already had made detailed observations of the Canal du Midi, whose course through mountains and across rivers was more relevant for American emulation. Like it or not, he and Adams had no alternative but to seek money from the banker-brokers of the Amsterdam Exchange. One of the Van Staphorsts probably repeated for Jefferson the tour he gave Abigail Adams of this center of the city's financial life. The Exchange presented a great spectacle: a large square enclosed by a piazza in which between noon and two o'clock ten thousand or more thronged to buy or sell almost any commodity or service. Their mingled cries, shouts, and conversation sounded, Mrs. Adams said, "like the swarming of bees."[18] As for the bankers themselves, Jefferson's protégé, William Short, who came to know them better than did any other American of his time, said they were "very dull men, the sum of whose ideas consists in a few constant habits—obstinate, incapable of being influenced."[19]

First, Adams introduced Jefferson to Jacob and Nicholas Van Staphorst, Jan Willink, and Nicholas Hubbard, who would float loans. Jefferson then met bankers and brokers like George Grand and Jean de Neufville, who they hoped would subscribe to loans. Almost all, if not all, of them belonged to the anti-Orange Patriot party. While attending to public matters, Jefferson took occasion to settle his own accounts by letters of exchange drawn on the Van Staphorsts: extensive purchases of books; John Stockdale's bill for printing *Notes of Virginia*; advances by the artist John Trumbull for sundry purchases at London; his secretary William Short's salary; expenses listed by his butler Petit for running the Hôtel Langeac; his girls' fees at the Panthémont school; and, of course, his own expenses at Amsterdam.[20] Perhaps Jefferson's sanguine forecast of American growth and prosperity led him to consider his own prospects so optimistically that he did not realize how greatly he was burdening his own future.

When John Adams guided Jefferson to places of cultural or historic interest in the Netherlands, he drew upon his own experiences between 1780 and 1786. Because Jefferson always counseled others to seek out an eminence from which to see a city soon after their arrival, he must have done as the Adamses did in 1780: ascend to the roof of Amsterdam's statehouse to study the complex pattern of the city's canals and streets, as well as the fine prospect of the sea, city, and ships in the harbor. Dutens said in his guidebook that this was a "superb" building and noted especially among its paintings Rembrandt's celebrated "night scene." It is probable that, like the Adamses, Jefferson also saw there the civic paintings and the armor of the Dutch admirals. Considering Jefferson's interest in the Jewish faith and in architecture, he must have been glad that the usual tourist round gave him an opportunity to inspect Amsterdam's great Sephardic synagogue, which served the large Jewish quarter of the city.[21]

Sharing the costs of relays for Jefferson's carriage, the two Americans returned to The Hague, where Jefferson saw for the first time its government buildings and especially the Mauritshuis, which originally had been the residence of the Prince Jean Maurice of Nassau-Orange. A decade before 1788, Prince William V had added a long gallery and employed a German painter, T. P. C. Haag, to supervise his family's works of art, assembled over a span of two centuries. This collection of old masters was as large and rich as any that Jefferson had seen in France or England.

135

Because the kingdom of the Netherlands recovered in 1815 about 100 of the 160-odd pictures that the French Republic's army had removed in 1795, one can identify many of the works of art that were at The Hague in 1788 for the delectation of such genteel folk as Jefferson. Including paintings that were wrongly attributed and copies mistaken for originals, the collection included Jan Breughel the Elder's *The Rest While on the Flight into Egypt*, *Christ Delivering the Souls from Purgatory*, and *The Temptation of St. Anthony*; Correggio's *Jupiter and Antiope*; one by Pieter Breughel the Younger; four portraits by Hans Holbein the Younger; one by Nicholas Poussin; four by Rembrandt, including portraits of the artist *As an Officer* and *As a Young Man*, *Simeon in the Temple*, and *Susannah in the Pool*; six by Rubens, including portraits of *Isabella Brant* and *Helene Fourment*, and paintings representing *Alexander the Great*, *Cutting the Gordian Knot*, *The Departure of Adonis*, *Eve Offering Adam the Forbidden Fruit*, *The Naïades Refilling the Cornucopia of Abundance*, and *Venus and Adonis*; Andrea del Sarto's *The Offering of Abraham*; fourteen by Jan Harvis Steen; four by David Teniers the Younger; van der Werff's *The Flight into Egypt*; Titian's *Venus Blindfolding Amor*; two by Willem Van de Velde; four by Sir Anthony Van Dyke; four by Claude Joseph Vernet; Paolo Veronese's *Christ and the Woman Taken in Adultery*, *Madonna and Child in a Landscape*, and *Maternal Love*; and eight by Philips Wouvermans. Among the works of sculpture was a copy of the Laocoön group.[22]

Adams took Jefferson to Haarlem to visit the bankers Jan de Neufville
senior and junior at their country seat, near which Jefferson made a rough
sketch of the neoclassical house of the Anglo-Dutch financier Henry Hope;
he considered it the finest in the land and one of the finest in all Europe. Near
Haarlem the Americans were so beset by a plague of July flies that Jefferson
had his carriage fitted with netting. At Amsterdam, besides calling in a
barber often and having clothes washed, he bought china plates and cups,
hyson tea, a letter press, paper, quills, sealing wax, sheet music, toothpicks,
and a waffle iron. When he jotted in his accounts modest expenditures for
"drinkel," he had not been drinking strong liquors in a barroom, but only
tea at a teahouse.

Having concluded financial business to their satisfaction, Jefferson and
Adams parted. The latter left Amsterdam to embark at the Hook of Holland
for England. After writing to the commissioners of the treasury in America
of what he and Adams had accomplished, Jefferson called for and paid his bill
at the Wapping Van Amsterdam and set out for Germany by way of Utrecht.
Ever a careful recorder and analyzer of accounts, he calculated before he left
Amsterdam the expenses that he had incurred since leaving Paris, making
a careful differentiation between what was chargeable to the United States
and what constituted personal expenses. He was now ready to travel at his
own expense through the Rhineland to Strasbourg.[23] Rather than endure
again either the ferries or long road detours of the Netherlands, he took
passage for himself and a *valet de place* on a riverboat, called a *schuyt*, from
Amsterdam to Utrecht. The best space on such craft was on the roof, where

gentlemen usually rode, and the worst was in the *ruim*, or hold, often occupied by drunken *boers*, or farmers.[24]

On March 30, 1788, Jefferson's trip from Amsterdam to Utrecht was one of "remarkable pleasantness." Bucolic scene succeeded bucolic scene: on fields of rich black mold, lower than the water level of the canal and interspersed by pastures and grazing cattle, there were occasional country houses that bespoke "the wealth and the cleanliness of the country," even though "generally in an uncouth taste . . . exhibiting no regular architecture." At Utrecht he lodged and supped at Aubelette's Tavern. Because of the recent strife between the Patriots and the Monarchists, the university and its law school were probably still closed at the time of his visit. Jefferson's only comment on the sights of the city was that the cathedral's spire was "remarkable for its height." Farmer Jefferson deduced that between Utrecht and the border between the Netherlands and the Holy Roman Empire the soil was too poor and sandy to support good crops of wheat, but he was interested in how the numerous farmhouses and their kitchen gardens were protected from cold winter winds by thick hedges of beech and apple trees. Since he had sent his coachman Espagnol and the carriage ahead by a freight boat to Utrecht, all was in readiness the next morning to make an early departure for Nijmegen, the fortress city guarding Holland from the German states just before the Rhine branches. They dined and spent the night at Chez un Anglois Inn on Nijmegen's Place Royale. Paying to see the sights, Jefferson pronounced the views of the Rhine from its hills "sublime." He commented that the local tradition associating its *slot*, or château, with Julius Caesar "must be apocryphal."[25]

Jefferson was glad to leave the Netherlands on April 1, 1788. He found nothing to admire about Dutch agriculture and flat cities of narrow streets. Although a lover of art, he liked only the most modern of Dutch or Flemish pictures. Seventeen eighty-eight was for the United States a year of hard times and hard bargains. He knew that the Dutch were his country's largest trading partner after Great Britain, and he hoped that increasingly friendly relations between the United States and the United Netherlands would bring each material gains. But the country was too dispiriting a place for such a lover of liberty as Jefferson. He and John Adams might have been critical of their High Mightinesses of the Estates General, who before 1787 had presided somewhat inefficiently over the neutrality-loving, free Dutch Republic, but Jefferson did not enjoy seeing it replaced by a hereditary monarchy propped up by Prussian bayonets, abetted by George III of Great Britain, and following pro-British policies. Sadly, he had seen France abandon her promise to support the Dutch Republican party when only France could have saved Dutch liberties. Alas, the impending bankruptcy of the French kingdom left no alternative.

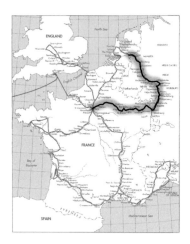

12 *In the Rhineland and from Strasbourg to Paris*

JEFFERSON'S DECISION TO RETURN TO PARIS FROM THE NETHER-
lands by way of the Rhine valley and Strasbourg rested in part on his desire
to investigate trading opportunities and to learn of improvements in agriculture, mechanical contrivances, and manufacture that might benefit
Americans. He also conformed to his habit of seeing the principal architectural and artistic works in towns and cities on his way. This was an arduous
journey even for a forty-three-year-old man whose health was generally
good, except for headaches and his right wrist, which still gave him occasional arthritic pain. For most of his trip Jefferson followed the routes suggested in Louis Dutens's guidebook. He also relied on the advice of friends
in making practical arrangements for his travels. The Van Staphorsts and
Willinks provided letters of credit and the names of banks and inns along his
route. John Trumbull provided a helpful account of his own journey in the
valley of the Rhine two years earlier by boats and post wagons. The way that
Jefferson traveled in Germany differed little from the way he traveled in
France and Italy, except that east of the Rhine the Prince de Turn-et-Taxis
operated the system of providing relays of horses as a private, not a state,
monopoly. Jefferson paid German postilions a backhanded insult when he
said that they were "incorruptible by money, by fair words or foul. . . .
Nothing on earth can induce [them] to go out of a walk." Having very little
command of the German language, he was forced to rely on his valet
Espagnol's lingua franca of the stable and the road.[1]

On April 1, 1788, acting on advice that he later regretted following,
Jefferson paid the horse hirer at the Nijmegen post house to hitch only three
horses to his carriage instead of four. In doing so he hoped to circumvent the
fee policy of the Turn-et-Taxis monopoly, which was calculated on the num-

ber of horses used at the first post house in Germany. While a pair and a cock horse for use on hills and in mud and sand might have sufficed on French roads, Jefferson's difficulties on bad German roads proved that not to engage two pair was an economy of neither time nor money.

At Nijmegen Jefferson saw a ferry system he already had observed on the Po River in Italy and was to see again at several places on the Rhine. He described it variously as one based on "vibrating boats" and on a "pendulum" movement. At Nijmegen seven "little barks" supported a platform for vehicles and horses; motive power was given by the river's own current; and a rope was stretched diagonally across the river to guide the whole.[2] Crossing the border near the Prussian village of Kranenburg, Jefferson commented that although the soil and climate were the same, he passed "from ease and opulence to extreme poverty," where "the fear of slaves is visible in the faces of the Prussian subjects," who lived under a "despotism." He thought the crop fields "wanted manure, being visibly worn down." Kleve was Jefferson's first stop for a relay of fresh horses. Staying overnight at the post house inn, he found the place to be "little more than a village," with neither a showy palace built in imitation of Versailles nor the prosperous industry that often accompanies thrift. Instead, the great, brooding medieval tower of Kleve looked down on a bleak town whose shop windows were devoid of goods or food and whose inhabitants seemed ill-dressed, starved, furtive, and depressed. Because of his wartime experience as governor of Virginia with Hessian prisoners, he was partially prepared for such conditions in Germany. Contributing further to this dispiriting introduction to the German states, snow and rain made the road so bad that after breakfasting at the next stop, Xanten, Jefferson bought some tools in anticipation of digging the carriage wheels out of a morass.[3]

On April 2, between Xanten and Duisburg, Jefferson's interest in ancient history and a misleading comment by Dutens led him into fruitless inquiries concerning the site where Herman the German in A.D. 9 had overwhelmed the Roman general Varus and his legions. In these two towns Jefferson could find no one who spoke any language that he did. Evidently, he confused the Teutoburg Forest site of Varus's debacle, about a hundred miles east of the Rhine, with the system of Roman frontier forts and encampments that Drusus Germanicus had established in 10 B.C. on the west bank of the Rhine, of which Xanten is a minor but excellent example. Perhaps viewing the ruins of Xanten's medieval crenelation and machicolation through snow flurries blinded Jefferson to their Roman foundations. Considering his admiration of the literature that presents Ossian as a Gaelic hero and considering his frequent comparison of the mythical Teutonic sources of Anglo-American liberties with the facts of Roman and Norman tyranny,[4] it is too bad that Jefferson was not also acquainted with the *Nibelungenlied*, according to which Xanten was the birthplace of Siegfried. Jefferson passed through the town of Rheinburg without noticing its Roman remains or commenting on its Rathaus. Jefferson estimated the Rhine to be about a quarter-mile wide at this point. To reach the small river port of Duisburg he crossed the Rhine in "a scow with sails" in eight or ten minutes, thanks to a good breeze. He spent the night of April 2 at Essen, then only a prosperous market town. The next morning he traveled to Düsseldorf, described by Dutens as a fortified town of ten thousand. Of course no one could have foreseen that the industrial revolution would transform these country towns into great cities in the next century. Jefferson was pleased to observe that their buildings were in good repair, but he did not bother to inspect either the Münster at Essen or Duisburg's church associated with the geographer Mercator.

Jefferson spent the night of April 3 at Düsseldorf at the Zwei Brukker Hof, of which Herr Zimmermann was the proprietor. "The best tavern I saw in my whole journey" was Jefferson's encomium on this long-vanished hostelry. The little city's Rathaus was the sort of building that Jefferson approved of, and he commented favorably on the neoclassical schloss of the Elector of Cologne. In them and in the Jagerhof, on the edge of town, the Elector Karl Theodore had left an enlightened mark, though not quite so self-congratulatory as his anonymous gift to the city of an equestrian statue of himself.[5] Since Jefferson usually relied on the advice of artist friends,[6] he knew from John Trumbull, more than from Dutens, that a visit to the Elector's gallery "would well repay the trouble." Düsseldorf's glory, Jefferson exclaimed, was the Elector's collection of paintings. He visited the gallery twice, tipping its servants well. He pronounced it "sublime" and "equal in merit to anything in the world . . . [and] worth repeated examination." Trumbull had alerted him to the fact that "the finest part" of the collection was the works by Rubens,[7] one of which was *The Last Judgement*. Among other pictures were a *Magdalen* by Carlo Dolci, a *St. John* by Raphael, an *Annunciation* by Guido Reni, and a *Madonna* by Zanetti.[8]

Jefferson did not concur in Trumbull's selection of favorite pictures. Admitting that he was no connoisseur of art, Jefferson wrote to Maria Cosway that he preferred the works of the minor late-seventeenth- and early-eighteenth-century Dutch painter Adrian van der Werff and the Italian painter Carlo Dolci, of the same period, to "the old faded red things of Rubens." Presumably, Jefferson had been prejudiced against Rubens's series of paintings celebrating Marie de Medici, which he and Mrs. Cosway had seen at Paris in the Luxembourg Palace. At Düsseldorf he singled out for praise Adrian van der Werff's painting of Abraham, Sarah, Hagar, and Ishmael, saying that it was so "delicious" that "I would have agreed to be Abraham, though the consequence would have been that I should have been dead five or six thousand years." Trumbull, on the other hand, wrote later in his *Memoirs* that van der Werff's and Dolci's were, "of all the celebrated pictures I have seen, . . . the very worst—mere monuments of labor, patience and want of genius."

We cannot know whether Jefferson would have been swayed by Trumbull's condemnation of van der Werff and Dolci. The ideological subject matter of paintings was so important to Jefferson that it is unlikely that he cared for any picture celebrating a monarch. Certainly he withheld approval of even great artists if they idealized a foolish king like James I of England, a dictatorial one like Louis XIV of France, or a perpetrator of the massacre of religious opponents such as Henri II's queen. Although he wrote Maria Cosway that he was "but a son of nature, loving what I see and feel, without

Sarah Fürt Hagar zu Abraham and *Die Verstossung Hagars*, 1701, paintings by Adrian van der Werff (1659–1722). John Trumbull chided Jefferson for his extravagant praise of van der Werff's scene portraying Abraham's dismissal of Hagar.

being able to give a reason, nor caring much whether there be one," he had at least once modified his artistic opinion after an exchange with a professional artist, Sophie de Tott.[9]

In continuing on his way to Cologne, Jefferson decided not to "go off the road" in order to visit the Elector's rococo schloss at Benrath. On recrossing the Rhine he had to pass through Zons, another ruined medieval fortified town whose medieval walls and towers rested on Roman foundations laid up by Drusus Germanicus. Jefferson later urged American tourists upon entering Westphalia to "take notice" of the region's "celebrated ham," whose curing by salt, pepper, and smoke was the same as in Virginia. If he was amused by the name of the inn where he dined and lodged in Cologne—the Holy Ghost, presided over by the hospitable Herr Ingel—he did not say so. Jefferson paid a barber to shave him and fix his hair. He noted in his journal that Cologne was a walled city, but he was silent about its buildings, probably agreeing with Trumbull that they were "ill-built." Jefferson did not approve of vast cathedrals like Cologne's St. Peter's, which had been built at the expense of a tax-ridden and credulous populace. He probably thought it a good thing that the citizens of Cologne had long before expelled their archbishop and left one of the cathedral's two spires unfinished. A resolute apostle of religious freedom, Jefferson was keenly aware of the religious contradictions of the city. Although antiepiscopal, it had 250 Roman Catholic churches. And the Roman Catholics, although they insisted on their own freedom, permitted only one Protestant church, and that of recent license.

It was at Cologne that Jefferson made his principal investigation of commercial opportunities on the Rhine. On a quay worthy of a seaport town, he discovered that most of the city's exports went to Rotterdam,

including "a good deal" for transshipment to America. He decided that its
commerce was principally in the hands of Protestants, even though they
were "extremely restricted" and "oppressed by every form of government
which is Catholic and excessively intolerant." German products that particularly caught his fancy were millstones and wine, about both of which he
resolved to learn more. He soon concluded that the so-called millstones of
Cologne were neither quarried nor finished there. Eventually he learned
that they were made of tufa, a volcanic rock that was quarried and finished
at the nearby river town of Andernach. Many told him that Cologne was the
"most northern spot on the earth on which wine is made" and that Rhenish
vineyards were planted with vines developed from stock imported long ago
from the Loire, Alsace, and Champagne. Concerned about the possible
effect of North American climatic conditions on European vines, Jefferson
considered it auspicious that the Dutch had taken Rhenish vines to the Cape
of Good Hope to start viticulture there. Hoping for the best, he purchased
from a Cologne wine merchant named Jean Jacques Peuchen cuttings to
tend at Paris until he could send them to Virginia.

On April 4 Jefferson left Cologne for Bonn, where he changed horses
and took breakfast at the Court of England Tavern. Without commenting
on the city's being undefended by walls or on its educational institutions, he
inspected the archbishop of Cologne's mid-eighteenth-century electoral
palace and administrative capital before driving up the quadruple avenue of
horse chestnuts of the Popeldorfer Allée on his way out of town. Bypassing
the Elector's summer retreat, Schloss Augustusburg at Bruhl, he satisfied his
curiosity about millstones at Andernach, changed horses at Remagen, and
continued on his way.[10] Up to this point he had considered the roads better

than the weather, but now the situation reversed. Unfortunately, wrote Jefferson, recent snows and rains had left the roads "worse than imagination can paint" all the way to Frankfurt, ninety miles away.

When Jefferson reached Coblenz on April 5, he spent the night at L'Homme Sauvage, where he found his landlord "most obliging" in informing him about the merits of Moselle wines. Probably relying upon him, Jefferson advised American tourists to request six-year-old Moselle from the winery of Baron Breidbach Burresheim, the grand chamberlain and bailiff of Coblenz, whose grapes grew on the mountain of Braunberg. Jefferson considered this wine, in comparison with several others of the region, "quite clear of acid, stronger, and very sensibly the best." He also commended to tourists Coblenz's fine breakfast rolls, which, he noted, Philadelphians mistakenly called French instead of German. Jefferson liked the palace and administrative center that the Elector of Trèves had completed at Coblenz in 1786, not for its heavy, severely regular and symmetrical assemblage of neoclassical blocs and quadrants, but for its heating system, provided by hot air drawn through tile tubes from furnaces below. When he advised other Americans to visit the schloss across the Rhine from Coblenz, it was because of its fine views of the river and city rather than because of its ponderous fortifications.

From Coblenz, Jefferson was ferried across the river on still another "pendulum boat" in order to follow the post road up the Lahn River valley toward Frankfurt. He described this route as "a barren desert" of reddish soil and rock interspersed with patches of maize, vines, and forests of oak and beech. In his more prosaic accounts, he said the road passed through "tremendous hills," but to Maria Cosway he said the route was "as mountainous as the passage of the Alps." He breakfasted at the half-timbered village of Nassau, whose meager comforts he contrasted with the opulence of "the House of Orange to which it belongs" and drove through Bad Schwalbach and Wiesbaden as quickly as possible. Spring was long in reaching Germany that year. It was too early for the season at the spas. Under different circumstances he might have paused long enough to soak his wrist in their hot mineral waters. Instead, he hurried on to Frankfurt, which he reached on April 6. The reason for his haste was his desire to meet there an old friend and to travel with him for several days in that vicinity.[11]

This friend was Major the Baron Geismar, who had been one of the officers surrendered at Saratoga as a result of the convention drawn up by the American and British commanders. The so-called convention troops had been interned at several places before they were quartered at Charlottesville in January 1777. Most of the four thousand men had been German mercenary soldiers, and Geismar had commanded a brigade enlisted from his home district of Hanau in the state of Hesse-Kassel. In Virginia the enlisted men and some officers had lived in barracks, but other officers had taken advantage of a lenient parole system to rent houses in the vicinity of Monticello. Geismar was one of these. He had become an intimate of Thomas and Martha Jefferson, exchanging visits, supper parties, amateur theatricals, and musical evenings, during which Jefferson played the violin, Mrs. Jefferson the harpsichord, and Geismar the viola. As governor of Virginia,

Jefferson had tried to facilitate the baron's early exchange on grounds that he was the only child of an aged parent whose ill health placed the son's patrimony in danger.[12] When negotiations with the British stalled, Geismar had been paroled to New York in November 1780 preparatory to his passage to Europe. Before leaving Albemarle, the good baron had given Jefferson "all my musik" and had thanked him profusely for the many "civilitys and kindness shown to me during my stay."[13] As one who had played music with Martha Jefferson at Monticello, Geismar was one of the small, inner circle of Thomas Jefferson's friends. He was one of the two people known to have addressed him as "Mon Cher."[14]

Major Geismar was now an officer of the garrison at Hanau and an official of the court of Landgrave and Hereditary Prince Wilhelm of Hesse-Kassel, who had inherited Hanau in 1785. Because the prince's castle at Kassel was too old-fashioned and too far from the metropolis of Frankfurt, Prince Wilhelm held court mainly at Schloss Philippsruhe, on the road from Frankfurt to Hanau and surrounded on two sides by the River Main. A German derivative of Versailles, it had great gilded salons and clipped *allées*.

In Europe Jefferson had corresponded with Geismar since 1785.[15] In an enthusiastic reply to Jefferson's first letter, the baron had urged Jefferson to visit Hanau: "You will be welcome, Mon Cher, in our part of the world." Although professing devotion to Prince Wilhelm, he had declared: "I shall always be a true Republican and above all a good American. . . . Come spend a while with us. Together we will tour the better part of Germany." And perhaps, he said, they would even go to Italy together.[16] While Jefferson was in Amsterdam in March 1788, he accepted Geismar's

145

Marktplatz von Frankfurt am Main um 1750, engraving. Baron von Geismar met Jefferson here before taking him on a tour of castles and vineyards.

Ehemaliger Gasthof zum Roten Haus auf der Zeil, 1769, engraving by J. M. Zell. The Roten Haus was Jefferson's hotel at Frankfurt.

invitation to meet at Frankfurt.[17] Aware for the first time that Jefferson was a widower, Geismar's sentiments matched Jefferson's perfectly: "A handshake by a hearty friend says more of condolence than all the quills of the universe."[18]

Since Jefferson had told Geismar that he would lodge at Herr Dick's stylish Roten Haus Hotel at Frankfurt, the baron made arrangements with its proprietor to inform him as soon as Jefferson arrived. This was a fortunate choice of inns, because Dick's son knew some English and French. Jefferson found that his *hotelier* was also a great wine merchant who kept a fine cellar, from which reputable guests were permitted to taste some of his "genuine Hoch, and of the oldest." Wishing to appear at his best for his friend, Jefferson called in a barber on April 7, 8, and 10, when he presumably was shaved and had his hair washed and powdered. While Espagnol saw to repairing the cabriolet, Jefferson hired a local carriage. He attended the theater on April 7 and 8, bought books, and placed an order to have a topcoat made on the ninth. In addition, he employed as *valet de place* one of Herr Dick's employees, Arnaud, who accompanied him and Geismar on their peregrinations for four or five days of sightseeing at Frankfurt, Hanau, Mainz, and the great vineyards of the Rhine.

Jefferson made no description of Frankfurt in his "Hints to Americans Travelling in Europe," but in his "Notes of a Tour through Holland and the Rhine Valley" he was more expansive. He was heartened to see the fine "mulatto" land of the countryside, planted in corn, vines, and fruit trees and giving "the appearance of wealth." The "commercial town" of Frankfurt was a little republic, or more properly speaking, a Free City of the Holy Roman Empire. Free of onerous taxation, it was hospitable to commerce, manufacturing, and banking. Although officially Lutheran, Frankfurt was tolerant of both denomination and faith. Its annual fairs in April and October made it a trading center for much of Germany. Periodically it enjoyed the ceremonious and lucrative election of a Holy Roman Emperor. Among the main sights that Geismar showed his visitor was the Romerburg Building, in which the election of emperors took place. No matter how much Jefferson the architect disliked Gothic architecture, Jefferson the political scientist must have been interested in this remarkable institutional structure. Surely he liked the nearby modern palace of the Prince de Turn-et-Taxis, both a residence and headquarters for the monopoly of posts and relays. As Geismar had ample entrée, it is not unlikely that he took Jefferson to call on some of the notables of Frankfurt in their Louis Seize drawing rooms. Besides tasting wine and accumulating oenological lore, Jefferson also inspected the cast-iron stoves made there. Later, he ordered two of them in different sizes, each representing an urn resting on a column.[19]

Since Baron Geismar later introduced to the Court of Hesse-Kassel at Philippsruhe Jefferson's protégés Rutledge and Shippen, he undoubtedly did Jefferson the same honor. Jefferson wrote William Short that he met there "many" of the Hessian officers he had known in Virginia. In private he was critical of conditions at Hanau, but he was careful to keep his opinion to himself so as not to embarrass his host. Noting the difference in the apparent effects of government as soon as he passed from the Free City into the principality of Hesse, he wrote that Frankfurt was filled with "life, bustle and motion," while in Hanau there was only the "silence and quiet of the

Prospekt des Fürstl, Taxischen Pallasts, ca. 1745, engraving by Johann Michael Eben. Jefferson complained about the rates the Prince of Turn und Taxis charged for post horses in Germany, but he must have admired the nobleman's residence and headquarters at Frankfurt.

NON VESTEM SED VESTIS FARCTUM.
HANAW.

View of Hanau, engraving. Hanau was
then part of Hesse, in whose court
Geismar was an official.

mansions of the dead. Nobody is seen moving in its streets; every door is
shut; no sound of the saw, the hammer, or other utensil of industry. The
drum and fife is all that is heard. The streets are cleaner than a German floor,
because nobody passes them."[20]

Yet, Hanau's ruler permitted Calvinists to worship publicly, whereas
Frankfurt did not.[21] Because Hanau's populace was divided almost evenly
between Roman Catholics and Lutherans, there was great religious tolera-
tion. Because the town was renowned for its goldsmiths, one may assume
that there was also banking, an assumption that is reinforced by Geismar's
statement that Prince Wilhelm's father had "left his coffers full" from an
annual tax harvest in addition to what he received for providing mercenary
troops to other rulers. Whether such gold and banks provided credit for any
but state enterprises is doubtful. Although Jefferson did not assert directly
that too heavy a tax load was exacted of Hessians, he did say that he saw more
beggars in Hesse-Kassel than anywhere else in Germany. An unbending foe
of despotism, he attributed the greater profusion of game in Hesse than in
the environs of Frankfurt, not to the ruler's desire to hunt game for sport,
but to his disarming of potentially rebellious subjects.

A quarter-mile northwest of Hanau the Virginian found Wilhelmsbad,
not only the country seat of the Prince-Landgrave of Hesse-Kassel but an
early spa that Jefferson declared "well worth visiting." Although it was early
in the season, he may have taken its waters. In an unusual act, he sketched
a plan of the "clever" ruin nearby: a *folie* representing the remains of an old
castle, consisting of a two-story round tower with one-story squared towers
at its sides. He did not profess to like it as much as the trefoil *folie* he had seen
and sketched in England. At Wilhelmsbad he also admired a mock hermitage furnished with modest articles of furniture and supplies in which there
was "a good figure of a hermit in plaister, coloured to the life." He applauded
even more the originality and fine execution of a sentry box covered over
with bark so as to look exactly like the trunk of an old tree.

With his friend as cicerone and his own *valet de place*, Arnaud, to
attend them, Jefferson and Geismar made a tour of the wine country near
the confluence of the Main and the Rhine. They first went to Hadesheim
and Hochheim. At the latter Jefferson ordered one hundred vine cuttings
to be delivered to Paris. After spending the night of April 11 at the river
port of Rudesheim, they inspected the famous vineyards nearby. When

View from the End of the Pleasure Garden
at Philippsruhe through the Grand Allée.
The Prince of Hesse taxed his subjects
heavily and sold their military services to
maintain a diminutive Versailles.

they visited the Marco Brünnen winery near Mittelheim, they passed by
the village's sixteenth-century Rathaus without comment. They had to go
through the village of Oëstrich, but they gave no description of its mid-
seventeenth-century weighhouse. Rudesheim has always been the area's
largest river port for the shipment of wine whose correct appellation is
Riesling, though the name Hock is commonly used. Jefferson bought
there several bottles of wine and fifty vine cuttings, but he made no comment about the town, its wine presses, or its old fortifications. He was
happy to go to the Schloss Johannisberger, "where the most celebrated
wines are made." There he tasted wine with his friend and observed the
way the vineyards were planted and how the grapes were pressed. Higher
up on the slopes, the owners of the schloss had constructed a sham medieval castle to enliven the skyline. Now the sham has become a "real" castle,
whose name is given to a lesser Riesling. From Rudesheim, Jefferson's little
party took a boat down the river to Mainz. It was only a short distance to
the beginning of the Rheingau, the passage between cliffs that have reminded many of the Hudson's palisades. Jefferson regretted that he had
not seen the natural beauties of the Rhine between Coblenz and Mainz by
boat, as had Trumbull. He seems to have given no thought to either the
Roman or contemporary sights of Mainz.[22]

The leave-taking between Jefferson and Geismar must have been as
emotional as these eighteenth-century men of the Enlightenment permitted of themselves. Despite their speaking of traveling together in Italy and
the baron's hope of visiting Jefferson at Paris, each seems to have realized
that this was their final adieu. Their firm handshake and unspoken words
about happy times in Virginia were matched by their optimism for the

future of mankind and vows of friendship so long as "on this side of the Styx."[23] At the same time Jefferson distributed to Arnaud and other servants generous tokens of his appreciation for their good services.

On April 11 Jefferson did not make an early departure from the Hôtel de Mayence in the old, walled city of Mainz, where he stayed at the Three Crowns Inn. That city's institutions were even more at odds with Frankfurt's republican liberties than Hanau's had been. The imperial city drew trade away from Mainz, then in the last decade of its misrule by the Elector Karl Theodore von Dahlberg and the archbishop of Trèves, Frederich Karl Joseph d'Erthal, whom the citizens of Mainz expelled in 1792. Until then commerce languished in Mainz, but its cathedral was rich. Near the Romanesque Dom, the bibliophile Jefferson must have seen the house where Johann Gutenberg had conducted his printing and publishing business, but he commented neither on it nor on the nearby Rathaus, each exuberantly Gothic and benighted in the eyes of such an eighteenth-century neoclassicist. Nor did he comment on the seventeenth-century baroque splendor of the Prince-Bishop's palace. That he said nothing about Mainz's Roman oldest tower, which soldiers of the XXII Legion had built in 1 B.C. to honor the memory of Drusus, can be explained by the necessity of gaining special permission of the military commander of the Zitadelle, within whose precincts the tower was located.[24]

It was only two stages from Mainz to Worms through the river plain, which began as rich, black soil. The road often degenerated into a river of sand through which twenty-horse caravans sometimes struggled. In the districts of Laudenheim, Bodenheim, and Nierstein, Jefferson saw that the steep southeastern slopes were planted with grapes and learned that they produced white wine of the second quality. By the time he reached Oppenheim, the hillsides had changed color from gray to red, although the best soil of the river plain remained black as far as Worms, where it became so sandy that it was fit only for planting pine trees. While a fresh team of horses was being assembled at the post house Zum Swanen, Jefferson ascended to the top of Oppenheim's Katherine Church, located on the chief eminence between Mainz and Worms. It is no surprise that he wrote nothing about the latter city's great Romanesque cathedral and bishop's palace. It is hard, however, to understand how this oenophile failed to comment on the vineyard engulfing the Liebfrauen Kirche that gives its name to the local mother's milk. It was with undoubted pleasure that Jefferson, having dined, himself quit Worms through its southeastern gate, whose Roman character has been enhanced in mid-twentieth-century reconstruction. After all, he was only a dozen or so miles away from one of the eighteenth century's model cities, Mannheim, which he reached on April 14.[25]

At Mannheim, Jefferson put up at the Cour du Palatin, a "good tavern," for a three-night stay. He called in a barber twice, went to the theater once, and bought a book.[26] Mannheim was a new, planned city, built when the Prince of the Palatinate abandoned Heidelberg as his residence and capital in 1720. Not so imaginative a city as some proposed by the French architect Ledoux,[27] its 1758 plan shows a relentless rectangular grid within star-shaped fortifications. Jefferson liked its geometry enough to tell Americans visiting Germany that they "must" go to Mannheim. He did not comment on the monotonous regularity of the city, its schloss, its grandiose state apartments, its Rathaus, or its neoclassical arsenal. He did say that the Prince Elector Charles Theodore's gallery of paintings was "more considerable than that of Düsseldorf, but has not so many precious things." He advised young Americans on their grand tour to follow his example by making a circuit of four excursions from Mannheim. Two of these were for agricultural purposes: to Kaeferthal to see rhubarb and wild boars and to Dossenheim to see Angora goats. The third was to visit Heidelberg, where Jefferson spent part of April 15.

To Jefferson, the schloss of Heidelberg, located high up its little mountain, was "the most imposing ruin of modern ages," even though then there was nothing "under cover" but the chapel. He thought that "its situation was so much the most romantic and delightful possible" that he would have been "glad to have passed days at it." Finding that the apple, pear, cherry, peach, apricot, and almond trees were all in bloom, he even professed that the climate was "like" Italy's. He was enchanted by the gardens that lie above the château, "climbing up the mountain in terasses." To Maria Cosway he wrote as soon as he returned to Paris:

> At Heidelberg I wished for you, too. In fact I led you by the hand thro' the whole garden. I was struck with the resemblance of this scene to that of Vaucluse as seen from what is called the château of Petrarch. Nature has formed both on the same sketch, but she has filled up that of Heidelberg with bolder hand. The river is larger, the mountains more majestic and better clothed. Art too has seconded her views. The château of Petrarch is the ruin of a modest country house; that of Heidelberg would stand well along side the pyramids of Egypt. It is certainly the most magnificent ruin after those left us by the ancients.

Nowadays it is difficult for a visitor to dismiss the extent of nineteenth-century restorations of the Heidelberger Schloss and to remember that in the early eighteenth century the Electoral Princes of the Palatinate had abandoned it after its repeated destruction by peacetime fires as well as by wars. It is moot whether Jefferson knew that some two hundred and fifty years before, Elizabeth Stuart and her husband Frederick V had employed Inigo Jones as their architect for a new wing to house a theater in which they could view Shakespearian plays. When Jefferson visited the ruined castle, he showed himself to be a quantifying and classifying man of his times: "I measured . . . the famous tun of Heidelberg," he wrote, recording the great wine keg's dimensions and capacity. "New built in 1751," it may have been, but, he announced with what was almost pride of discovery, "there is no wine in it now."[28] What most caught his fancy was the Heidelbergers' careful cultivation of trees. Poor soil near the town was planted in pines, but there were many peach and other fruit trees on the lower slopes of the mountain. The paths on the upper parts of the mountain formed a system of diagonals at an angle of about sixty degrees between horizontal ones at four levels, including a flattened summit. Later, in going over his notes, Jefferson wrote between the lines: "The paths . . . gave me the idea of making paths on Monticello."[29]

*Les Jardins de Schwetzingen de l'Electeur
Palatine, avec une Coupe des Maisons d'Hiver,*
engraving by George Louis Le Rouge.
Jefferson visited the Elector's gardens and
summer palace, halfway between Heidelberg and Mannheim.

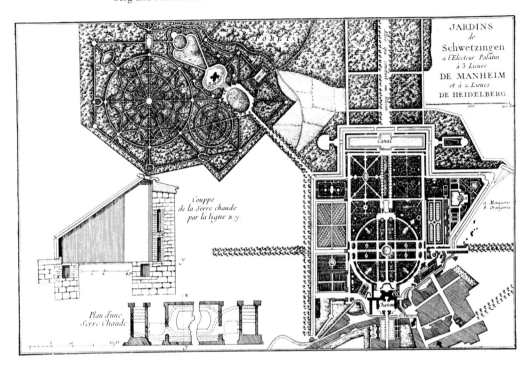

The fourth excursion from Mannheim that Jefferson recommended
was to Schwetzingen, the summer retreat of the Princes of the Palatinate.
The purpose of such a jaunt was not to examine the schloss, which mixes
seventeenth-century vernacular with baroque architectural elements. Nor
was it to view the rococo pavilion in which Mozart had given concerts and
which was the scene for the first presentation of *Iphigenea in Tauris*. His
reason for going there was to see the extensive grounds, comprising park,
folies, flower gardens, and waterworks, all of which could have inspired Watteau's *Departure for Cytheria*. Jefferson complained that Schwetzingen's formal, Franco-Italian garden demonstrated "how much money may be laid out
to make an ugly thing." The natural, English garden, however, relieved his
eye from "the straight rows of trees, [and] round and square basons. . . .
There are some tolerable morsels of Grecian architecture, and a good ruin.
The Aviary, too, is clever. It consists of cells of about 8 feet wide, arranged
'round, and looking into, a circular area of about 40 or 50 feet [in] diameter.
The cells have doors both of wire and glass, and have [, besides exotic birds,]
small shrubs in them." Jefferson concluded that although the gardens of
Schwetzingen were "among the best of Germany," they were "not to be
compared to the English gardens."[30]

On April 15 Jefferson crossed the Rhine to Speyer, where he found little "remarkable." By now he was sated with the Rhenish urban formula: medieval walls and towers on Roman foundations, a Gothic or Romanesque cathedral, a Rathaus, and a market square. Uninterested in cathedrals and having a low opinion of monarchs, he did not bother to see the tombs of three Holy Roman Emperors in the crypt of Speyer's Dom. He might have applauded when Speyer's citizens rebelled against their repressive Prince-Bishop a few years later and erected a tree of liberty.[31]

Recrossing the Rhine on April 16 in a scow propelled by oars, Jefferson reached Karlsruhe, the new capital of Baden, in time for an early dinner at the Prince Héréditan Tavern. He concluded that the margrave of Baden was "an excellent sovereign," judging from the appearance of his dominions. The town then seemed to be "only an appendage to his palace" located in the midst of a large, natural forest whose oaks were "the best trees" Jefferson had seen in Germany, even though they were cut by *allées*. Jefferson advised young tourists not only to visit the tower of Schloss Karlsruhe but also to "visit the gardens minutely. You will see in it some deer of an uncommon [spotted] kind, Angora goats, tamed beavers, and a fine collection of [both gold and silver] pheasants." Jefferson left Karlsruhe in the afternoon and passed rapidly through several towns on his way to France. There was little for him to remark upon at Rastatt except that it was "another seat of the Margrave of Baden," possessing a baroque schloss, a nice garden with a teahouse fondly believed to resemble a pagoda, and the usual mélange of Rathaus and market.[32]

Crossing the Rhine by a wooden bridge, he reached Strasbourg late the evening of April 16 to lodge at the ancient L'Esprit Tavern for three nights. This hotel was located near the Pont Saint Nicholas in the oldest part of the city, where the Rhine's tributary, the River Ill, gives the appearance of an Amsterdam canal. When Louis XIV had seized the city in 1681, during peacetime, the Alsatians retained through their guilds a share of the city's governance. It was not for reasons of reverence that Jefferson told Thomas Lee Shippen and John Rutledge, Jr., that one of the two things they must visit was its Gothic cathedral, whose 465-foot spire was "the highest in the world and the handsomest." "Go to the very top of it," he urged, even though by way of only a tolerable staircase, "in order to see the city in one *coup d'oeuil;* but let it be the last operation of the day, as you will need a long rest after it." He did not speak either of the cathedral's famous astronomical clock or of the celebrated funeral monument to Marshal Saxe in the Protestant church of St. Thomas. The latter depicted Saxe as descending to his tomb, whose door was held open by Death, while a symbolic France tried to detain him amid an ensemble of broken staffs and flags of the Austrian eagle, the English leopard, and the Dutch lion. Without recording it, Jefferson may have walked though the Place Broglie to visit the city's Aubette picture gallery. He made no mention of either Strasbourg's 300-year-old university, of which Goethe was a 1771 graduate, or her 350-year-old Protestant Gymnasium.

The other sight Jefferson insisted that young Americans see at Strasbourg was its Episcopal Palace, which he called the "palace of Cardinal de Rohan-Soubise."[33] He did not mean to direct travelers thither because of the structure's architectural merit, but only to feed their curiosity excited by the contemporary speculation over whether the cardinal had given a diamond necklace to Queen Marie Antoinette or to an impersonator in hope of amatory favors. When the cardinal refused to pay for the jewels, his trial showed to all how rotten the French high clergy and nobility were.[34] It was appropriate that books constituted Jefferson's chief pleasure at Strasbourg, where Johannes Gutenberg had made his first experiments 350 years earlier. He bought a number of books from Monsieur Koenig, who kept at the corner of the rue des Grands Arcades and the rue des Hallébardes what Jefferson pronounced "the best shop of classical books I ever saw."[35]

Often Jefferson's purpose was to note foreign practices whose introduction to America would benefit its inhabitants. Considering what he had seen in the Rhine valley, one must conclude that he had indeed addressed its arts, commerce, manufactures, and agriculture. He measured with care the Rhenish system of operating a bridge of boats. He bought iron stoves, remarked upon how there was a market for rhubarb as an alchemist's ingredient, and observed that the Rhinelanders had adopted cultivation of Indian maize and tobacco. He satisfied his curiosity about the area's method of curing and smoking hams.[36]

Jefferson was enthusiastic about the German people and especially about those between Mainz and Strasbourg. He wrote to William Short: "The neighborhood of this place is that which has been to us a second mother country. It is from the Palatinate on this part of the Rhine that those swarms of Germans have come, who, next to the descendants of the English, form the greatest body of our people. I have been continually amused by seeing here the origin of whatever is not English among us. I have fancied myself often in the upper parts of Maryland and Pennsylvania."[37] In his last letter to Baron de Geismar, Jefferson assured his friend that his journey in the Rhineland had been "prosperous" chiefly because of the grapevines to which the baron had led him. Not doubting that these would thrive in Albemarle County, he expressed the hope that if Geismar ever revisited Monticello, "I shall be able to give you there a glass of Hock or of Rudesheim of my own making."[38]

Nevertheless, the most valuable result of Jefferson's journey in the Rhineland was his improvement of the plow. On April 13 he had noted near Mannheim the very inefficient German method of plowing with oxen made to "draw by the horns" rather than by their shoulders or bodies. A fortnight later in Alsace, he found that although "oxen plough here with collars and hames," it was still inefficient because the plows were so poor. After rumination, he wrote at Nancy on April 19 his first scheme for a scientifically designed moldboard for a plow that would turn a furrow deep and true enough to use soil efficiently. Since he already knew about Du Hamel's improved plow, only Jefferson's mathematical calculations for the curvature and dimensions of the moldboard were new, and these scientific characteristics distinguished his contribution from those of the French empiricist.[39]

On April 20, 1788, Jefferson left Strasbourg for Paris. At first his route took him north. He stopped three times for fresh relays of horses and postilions before spending the night at Phalsbourg, where he supped and breakfasted. The next day, four short stages brought him through the Vosges Mountains. During the remainder of his journey to Paris he was delighted by the blossoming of apple, cherry, and peach trees along the way. He dined and was barbered two posts before Nancy, which he called "a neat little town" with "agreeable environs." Jefferson was too preoccupied with his thoughts about plows and plowing to give much heed to the city of Nancy.[40] He lodged on the Place Stanislaus, arriving in time to engage a *valet de place* and to drink chocolate. Before supping, he made a circuit of the square, admiring the regular façades of the buildings and the *allées* and gardens near the château constructed by Louis XV's father-in-law, Stanislaus, the ex-king of Poland. One possible reason that Jefferson did not praise Nancy more was that he may have suspected that its rococo delights had been achieved at the expense of impoverishing the populace of Lorraine, whose roads, he noted, were "strung with beggars." After breakfast on the twenty-first, Jefferson set out again in his carriage, reaching St. Dizier in time to sup and lodge at the Hôtel de la Poste. The next day he passed through three posts before he paused at Châlons-sur-Marne long enough for an early dinner and to be barbered.

Jefferson arrived at Monsieur Coussin's Hôtel de Rohan at Epernay to lodge the night of April 22. Then, as now, Epernay was the center of Champagne's wine district. With Coussin's guidance, he toured the great vineyards and sampled some of their products. The vicinity of Epernay, he wrote, was "precisely the canton where the most celebrated wines are made." He noted that the soil on the preferred southern slopes of a range of little mountains was composed of "meagre mulatto clay mixed with small broken stones, and a little hue of chalk" and was "very dry." Jefferson sketched a map, locating and commenting on the wine villages in the vicinity of Epernay.

He observed that most of the grapes were purple and that white grapes were planted only on poorer soil. The vines were planted two feet apart, but they later spread, so that there was a plant for every square foot. Each vine rested in a hole one foot deep, filled with compost so that two buds showed above the surface. Very little fertilizer was used. Vines were staked and tied with straw. A fine vineyard utilized land worth 3,000 francs an arpent and yielded about 2,400 bottles of wine. An inferior one utilized land worth 1,000 francs an arpent and yielded about 1,000 bottles. Because Jefferson wished to acquire precise knowledge of the different kinds of wine produced in this province, he made very thorough notes.

The district of Champagne produced two kinds of white wine. Jefferson wrote that the *mousseux*, or sparkling, variety was "little drank in France but are alone known and drank in foreign countries." That was only one of the reasons, however, why sparkling champagne was worth an eighth more than what the still, or *non-mousseux*, cost; the winemaking process accounted for the rest. In September pickers gathered the grapes for making sparkling champagne. About one-third of the grapes were considered to be of the first quality, but only one-eighth of a bunch was selected for the sparkling wine. The vinters next pressed the grapes "very lightly" for about an hour, "without treading them or permitting them to ferment at all." The grapejuice was allowed to stand for forty-eight hours in bottles that were uncovered except for a napkin over the mouth. It was then corked and stored until March, when the vinters decided whether the stock would make the famous "brisk," or sparkling wine. If so, they decanted it into other bottles between March and June, allowing its natural sugars to develop into sparkling wine. If not, they kept the stock until September, when it was decanted to become still wine. Besides learning that sparkling wines are "in perfection from 2 to 10 years old and will even be very good to 15," Jefferson picked up lore about famous late-eighteenth-century vintages, but before he could have absorbed it, he bought sixty bottles of still white wine at the first vineyard he visited, that of Monsieur Dorsay at the village of Aij. Jefferson made notes of the other vineyards of the area, including that of the Benedictine monks who supplied the wine for the king's table, for which they charged two-fifths more than Dorsay. Jefferson wrote that although the Benedictines' red was the best in Champagne, their white "is hardly as good as Dorsay's."[41]

On his departure he paid Coussin for his wine and instructed that it be delivered to the back door of the Hôtel Langeac at Paris, in order to avoid paying a municipal tariff at the Grille de Chaillot. A very early start on the twenty-third enabled Jefferson to breakfast at Château-Thierry, to reach Meaux in time for an early dinner at the Hôtel Royal, and, after two more stages, to reach Paris the evening of April 23, fifty days after he had left the French metropolis.[42]

EPILOGUE:

Apostle of European Culture

SINCE AT LEAST 1788 JEFFERSON HAD SOUGHT LEAVE FROM HIS post at Paris so that he could go to Virginia for business and family reasons. He wished to take his daughters home, where they would enjoy a Protestant and republican environment as well as meet young men who would be suitable husbands. When he finally left the French capital in September 1789, he accomplished a relatively painless transition from the Hôtel Langeac to Monticello for himself, his two daughters, two slaves, two carriages, and at least eighty-six cases and containers.

On September 26, 1789, Jefferson and his daughters Patsy and Polly, in his new, London-made carriage, and their slave-servants James and Sally Hemings, in his old phaeton, departed from Paris for Le Havre. Delays on the road caused by a broken axletree and the loss of a wrought-iron tire from one of the wheels proved of little consequence, because a contrary wind kept their Channel ship, the *Anna*, in port. As in 1784, the Jefferson party lodged at Le Havre in Mahon's Hôtel l'Aigle d'Or.[1] Because he now possessed so much knowledge of other European ports, it is a pity that Jefferson did not compare them with Le Havre, a city of more than twenty-five thousand. Arthur Young thought that Le Havre was "fuller of motion, life, activity than any place . . . in France." When Jefferson walked around the harbor with Nathaniel Cutting, he professed to be "astonished at the extent and magnitude of the public works." He predicted that Louis XVI's improvement of the harbor by a mole and two quay-lined basins large enough to accommodate hundreds of merchant ships would make it the "first seat of commerce in France."[2]

During a ten-day wait for favorable winds, Jefferson attempted without success to visit the superintendent of the saltworks across the Seine estuary at Honfleur, where he recently had secured for American sea captains the privilege of buying salt cheaply and almost duty-free. He and "his two lovely daughters" consorted much with Cutting on walks and carriage drives. While they took tea together, the minister explained in detail his advice to the American explorer John Ledyard about how to determine degrees of latitude and that he tattoo on himself the most important notes of his travels.[3] Among Jefferson's small purchases on the eve of departing for Le Havre was an ottoman upholstered in *velours d'Utrecht*.[4] This was probably a thoughtful and rather expensive gesture to provide the eleven-year-old Polly with a comfort she had lacked coming over, a place other than a wooden bench on which to sit. Another purchase was a shepherd dog, "big with pups," with which the Jefferson girls could play on shipboard and which later could be put to useful purpose at Monticello.[5]

When the wind finally shifted, the party embarked, on October 7, for Cowes, where they would meet a ship bound for America. According to Jefferson, during the passage from Le Havre "it was blowing almost a tempest" for twenty-six hours of "boisterous navigation and mortal illness." Cutting, who accompanied them, confirmed in his diary that the Jeffersons had indeed become "exceedingly seasick," although he himself thought that the breezes were no more than "fine" or "fresh." Captain Wright brought the *Anna* into Cowes at 2:00 A.M. on October 8 and anchored near the mouth of the Medina River.[6] Because the same wind that enabled the *Anna* to sail westward from Le Havre prevented other ships from sailing southwestward from the Thames estuary, the Jeffersons had to wait at Cowes until October 17 for their transatlantic ship to arrive.[7] The *Clermont*, reputedly a "good sailer" with "excellent" accommodations, was beginning its fourth voyage under its "capable and obliging" captain, Nathaniel Colley of Norfolk, Virginia.[8]

Mainly because Jefferson had insisted on a direct voyage to Virginia, but also because he did not wish to be separated from his extensive baggage, he had reluctantly abandoned his scheme to engage only staterooms and to share the saloon and dining table with other passengers. Instead, he had authorized Trumbull to engage meals for his party, all the *Clermont*'s passenger space, and room enough for his carriages and baggage as well as for an unspecified number of containers of plants and vine cuttings.[9] Even though most of Jefferson's furniture was left at Paris, he took with him chairs, china, clothing, silver, sofas, oil paintings, portrait busts, and the large marble neoclassical altar pedestal that Madame de Tessé had given him as a going-away present.[10]

Until the Jeffersons' ship could sail, they spent much of their time at the Fountain Inn, whose proprietress, Mrs. Symes, clucked over her clientele in a matronly fashion. In addition to long, conversational walks with Jefferson at Cowes, Cutting accompanied the Jeffersons on an excursion to the town of Newport, which the British writer on picturesque beauty, William Gilpin, described as "large" and "handsome." Although they did not examine Newport's free school, in whose great room the beleaguered Charles I had treated with the commissioners of Parliament,[11] they visited Carisbrook Castle. Whether Sir George Cary, the castle's governor in Elizabethan times, was related to the Carys of Virginia did not matter: Jefferson recorded their visit to "Carysbrook" as if there were no doubt of the relationship.[12] The castle was, of course, famous for having served as a prison for Charles I. If Jefferson ruminated on Charles's fate, he alluded neither to it, nor to the castle's antiquity, nor to its extensive fortifications.[13]

The Jefferson girls found opportunities to buy a number of "trifles"—galoshes, muslin, pillows, shoes, spices, tape, and washbasins, not to mention "butcher's meat" for their mother dog.[14] Cutting observed how the "worthy" Jefferson instructed the "lovely" Polly in Spanish by reading with her about the conquest of Mexico. Cutting agreed with everyone else who met her that Maria possessed a "perfect pattern of good temper" and a frequent "engaging smile." Based on her "cheerful attention" and early progress in her studies, he predicted that "when her faculties attain[ed] their maturity, she w[oul]d be the delight of her friends and a distinguish'd ornament to her sex." He remarked that the "amiable . . . , tall and genteel" Martha, aged seventeen, retained all "that winning simplicity and good humour'd reserve that are evident proofs of innate Virtue and an happy disposition," despite her education in a convent and residence in a country "remarkable for its levity and forward indelicacy of manner."[15] That Cutting commented hardly at all about Jefferson may be interpreted as proof that the statesman had attained stature of such mythological proportions as to delude Americans into thinking that he had never been anything but a cosmopolitan, learned, and wise man. As Jefferson had remarked of Thomas Lee Shippen after his grand tour, he himself was going home to America "charged like a bee with honey," honey gathered in the course of the most extensive European travel by any American of his time.

The unfavorable winds that delayed the *Clermont*'s sailing for Virginia brought to Cowes the *Montgomery*, bound for New York with John Trumbull among its passengers. Soon after the *Montgomery* anchored, the young artist went ashore to join the Jeffersons at tea at the Fountain Inn.[16] When the wind shifted on October 22, Captain Colley took the *Clermont* out in a fleet of about thirty ships. For a day the two ships sailed close enough for Jefferson and Trumbull to converse. All three Jeffersons were seasick for the first five days, after which the skies were sunny, the ocean calm, and the weather fine. When the *Clermont* reached the Virginia capes, however, mist and fog were so thick that no pilot came out to meet it. Captain Colley himself took his ship into Chesapeake Bay and anchored off Norfolk, ending a voyage of twenty-nine days. Prematurely Jefferson wrote to William Short of his relief that, in addition to getting his daughters, plants, shepherd dogs, and baggage safely to port, "I have now passed the Atlantic twice without knowing what a storm is." His troubles were not long in coming, however. Sudden, strong winds caused the ship to drag anchor, lose her topsails, and almost collide with another vessel. Soon after the Jeffersons disembarked, a fire broke out aboard ship. Fortunately, the flames were extinguished before they reached the Jeffersons' baggage. When the distraught passengers landed at Norfolk and went to Lindsay's Hotel, they found that all the rooms were taken. The Jeffersons were blessed with good fortune: some gentlemen gave up rooms for their occupancy.[17] Such generosity by his countrymen must have warmed Jefferson, who sometimes so pined for the amenities he had enjoyed at Paris that he felt that he "but half exist[ed]" in America.[18]

Meanwhile, William Short had become U.S. chargé d'affaires at Paris, attending to the official business of the legation, as well as residing in and overseeing the domestic staff of the Hôtel Langeac. Jefferson had been so intent on resuming his legation in the spring of 1790 that he had paid the upholsterer Mathieu to recover furniture and to install looking glass in his rented *hôtel*. When, after his arrival in the United States, Jefferson acceded to President Washington's request that he accept the position of secretary of state, it fell to Short to terminate Jefferson's lease of the building in Paris, pay off its staff, and supervise the packing of Jefferson's books, clothes, and fine furniture for shipment to Philadelphia and to Monticello. In addition, he had to sell Jefferson's three horses and inconsequential household furniture. Although Short had an official duty to do some of these things, Jefferson's "adoptive son" did many others out of affection.[19] Nathaniel and John Brown Cutting, American merchants on both sides of the English Channel, and the artist John Trumbull, who himself was preparing to return to the United States from England, for all of whom Jefferson had frequently served as host and benefactor, provided lesser assistance. In 1789 the minister had sent most of his baggage by boat down the Seine to Le Havre, where Nathaniel Cutting arranged its shipment to England. John Brown Cutting and Trumbull engaged both the Jeffersons' cross-Channel and transatlantic passage, besides obtaining from the British prime minister, William Pitt, a waiver of customs inspection of his baggage while it was in transit.[20]

AS ARTHUR YOUNG WROTE IN THE PREFACE TO HIS *Travels in France*, any comprehensive description of that country demanded an unprejudiced investigation by someone who was both a farmer and a politician.[21] Jefferson was just such a man. If he had published in the 1790s a report of what he had observed during the last years of the ancien régime, it might have rivaled Young's account of western Europe on the eve of revolution. Although in the countryside Jefferson had taken careful notes on the laborers, soils, crops, livestock, and fish of the localities he visited, it is an exaggeration to denominate him an agrarian, an appellation that he himself encouraged in the self-deprecatory mode of his friend Dr. Franklin.[22] Nor was Franklin a mere Quaker or Jefferson a mere farmer. These were generally fashionable poses of the era, but they were also appropriate to and useful for the foreign representatives of their emerging country. Although Jefferson listed agriculture ahead of architecture in his "hints" to Americans traveling in Europe, that sequence was more alphabetical than preferential. When he advised young Americans on how and where to spend their time in Europe, he suggested that they allocate most of their time to its great cities.[23] More an urbanist than he admitted, Jefferson spent 68 percent of his time in cities between 1775 and 1800.[24] He prized urban cultural opportunities, even though he customarily made light of his sightseeing at art galleries, museums, and palaces. As Fiske Kimball said eighty years ago, Jefferson's travels made him "the first American connoisseur and patron of the arts."[25]

With the possible exception of John Quincy Adams, Jefferson traveled more extensively than any other president of the United States before the age of the airplane. In England, France, northern Italy, Belgium, the Netherlands, and the Rhineland of Germany he found opportunities to converse with high and low, although he was on close terms with only a few prominent commoners and liberal nobles.[26] Aside from being a diplomat, Jefferson was one of America's chief experts on European affairs. From his experience at the court of Versailles he learned from such masters as Vergennes and Montmorin how European diplomacy was conducted. There and on his travels, he learned how a great country should be administered. A practical as well as an idealistic statesman, he was able to win unprecedented advantages for American shippers between the French West Indies and French home ports, in part because he had studied the conditions of trade at Bordeaux, La Rochelle, and Nantes.[27]

For all his hopes that the Atlantic would be a barrier against the evils of the Old World, Jefferson celebrated Europe's cultural legacy to America and strengthened the rapport between the United States and France. The latter proved to be of greater long-term significance than were the trade concessions. While Jefferson contributed to reshaping the international language of liberalism to embrace the American experience, he became the foremost apostle to the United States of European culture. His entire viewpoint was broadened and heightened by his European experiences and friendships.

Gilbert Chinard's inference of the 1920s that before Jefferson left his native land he had already made up his mind about what Europe, and especially France, had to offer persists even today.[28] Too many pass too lightly over the fact that Jefferson was the first American to say that after his own country, his "choice" of a place to live was France, that "great and good country" so eminent in character, hospitality, and science.[29] Not even Dumas Malone in *Jefferson and His Time* or Merrill D. Peterson in *Thomas Jefferson and the New Nation* dispels completely the false notion that Jefferson's genius was developed almost in isolation from Europe. While they rightly emphasize that Jefferson returned to America in 1789 more convinced than he had been in 1784 that the United States should abstain from European political quarrels, they inadvertently allow their readers to extend political to cultural isolationism. Because Malone and Peterson have depicted Jefferson throughout his life span, their appreciation of how Europe exercised a lasting cultural influence on him is dissipated. Malone stated that when Jefferson posed for the artist Mather Brown in 1786, he was a man of fashion. In spite of his authorship of the Declaration of Independence, perhaps as many French as American leaders recognized him as a political and cultural sage in 1789.[30]

Jefferson so greatly expanded his world-view during his years in France that he lost whatever remained of a colonial viewpoint. He now saw with great clarity that the United States and western Europe shared one culture, a whole culture that was not divided into a yin of political economy and a yang of fine arts. As he adopted new cultural attitudes, he shed old cultural shibboleths. A resolute republican and a convert to the neoclassicism of Charles Louis Clérisseau, he did not pay obeisance to the shabby grandeur of Versailles. Because lovers of royal panoply and oldfashioned Francophiles have had difficulty in understanding that Jefferson rejected this icon, they have sometimes implied that he never gained more than a superficial appreciation of French culture and was, indeed, an apostle of frontier America, little influenced by his European experience.

Before 1784 Jefferson's preferences in architecture, painting, and sculpture had been based almost entirely upon his reading. During his diplomatic service he was able easily to acquire for the first time French books to complement those he possessed in English. From these, this scholarly man might have reached much the same conclusions concerning the fine arts that he did by personal observation and consultation with French connoisseurs in preferring Louis Seize to Louis Quatorze, Clérisseau to Palladio, Haydn and Mozart to Lully, David to Watteau and Fragonard, Ossian to Racine, toille de Jouiy to brocade, natural to powdered hair, the simple to the grandiose. His tastes changed as he came to know the French language and French concepts of the fine arts. What he saw of the fine arts in Europe and his discourse with architects, musicians, and painters raised his standards and led to a sea change in his thought. Now accepting variation from previously restrictive rules, he gained a broader cultural vision and an improved perspective, which permitted him to move easily between details and the meaning of their whole. By 1790 his cultural evolution had brought him so far beyond most Americans that the ultra-Federalists of the 1790s had some reason for perceiving him to be un-American.

In four and a half years his architectural and artistic tastes had become more modern, more chaste, less formal, and perhaps more practical. Charles Louis Clérisseau had a great influence on Jefferson's tastes in art and sculpture, as well as in architecture. Jefferson could not have failed to see how Clérisseau's engravings of the "antiquities" of southern France had influenced such artists as Hubert Robert to combine naturalism with neoclassicism. This helps explain Jefferson's conclusion that architecture was "the most important" of the fine arts.[31] Although Fiske Kimball in *Thomas Jefferson, Architect* called attention in 1916 to Jefferson's interest in all the fine arts, it is in architecture that Jefferson's interest has been most renowned. Unfortunately, Kimball could not know in 1916 what we today know of Clérisseau. He exaggerated, to say the least, in stating that Jefferson "had arrived at the fundamental scheme" of the Virginia state capitol "before he ever left [America] and long before he met Clérisseau, the French architect who helped him with the model."[32] Jefferson deserves the credit he has long received for the concept of adapting the Graeco-Roman temple for a seat of government, but Clérisseau was at least the co-architect of the Virginia state capitol.[33]

Although Jefferson was confident of his own talents as an amateur architect, he habitually secured for important projects professional architects and builders, besides Clérisseau, Benjamin H. Latrobe and Robert Mills in later decades. He acknowledged their professional advice.[34] Inadvertently, Kimball encouraged subsequent writers on architecture to over-emphasize Jefferson's classicist rigidity stemming from bookish Palladian-ism and to underemphasize his adoption of the Louis Seize style that made Monticello after 1790, to say nothing of Poplar Forest, more modern, more modest, more utilitarian, and more comfortable. Jefferson did not imprison himself or his friends in inconvenient neoclassical temples whose suites of rooms lacked privacy and independent communication. Even his classical capitals, dados, entablatures, friezes, loggias, pediments, and pi-azzas were not of the unrelenting character sometimes found in the deco-ration of Anglo-Palladian structures. Jefferson's references during the rest of his life to Palladio's *Four Books of Architecture* in advising friends or writing specifications for builders did not mean that he still considered the sixteenth-century Italian to be the ultimate authority in architectural matters; rather, he was only a convenient encyclopedic source. For such details he cited Antoine Babuty Desgodets's *Les Edifices antiques de Rome* nearly as often.[35]

Monticello is indeed an amalgam of all that Jefferson had read and seen. He based his arguments for a simple civic and domestic style not merely on aesthetics but on utility and expense. Prophesying that the United States would double its population every two decades, he insisted that so many buildings would be needed that they should be built in the most convenient form and of the least perishable materials.[36] Except for the Maison Carrée and Versailles, neither the French nor the Italian build-ings that Jefferson actually viewed received attention from scholars before the 1940s.[37] He never saw a building designed by Andrea Palladio. If Jef-ferson had ever made another trip to Italy, he might have seen some,[38] but in 1787 he did not feel that he had the time to travel an additional fifty miles to inspect a Palladian villa.

Around 1787 there occurred a far-ranging revolution in taste. While in the early 1780s there had been a confusion between the attributes of a philosopher-statesman and a dilettante, by 1787 there had emerged, as a by-product of the cult of Nature, a sharper distinction between these categories of eighteenth-century men, as revealed in the way that many French and English leaders of affairs, thought, and fashion saw themselves. The demar-cation between the serious and the dilettantes injected into popular culture the requirement of both an inner presence and the outer expression of stern, moral purpose. One focus in this revolution of taste and manners was the French Salon of 1787.[39] Jefferson attended this display of paintings in the Louvre and joined in the praise of David's *Death of Socrates*. In discussions of celebrated paintings with professional artists such as Maria Cosway, Sophie de Tott, and John Trumbull, Jefferson improved his ability to criticize works of art. After 1787, the more he saw of modern painting, in art shops as well as in museums, the less important the items on his early want list became. Somewhat in the vein of one of his favorite poets, William Shenstone, he wrote Sophie de Tott that he despised "artificial canons of criticism": when he read a work in prose or poetry or saw a painting or a statue, he only asked "whether it gives me pleasure, whether it is animating, interesting, attach-ing? If it is, it is good for these reasons."[40] When on rare occasions he took notes about paintings, his concern was not so much art for art's sake as it was the subject matter and the possibility of obtaining painted or engraved copies with which to embellish his house. Although the idealism of the author of the Declaration of Independence was genuine, most aspects of Jefferson's taste were consonant with those of fashionable European collectors, who idealized the simplicity of ancient Greece and the early Roman republic.

He was not slow, however, to enhance his appearance as a statesman of the new age. In 1786 Jefferson was willing to have Mather Brown portray him in a frilly jabot and with powdered and curled hair—a costume then appropriate both for a serious diplomat and for a dilettante. In performing official duties, Jefferson was as punctilious in his attire as in seizing the customary "smooth handle" of usage.[41] Since powdered hair or wigs were de rigueur at Versailles, it is not to be believed that he ever went to the French court without powdered hair. To judge from the many entries he made in his accounts about paying barbers while on his travels, he must sometimes have worn his hair powdered and curled even on his excursions. By 1788 conventions began to change; it was becoming impossible to reconcile such a frivolous appearance with the stern, moral purpose expected of a statesman. Now it was considered imperative that a serious man's wisdom be reflected in his "natural" outer appearance. Just as the court of Versailles was becoming increasingly irrelevant, so was the dress of the courtier.

Rarely was the transition from the old to the new conventions of dress better demonstrated than in the contrast between the four portraits of Jefferson that John Trumbull painted in 1788.[42] These suggest that Jefferson was undecided about how he wished to appear. At the risk of straining the limits of fair interpretation, it is as though he chose to differentiate between his private and his public image in a paradoxical way: the private man was more fashionably formal, in curled and powdered hair, while the public man was more humbly informal, with his hair *au naturel.* Trumbull painted the public man first, directly onto the canvas of what today is called the "small" *Signing of the Declaration of Independence.* Afterwards he painted three miniature copies of Jefferson's portrait on wooden panels so that Jefferson might give them as remembrances to three ladies—Angelica Church, Maria Cosway, and Patsy Jefferson. But these miniatures, depicting him as the fashionable man these ladies knew him to be, differed from the original in significant ways. The miniatures were likenesses of the present man; the original was of the mythic Jefferson of the past and the future, the author of the Declaration, the party leader, the president, and the sage.

The three miniatures and Brown's portrait reflected Jefferson's fashionable, courtly exterior, just as Brown's contemporaneous portraits of John Adams and of Charles Bulfinch did of those men. Preferring not to be seen as a dilettante, however, Jefferson adopted the view that Brown's was not a worthy likeness. In 1789 the shift of fashion to "natural" ways of wearing one's hair and of dressing allowed Jefferson to combine his inclinations with his observance of fashion. Except when he was on obligatory visits to Versailles, he now wore his graying, sandy hair without powder, and he soon ceased curling the ends into a roll, in order to make an outward affirmation of chaste republicanism. In originally painting Jefferson's hair *au naturel*, Trumbull was at the same time both retrospective and prescient. Posterity has rewarded him by being a little incredulous that Jefferson ever looked differently than as Trumbull represented the author of the Declaration.

William Short did not address the style of Jefferson's hair in 1776 or 1786 when he wrote Trumbull that although Brown's portrait of Adams was considered "an excellent likeness," it was generally supposed to be an "étude" and had "no feature like him." Trumbull thought that Brown's picture of Adams was "very like him," although he did "not think so well" of Jefferson's likeness.[43]

Remarkably, some in the twentieth century who profess to admire Jefferson's taste in architecture condemn his taste in painting and sculpture. They castigate him for occasional excessive praise of some mediocre neo-classical paintings that in his day were the rage throughout the Western world and for referring once to "the old red faded things of Rubens."[44] They overlook Jefferson's standards of selectivity. Whether he liked or disliked an artist's works depended largely on their subject matter. He did not admire those that praised kings, queens, and monarchies, as did Rubens's series of paintings of Marie de Medici in the Luxembourg Palace and of James I in the Banqueting House at Whitehall. That he thought differently if the subject matter were a morality tale from the Bible or ancient history is shown by the presence at Monticello of a copy of Rubens's *Diogenes and His Lantern*. There were also copies of three of Raphael's paintings at Monticello, plus prints and engravings of scenes from Cervantes and Shakespeare.[45] Perhaps the most convincing factor in assessing Jefferson's appreciation of art is that on at least one occasion he retracted his extravagant praise of a picture when the professional artist Sophie de Tott showed him why he should think less highly of it.[46]

Jefferson's collection of oil paintings numbered about seven dozen. There were about four dozen portraits, two dozen biblical scenes, and a dozen mythological subjects. None were landscapes. His interest in portraits of the founders of America was whetted by having viewed in royal European collections pictures of kings and national heroes. Besides the founders of the American Republic, Jefferson's notables were explorers such as Columbus, Cortez, Magellan, Raleigh, and Vespucci and natural philosophers such as Bacon, Locke, and Newton. Among the portraits, other than those of his family, were those of John Adams by Mather Brown, La Fayette by Joseph Boze, Franklin by Joseph Siffrède Dupléssis (long thought to be by Jean Baptiste Greuze), Madison by Robert Edge Pine, Thomas Paine by John Trumbull, and Washington by Joseph Wright. Of Jefferson's pre-1784 want list of seven pictures, he got only one: a copy of Sebastiano Ricci's biblical scene *Jeptha Meeting His Daughter*. Of the thirteen sculptures, he got none. Eventually, he had a baker's dozen of busts (seven of which were by Jean Antoine Houdon) portraying such worthies as John Adams, Alexander I of Russia, Benjamin Franklin, Alexander Hamilton, Andrew Jackson, John Paul Jones, La Fayette, James Madison, Napoleon, Anne Robert Jacques Turgot, and Voltaire. In addition, there was his own bust by Giuseppe Ceracchi. Two original works of sculpture of considerable merit were a marble statue of a reclining Ariadne and the great, multicolored, marble pedestal that Madame de Tessé had presented to him as a farewell gift.[47]

There have been recovered for display at Monticello seven of Jefferson's collection of forty-six portraits, four of his twenty-seven biblical scenes, and one of his fifteen mythological scenes. Most of these paintings have been rehung in the parlor, where once there were forty-eight. According to the standards of his day, and especially in the young United States, Jefferson had a considerable art collection,[48] even though, except for portraits, few of his paintings were originals. Then the greatest works of the old masters were in royal collections, just as today they are in museums. It is a fact, however, that when Jefferson could obtain an original work by a contemporary artist, such as Duplessis, Houdon, the Peales, or Trumbull, he did so. When he placed his pictures and statues at Monticello, they were unusual, if not unique, in America as to kind, variety, and manner of display. By no means did he despise engravings. He displayed at Monticello the engraved copy of Trumbull's *Death of Montgomery* that he had bought from the artist at Paris. Echoing Baron Grimm's approval of John Trumbull, Jefferson declared that he was "one of the best men and greatest artists in the world" and "superior to any other historical painter of the time except David."[49]

Another international vogue in the eighteenth century, in addition to collecting paintings and sculpture, was collecting antiquities, especially archaeological discoveries from Herculanaeum, Pompeii, and Rome, for which princes of church and state competed. Long interested in recovering Indian artifacts and fossilized bones of animals, Jefferson exhibited examples of them in the reception hall of Monticello in what was an unstated rivalry with European collectors.[50] Knowing that he could never compete in collecting examples of Mediterranean antiquity reinforced his enthusiasm for collecting antique Americana and for demonstrating the uniqueness of many animal species in the New World. Although it is probable that Jefferson would have bought more works of art if he had returned to France in 1790, it is unlikely that they would have differed greatly from what he already had acquired between 1784 and 1789. Because his tastes had changed with the times, it is doubtful that he would have sought anything on his pre-1784 want list.

Although the Commonwealth of Virginia never acted on Jefferson's plea, while he was governor, that it establish an art gallery and fund it annually as part of a scheme of general education,[51] he later enjoyed greater success in the establishment of the federal capital at Washington. Benjamin H. Latrobe later complimented Jefferson on having "planted the arts" in the United States through his sponsorship at Washington not only of buildings that were monuments to judgment, zeal, and taste but also of the "first sculpture that adorned an American public building."[52] Because there were at the end of the eighteenth century surges of internationalism that for a while transcended nationalism, it may be idle to discuss whether Jefferson was more remarkable for introducing American political ideas into France than for introducing French cultural ideas into the United States. The data he dutifully compiled concerning European bridges, cities, canals, commerce, harbors, millstones, olives, rice, roads, stoves, viticulture, and vari-

La Bastille dans les premiers jours de sa Démolition, 1789, painting by Hubert Robert (1733–1808). Jefferson went twice to see the demolition of the old fortress-prison and contributed to a fund for the widows of those who fell in taking it.

ous crops and fruits were almost wholly without effect. Jefferson was, however, the person who did most to transmit from France to the United States a European culture that was independent of Great Britain. His establishment of a multifaceted rapport between the United States and France was his most important accomplishment between the writing of the Declaration of Independence and becoming president. Indeed, he was the United States' greatest apostle of European culture.

NOTES

Throughout the notes I employ the following abbreviations for Jefferson's travel records and published editions of his papers:

Account Books, ViU
Thomas Jefferson Account Books (1767–1826), Photocopy, Manuscripts Collection, Alderman Library, University of Virginia, Charlottesville

Papers
The Papers of Thomas Jefferson, ed. Julian P. Boyd et al., 25 vols. to date (Princeton: Princeton University Press, 1950–)

Writings (Ford)
The Writings of Thomas Jefferson, ed. Paul L. Ford, 10 vols. (New York: Putnam's, 1892–99)

Writings (L&B)
The Writings of Thomas Jefferson, ed. Andrew A. Lipscomb and Albert E. Bergh, 20 vols. (Washington, D.C.: Thomas Jefferson Memorial Foundation, 1903–5)

PROLOGUE: AN AMERICAN FOR PARIS

1. Francis Hawcroft, *The Grand Tour and Milord Inglesi* (Norwich, 1959); Jefferson to Charles Bellini, Sept. 30, 1785, *Papers*, 8:568–69.
2. Jefferson, "Autobiography," *Writings* (Ford), 1:149.
3. Howard C. Rice, Jr., *Thomas Jefferson's Paris* (Princeton: Princeton University Press, 1976).
4. Dumas Malone, *Jefferson and His Time*, 6 vols. (Boston: Little, Brown, 1948–81); Merrill D. Peterson, *Thomas Jefferson and the New Nation* (New York: Oxford University Press, 1970).
5. See Gilbert Chinard, *Thomas Jefferson: Apostle of Americanism* (Boston: Little, Brown, 1939); and Merrill D. Peterson, *The Jefferson Image in the American Mind* (New York: Oxford University Press, 1960), 400, 408, 411–17, 437. See also Malone, *Jefferson*, 1:53, 73–74, 78, 2:xiv–xx; Peterson, *Jefferson*; Marie Kimball, *Thomas Jefferson*, 3 vols. (New York: Coward-McCann, 1943–50); Fiske Kimball, *Thomas Jefferson, Architect*, 2d ed., intro. Frederick D. Nichols (New York: Da Capo, 1968); and Frederick D. Nichols, "Jefferson: The Making of an Architect," in *Jefferson and the Arts: An Extended View*, ed. William Howard Adams (Washington, D.C.: National Gallery of Art, 1976), 159–85.
6. Bellini to Jefferson, Feb. 13, 1782, *Papers*, 6:150.
7. Jefferson to Bellini, Sept. 30, 1785, *Papers*, 8:569. See also François-Jean, marquis de Chastellux, *Travels in North America in the Years 1780, 1781 and 1782*, trans. and ed. Howard C. Rice, Jr., 2 vols. (Chapel Hill: University of North Carolina Press, 1963), 2:390.
8. Helen Cripe, *Thomas Jefferson and Music* (Charlottesville: University Press of Virginia, 1974), 6, 14, 21, 27, 88–93, 97–128.
9. Graham Hood, *The Governor's Palace at Williamsburg: A Cultural Study* (Williamsburg: Colonial Williamsburg Foundation, 1991), 20–325 passim. The inventories for three Virginia governors (Botetourt, Fauquier, and Dunmore)

specify Sir Peter Lely and Allan Ramsey as artists and at least thirteen oil paintings and ninety-eight prints (ibid., 287–98). Hood also prints the inventories for Governor Eden of Maryland and Governor Tryon of New York, showing them collectively to include one painting by Charles Willson Peale, one by Van Dyke, three historical scenes, and two dozen landscapes (ibid., 299–302). Harold E. Dickson and Seymour Howard conclude that Dr. John Morgan of Philadelphia showed Jefferson his art collection (Dickson, "Th. J. Art Collector," in Adams, *Jefferson and the Arts*, 105–32; Howard, "Thomas Jefferson's Art Gallery for Monticello," *Art Bulletin* 59 [Dec. 1977]: 583–600. See also George Gilmer to John Morgan, May 11, 1766, *Papers*, 1:18). Julian Boyd did not take editorial note of Dr. Morgan's art collection or of his grand tour. Dr. Morgan might have shown Jefferson his oil copies of *Judith with the Head of Holopherphes*, Albani's *Bacchus and Cupid*, and his own portrait by Angelica Kaufmann, as well as drawings believed to be by Domenichino, Michelangelo, Raphael, Van Dyke, and Veronese. See Carl Bridenbaugh and Jessica Bridenbaugh, *Rebels and Gentlemen: Philadelphia in the Age of Franklin*, 2d ed. (London: Oxford University Press, 1962), 213–15.

10. Jefferson to Robert Skipwith, Aug. 3, 1771, *Papers*, 1:76–81.

11. John Page to Jefferson, July 20, 1776, ibid., 1:468; E. Millicent Sowerby, ed., *The Catalogue of the Library of Thomas Jefferson*, 5 vols. (Washington, D.C.: Library of Congress, 1952–59), 4:389 (hereinafter cited as *Jefferson's Library*).

12. Jefferson to Wilson Miles Cary, Feb. 6, 1785, *Papers*, 7:637; Sowerby, *Jefferson's Library*, 4:389–90.

13. Jefferson, "Statues, Paintings &c," notebook for building Monticello ca. 1770–71, Coolidge Collection of Jefferson Papers, Massachusetts Historical Society, Boston, reproduced in Kimball, *Jefferson, Architect*, 135–36, fig. 79. In combining the lists for 1771 and 1782, I follow Fiske Kimball, "Jefferson and the Arts," *Proceedings of the American Philosophical Society* 137 (July 1943): 241–43, which Marie Kimball summarized in *Jefferson*, 1:154, as did Eleanor D. Berman in *Thomas Jefferson among the Arts* (New York: Philosophical Library, 1947), 77. Fiske Kimball concluded that Jefferson compiled his 1771 and 1782 lists on the basis of François Perrier's *Segmenta nobilium signorum e statuarii* (Rome, 1638), Jonathan Richardson's *Essay on the Theory of Painting*, and Joseph Spence's *Polymetis*. He believed that some of these were lost when Shadwell burned.

14. Bellini to Jefferson, Feb. 13, 1782, *Papers*, 6:150. Jefferson's 1782 want list included oil copies of the following: LeSueur's *Stoning of St. Stephen*; Raphael's *St. Paul Preaching at Athens*; Salvator Rosa's *Belisarius Begging Alms* and *The Prodigal Son*; Rubens's *Susanna and the Two Elders*; Giuseppi Zocchi's *Jeptha Meeting His Daughter*; *Seleuchus and Stratonice*, perhaps by either Cortona or David; *St. Ignatius at Prayer*, perhaps by Murillo; a *Curtius Leaping into the Chasm*, perhaps after a sculpture; and works by unidentified artists, *Cocles Defending the Bridge*, *Diana Venetrix*, and *The Sacrifice of Iphigenia*.

Jefferson's 1782 want list for statuettes included the following: Giambologna's *Rape of the Sabine Women*; Pollaiulo's *Hercules Strangling Antaeus*; the *Antinous*, then being renamed *Meleager*; the *Apollo Belvedere*; *The Boxer*, a Roman copy after a Greek original, and *The Borghese Warrior*, a copy from Agasias's lost original; and *The Dancing Faunus* (or *Satyr*), *The Hercules Farnese*, *The Medici Venus*, *The Myrmillo Expiring* (or *The Dying Gaul*), *Spinaro*, and *The Two Wrestlers*. For details about the paintings and sculptures, as well as for their citations, see George G. Shackelford, "A Peep into Elysium," in Adams, *Jefferson and the Arts*, 238–39, 263–64; and Howard, "Thomas Jefferson's Art Gallery," 590–95.

15. William Short to John Hartwell Cocke, July 8, 1828, Cocke Papers, Uni-

versity of Virginia, Charlottesville. See also George G. Shackelford, *Jefferson's Adoptive Son: The Life of William Short* (Lexington: University Press of Kentucky, 1993).

16. Kimball, "Jefferson and the Arts," 141–43, 241; Sowerby, *Jefferson's Library*, 4:357–99.

17. Jefferson to Page, May 4, 1786, *Papers*, 9:445.

18. Kimball, *Jefferson, Architect*, fig. 79.

19. James A. Bear, Jr., and Frederick D. Nichols, *Monticello* (Monticello: Thomas Jefferson Memorial Foundation, 1967), 23–37; Nichols, "Jefferson: The Making of an Architect," 163–64; Charles Errard and Roland Frerard, Sieur de Chambrai, *Parallèle de l'architecture antique avec la moderne, suivant les dix principaux auteurs qui ont écrit sur les cinq ordres*, in *Bibliothèque portative d'architecture*, ed. Charles Antoine Jombert, 4 vols. (Paris: Jombert, 1764); Antoine Babuty Desgodets, *Les Edifices antiques de Rome, mesurés et dessinés exactement sur les lieux* (Paris: Jombert, [1779]). Jefferson bought the first of these in 1802 and the second in 1791. See Sowerby, *Jefferson's Library*, 4:371–72, 380.

20. Joseph Addison, *Remarks on the Several Parts of Italy*, vol. 4 of *Miscellaneous Works* (1726; London: Tonson, 1767); *Guide pour le voyage d'Italie en poste*, 2d ed. (Genoa: Yvres Gravier Librairie, 1788); Carlo Bianconi, *Nuova guida di Milano per gli amanti delle belle arti sacre, e profane antichità Milanesi* (Milan: Nella Stampa Sirtori, 1787); Giacomo Brusco, *Description des beautés de Gènes et de ses environs* (Genoa: Yvres Gravier Librairie, 1781); Louis Dutens, *Itinéraire des routes les plus fréquentées, ou Journal des plusieurs voyages aux villes principales de l'Europe, depuis 1763 jusqu'en 1783* (Paris: Chez Théophile Barrois le jeune, 1783); Sowerby, *Jefferson's Library*, 4:28, 132–33.

21. Jefferson to Pierre Charles L'Enfant, Apr. 10, 1791, *Writings* (L&B), 7:162.

22. Jefferson to Marie Joseph Paul Yves Roch Gilbert du Motier, Marquis de La Fayette, Apr. 11, 1787, *Papers*, 11:283.

23. Thomas Jefferson, Account Books, ViU.

24. Jefferson to John Jay, Oct. 23, 1786, *Papers*, 10:484–85; Jay to Jefferson, July 27, 1787, ibid., 11:627–28.

25. Jefferson, "Hints to Americans Travelling in Europe," *Papers*, 13:264–76.

26. Abigail S. Adams, *Letters of Mrs. Adams, the Wife of John Adams*, ed. Charles F. Adams (Boston: Little Brown, 1840); John Adams, *The Diary and Autobiography of John Adams*, ed. Lyman H. Butterfield, 4 vols. (Cambridge: Belknap, 1961; hereinafter cited as John Adams, *Diary*); Katharine M. Roof, *Colonel William Smith and Lady: The Romance of Washington's Aide and Young Abigail Adams* (Boston: Houghton Mifflin, 1929); Hester Lynch Piozzi and Samuel Johnson, *The French Journals of Mrs. Thrale and Doctor Johnson*, ed. Moses Tyson and Henry Guppy (Manchester: Manchester University Press, 1932), 183.

27. Arthur Young, *Travels during the Years 1787, 1788 and 1789, Undertaken More Particularly with a View of Ascertaining the Cultivation, Wealth, Resources, and National Prosperity of the Kingdom of France*, 2 vols. (Dublin: Cross et al., 1793); François de La Rochefoucauld [-Liancourt], *Voyages en France (1781–1783)*, ed. Jean Marchand, 2 vols. (Paris: Librairie Ancienne Honoré Champion, 1932–38; hereinafter cited as Liancourt, *Voyages*).

28. In the 1790s Jefferson and Young exchanged plant seeds, using George Washington as their go-between. See Sowerby, *Jefferson's Library*, 1:330–32, 343–46; Kimball, *Jefferson, Architect*, 90–101; and Jefferson to Washington, [Aug. 3, 1791], *Papers*, 20:716–17.

1. Jefferson, Oct. 11, 1783, and July 1, 1784, Account Books, ViU.

2. Jefferson, July 5–25, 1784, ibid.; Patsy Jefferson to Eliza House Trist, [Aug. 24, 1785], *Papers*, 8:436–39.

3. Jefferson, July 25–31, 1784, Account Books, ViU; Jefferson to John Adams, July 24, 1784, and Jefferson to James Monroe, Nov. 11, 1784, *Papers*, 7:382, 508; Abigail Adams, "Diary of a Tour from London to Plymouth," July 20–28, 1787, in John Adams, *Diary*, 3:205.

4. Young, *Travels*, 1:160–62.

5. Roof, *Colonel William Smith and Lady*, 158. For Young's comment that the French relay service was worse than England's, see Young, *Travels*, 1:16.

6. Jefferson to Monroe, Nov. 11, 1784, *Papers*, 7:508; Patsy Jefferson to Eliza House Trist, [Aug. 24, 1785], ibid., 8:436–39; Young, *Travels*, 1:158–62.

7. Jefferson, Aug. 4–5, 1784, Account Books, ViU; Patsy to Eliza House Trist, [Aug. 24, 1785], *Papers*, 8:437; Young, *Travels*, 1:71–72, 158–62. Young noted monuments to Rollo, William I and Henry I of England, Henry V of France, and Richard Coeur de Lion, as well as the altarpiece *Adoration of the Shepherds* by Philippe de Champagne. The villages between Le Havre and Rouen were La Botte, Bolbec, Aliquiville, Yvetot, and Barentin.

8. Jefferson, Aug. 6–7, 1784, Account Books, ViU; Patsy Jefferson to Eliza House Trist, [Aug. 24, 1785], *Papers*, 8:437. These villages and towns were Vaudreuil, Gaillon, Vernon, Mantes, Bonnieres, and Meulan. In 1784 Mantes could best be described as a town. Today, the Michelin Company makes its tires there, and it is a city of more than forty-five thousand.

9. Jefferson, July 31–Aug. 6, 1784, Account Books, ViU; Jefferson to Maria Cosway, Oct. 12, 1786, *Papers*, 10:445.

10. Jefferson to Bellini, Sept. 30, 1785, *Papers*, 8:568–69.

11. Jefferson, Aug. 5–6, 1784, Account Books, ViU.

12. Jefferson to Jay, Jan. 3, 1783, *Papers*, 6:217–18; Jefferson to James Madison, Jr. (future president of the United States; hereinafter cited simply as Madison), May 25, 1788, ibid., 13:201–3.

13. Jefferson, "Hints to Americans Travelling in Europe," *Papers*, 13:268; see also Young, *Travels*, 1:16, 128–29.

14. Young, *Travels*, 1:128–29; Piozzi and Johnson, *French Journals*, 95, 175.

15. Guireaud de Talairac to Jefferson, Oct. 16, 1784, *Papers*, 7:442–43; Jefferson to Short, Sept. 30, 1790, ibid., 18:545. Jefferson persistently wrote "Têtebout" for Taitbout and sometimes "Tallyrac" for Talairac.

16. James A. Bear, Jr., *Report[s] of the Curator to the Trustees of the Thomas Jefferson Memorial Foundation*, 30 vols. (Charlottesville: Thomas Jefferson Memorial Foundation, 1954–84), 21:10–19, 12:25–26.

17. Jefferson, Jan. 10, 1787, Account Books, ViU. See also Partout to Jefferson, [Jan. 1787?], *Papers*, 10:296n; Philip Mazzei to Jefferson, Apr. 17, 1787, ibid., 11:98–99, 297. When Jefferson returned to America, he gave the *ecce homo* to Adrien Petit.

18. Marquis de Chastellux to Jefferson, Aug. 24, 1784, *Papers*, 7:410–11; Elizabeth Wayles and Francis Eppes to Jefferson, Oct. 13 and [14], 1784, ibid., 7:441–42; Dr. James Currie to Jefferson, Nov. 20, 1784, ibid., 7:538–39; John Quincy Adams, Jan. 29, 1785, *The Diary of John Quincy Adams*, ed. David G. Allen, 2 vols. to date (Cambridge: Belknap, 1981–), 1:218 (hereinafter cited as J. Q. Adams, *Diary*). Patsy's sponsor was the Comtesse de Brionne, the niece of the Abbess Béthisy de Mézières.

19. Auguste Louis Joseph Fidèle Armand de Lespinasse, Comte de Langeac, to Jefferson, Sept. 5, 1785, *Papers*, 8:485. Although the comte was a colonel of infantry, knight of the Royal Military Order of St. Louis, and royal governor of St. Nazaire and four other towns, his important position had been as captain of the guards of Monsieur, the Comte de Provence and future Louis XVIII, who lived at Paris as well as at Versailles. See also Louis Gottschalk, *Lafayette between the American and the French Revolutions, 1783–1789* (Chicago: University of Chicago Press, 1950), 28–29, 234–35; and Jean Dominique de La Rochefoucauld, "Genealogy Family Tree," in *Le Duc de La Rochefoucauld-Liancourt, 1747–1827* (Paris: Librairie Académique Perrin, 1980), 442–45 (hereinafter cited as La Rochefoucauld, *Liancourt*).

20. Kimball, *Jefferson, Architect*, 148–49; Howard C. Rice, Jr., *L'Hôtel de Langeac: Thomas Jefferson's Paris Residence, 1785–1789* (Paris: Lefèbvre; Monticello: Thomas Jefferson Memorial Foundation, 1947), 11–15.

21. Jefferson, Jan. 1784–Feb. 1785, Account Books, ViU.

22. Jefferson, Jan. 28, Feb. 10–19, 1787, ibid.

23. Jefferson, Feb. 1, 1787, ibid.

24. Jefferson, Dec. 30, 1786, Jan. 10, 27, 1787, ibid.

25. Jefferson, Jan. 16, Feb. 10–19, 1787, ibid.

26. Jefferson, Sept. 4–Nov. 9, 1786, ibid.

27. Jefferson, Jan. 1, 1788, ibid.; Mrs. Adams to Mrs. Cranch, July 16, 1787, in *Letters of Mrs. Adams*, 377; Jefferson to Chastellux, [Oct. 1786], *Papers*, 10:498; Roof, *Colonel William Smith and Lady*, 152–53.

28. Jefferson, Jan. 10, 28, Feb. 18, 1787; Dec. 12, 1788, Account Books, ViU; Chastellux to Jefferson, Aug. 24, 1784, *Papers*, 7:411; Jefferson to Mary Jefferson Bolling, July 23, 1787, ibid., 11:612. Now opposite the Russian Embassy, the Abbaye's school buildings are French government offices, and its chapel is a Protestant temple. Madame de Béthisy de Mézières (1743–94) ceased being the abbess in 1790. Besides the students, there were at the Abbaye orphans, widows, and ladies separated from their husbands. Among the latter had been Josephine de Beauharnais, the future empress.

29. For his purchase of a guitar, see Jefferson, Sept. 5, 1785; for the girandoles, see Dec. 1, 1787, at which time he also bought sets of red china and glassware. See also Jefferson, Jan. 28, and Feb. 1, 10, and 19, and Dec. 1, 1787, Account Books, ViU.

30. Claude Balbastre (1729–99) studied under the composer Jean Philippe Rameau. Balbastre's published works include *Pieces de clavecin* (Paris, 1759), *Recueil des noëls, formant quatres suites avec des variations puir le clavecin et piano forte* (Paris, ca. 1762), and *Sonates en quattor pour le clavecin ou le forte piano avec accompagnement de deux violons, une basse et deux cors ad libitum* (Paris, 1780). Among his arrangements was an elaborate setting for *La Marseillaise et l'air Ça Ira*. He became one of the four organists of Notre Dame de Paris. See Sir George Grove et al., *Dictionary of Music and Musicians*, 10 vols., 5th. ed. (London: Macmillan, 1954–61), 1:368–69. There is no mention of Balbastre's arrangement of the *Marseillaise* in Julien Tiersot, *Rouget de Lisle: Son oeuvre, sa vie* (Paris: Librairie Delagrave, 1892), but see program of Smithsonian Chamber Players, Radford College, Radford, Va., 1989.

31. Jefferson, Feb. 8, 1786, Oct. 10, 1787, May 15, 1788, Account Books, ViU. On several occasions Gouverneur Morris dined *en famille* with the three Jeffersons. See Gouverneur Morris, *A Diary of the French Revolution*, ed. Beatrix C. Davenport, 2 vols. (Boston: Houghton Mifflin, 1939), 1:8, 29, 166.

32. Jefferson, Jan. 8, 1787, Account Books, ViU; Silvio Bedini, *Thomas Jefferson: Statesman of Science* (New York: Macmillan, 1990), 135.

33. Jefferson, Jan. 16, Apr. 8, 17–20, 1789, Account Books, ViU.

34. Jefferson, Mar. 1, 1785, Mar. 13, 1789, Dec. 17, 1785, July 12, 1787, ibid.

35. Jefferson, Feb. 10-19, 1787, ibid. Jefferson called his personal goblet a cup. He lost some of these when robbers broke into the Hôtel Langeac and stole his candlesticks. See Boyd, note, *Papers*, 18:36.

36. Bear, *Reports*, 18:7–8, 20:11–12. After many delays in delivery of this model, William Short got it for Jefferson during his own excursion to southern France in spring 1789. Originally, Jefferson had intended to have Odiot make a silver ewer from the model.

37. Jefferson to John Trumbull, Aug. 5, 1789, *Papers*, 15:35; Jefferson, Jan. 16, 27, 1787, Account Books, ViU.

38. Jefferson to Martha J. Randolph, Dec. 23, 1793, *Writings* (Ford), 6:488.

39. See the epilogue.

CHAPTER 2. THE PARIS JEFFERSON KNEW

1. Thomas Jefferson, *Notes on the State of Virginia*, ed. William Peden (Chapel Hill: University of North Carolina Press, 1954), 164–65 (hereinafter cited as Jefferson, *Notes on Virginia* [Peden]). See also Jefferson to Currie, Aug. 4, 1787, *Papers*, 11:682; and Jefferson to Washington, Apr. 25, 1794, *Writings* (L&B), 9:283.

2. Jefferson's chronologies are found in *Papers*, vols. 1–7, 15–20; and Malone, *Jefferson*, vols. 2–5.

3. Jefferson to Thomas Mann Randolph, Jr., July 6, 1787, *Papers*, 11:557; Jefferson to John Rutledge, Jr., June 19, 1788, ibid., 13:262–64; Jefferson, "Hints to Americans Travelling in Europe," ibid., 264–76.

4. Jefferson, "Notes of a Tour into the Southern Parts of France, &c." (hereinafter cited as "Tour through Southern France"), ibid., 11:438; Jefferson to Short, Oct. 28, 1788, ibid., 14:42.

5. Jefferson to La Fayette, Apr. 11, 1787, ibid., 11:283–85; Gottschalk, *Lafayette between the American and the French Revolutions*, 310–11.

6. Abbés Arnoux and Chalut to Jefferson, Apr. 23, 1787, *Papers*, 11:303.

7. Jefferson, "Hints to Americans Travelling in Europe," ibid., 13:264–76.

8. Concerning Jefferson's devotion to and cultivation of peas, see Edwin M. Betts, *Thomas Jefferson's Garden Book, 1766–1824*, American Philosophical Society Memoirs, vol. 22 (Philadelphia: American Philosophical Society, 1944), 4, 22–23, 250, 610.

9. Jefferson to Monroe, Mar. 18, 1785, *Papers*, 8:43; Jefferson to Chastellux, [Oct. 1786], ibid., 10:498.

10. Rice, *Jefferson's Paris*, 102, 104. In 1777 the Comte d'Artois engaged Francis Joseph Bélanger (1744–1848) to build this *folie* in the midst of a forty-eight-acre English-style park. See M. L. Blumer, "Francis Joseph Bélanger," *Dictionnaire de Biographie Française*, ed. Michel Prevost et al., 17 vols. to date (Paris: Librairie Letouzey et Ané, 1933–), 5:1302–3.

11. Jefferson, Jan. 5, 1787, Account Books, ViU.

12. Kimball, *Jefferson, Architect*; Bear, *Reports*, 6:12, 14–15.

13. President Jefferson appointed Latrobe surveyor of the public buildings in 1803. Dr. William Thornton served as a commissioner of the District of Columbia from 1794 to 1802. See Saul K. Padover, *Thomas Jefferson and the National Capitol, 1783–1818* (Washington, D.C.: GPO, 1946), 513, 517.

14. Jefferson to Short, Apr. 2, 1785, *Papers*, 8:68.

15. Roof, *Colonel William Smith and Lady*, 80–81.

16. Jefferson gave money to the curé of Chaillot on Jan. 8 and 13, 1789. See Jefferson, Account Books, ViU; and Langeac to Jefferson, lease for Hôtel Langeac, Sept. 5, 1785, *Papers*, 8:485. Jefferson's Christ Episcopal Church, in Charlottesville,

was replaced by a Romanesque structure in the 1890s. St. Thomas's Episcopal Church, in Orange, Virginia, was built on Christ Church's plan in 1833. See Mary Rawlings, *The Albemarle of Other Days* (Charlottesville: Michie, 1925), 17.

17. Jefferson, July 2, 1789, Account Books, ViU.

18. Jefferson to David Humphreys, Aug. 14, 1787, *Papers*, 12:xxxiv, 32.

19. John Trumbull, *Autobiography, Reminiscences, and Letters* (New Haven: Hamlin, 1841), 107. Begun in 1626, the Luxembourg Palace was built on plans mainly by Salomon de Brosse with a design for a great garden by Boyceau. In 1750 its Medici Gallery became a museum.

20. Napoleon I replaced this gallery with a staircase. See Yvan Christ, "Luxembourg," *Dictionnaire de Paris* (Paris: Larousse, 1964), 309.

21. Buffon to Jefferson, Oct. 31, 1786, Mar. 27, Oct. 31, 1787, *Papers*, 9:130, 11:262, 12:194–95, 15:635. See also Jefferson to C. F. Michaelis and Others, Feb. 4, 1786, ibid., 11:111; the Reverend James Madison to Jefferson, Dec. 28, 1786, ibid., 10:642–43; and Benjamin Hawkins to Jefferson, June 9, 1787, ibid., 11:414. Buffon invited Jefferson and Chastellux to dine with him in February 1787.

22. *Letters of Mrs. Adams*, 285–87; Piozzi and Johnson, *French Journals*, 93, 173.

23. Jefferson to Madame de Tessé, Mar. 20, 1787, *Papers*, 11:226.

24. Marie Constans and Claude Ducourtail-Rey, *La Rue de Lille [et l'] Hôtel de Salm* (Paris: Institut Néerlandais for Délégation à L'Action Artistique de la Ville de Paris, Musée de la Légion d'Honneur and Société d'Histoire et de l'Archéologie de VIIe Arrondissement, 1983), 155–73; Adriaan W. Vliegenthart, *Bildersammlung der Fürsten zu Salm* (Apledoorn, The Netherlands: Walburg, 1981), 190–200. Prince Frédéric had seigneurial lands in northern France, in both the Austrian and the United Netherlands, and in the Rhineland. The Salm family was connected by marriage to the Bourbons, the Habsburgs, and the Hohenzollerns and to the houses of Hanover, Nassau, Savoy, and Stuart. Prince Frédéric belonged to the cadet branch, the Salm-Krybourg line. In 1781 he married a Hohenzollern princess, by whom he sired four children; she died in 1790.

25. Constans and Ducourtail-Rey, *Hôtel de Salm*, 155–73; Vliegenthart, *Salm*, 96–97.

26. Allan Braham, *The Architecture of the French Enlightenment* (Berkeley and Los Angeles: University of California Press, 1980), 109–10.

27. Jefferson to Cosway, Oct. 12, 1786, *Papers*, 10:444–45, 454; Young, *Travels*, 1:130–31.

28. Rice, *Jefferson's Paris*, 26, 31–35.

29. Jefferson, Dec. 22, 1787, Account Books, ViU; Young, *Travels*, 1:136.

30. Marie Catherine Sahut, *Le Louvre d'Hubert Robert* (Paris: Editions de la Réunion des Musées Nationaux, 1979), 3–9, 11–12, 14–15; James L. Connelly, "The Grand Gallery of the Louvre and the Museum Project: Architectural Problems," *Journal of the Society of Architectural Historians* 31 (May 1972): 120–32; Jean Starobinski, *1789: The Emblems of Reason*, trans. Barbara Bray (Charlottesville: University Press of Virginia, 1982), 105–18; Morris, *Diary of the French Revolution*, 1:17n, 374. Angiviller proposed conversion of the Louvre in 1777. Robert (1778–92) and his wife (1795–1806) lived under the Grand Gallery on the ground-floor level, which opened onto the Quai de Seine. His atelier was in the Vieux Louvre, between the cour Carrée and the rue de Rivoli. Angiviller also gave to his non-artistic younger brother, Comte Alexandre Sébastien de Flahaut, and his beautiful wife Adèle the use of such an apartment.

31. Jefferson to Trumbull, Aug. 25, 30, 1789, *Papers*, 12:xxxiv–xxxv, 69, 137; Rice, *Jefferson's Paris*, 31–35; William Howard Adams, ed., *The Eye of Thomas Jefferson* (Washington, D.C.: National Gallery of Art, 1976), 92–95, 108, 110, 128, 138,

144, 150–66. David's *Death of Socrates* is now in the Metropolitan Museum of Art in New York.

32. Jefferson to Madame de Bréhan, Mar. 14, 1789, *Papers*, 14:656.

33. Jefferson to Madame de Tott, Feb. 28, 1787, *Papers*, 11:187–88; Tott to Jefferson, Mar. 4, 1787, ibid., 198–99.

34. La Rochefoucauld, *Liancourt*, [442]; cf. Boyd, note, *Papers*, 10:158–59. See also Charles de Pougens to William Short, Jan. 11, 1830, William Short Papers, Library of Congress, Washington, D.C.

35. Morris, *Diary of the French Revolution*, 1:79, 106–7, 109–10, 218, 2:256.

36. Morris to William Carmichael, July 4, 1789, in Jared Sparks, *The Life of Gouverneur Morris, with Selections from His Correspondence*, 3 vols. (Boston: Gray and Bowen, 1832), 2:74. Although Morris was a Federalist senator from New York, he wrote Alexander Hamilton on December 19, 1800, that "because it was evidently the intention of our fellow citizens to make Mr. Jefferson their president, it seems proper to fulfill that intention" (ibid., 3:132).

37. *Journal de Paris*, Aug. 15, 1785, fig. 40 in Rice, *Jefferson's Paris*, 31.

38. Cripe, *Jefferson and Music*, 109–13, 119–20, 125–28. The musical ensemble of the Smithsonian Institution at Washington, D.C., uses the Balbastre orchestration. See also Simon Schama, *Citizens: A Chronicle of the French Revolution* (New York: Knopf, 1989), 598.

39. Jefferson, Sept. 2, 4, 7, 1784, Account Books, ViU. His first attendance was on Sept. 19, 1784. See also Jefferson to Cosway, Oct. 12, 1786, *Papers*, 10:445; Rice, *Jefferson's Paris*, 30–31; and Morris, *Diary of the French Revolution*, 1:35.

40. Piozzi and Johnson, *French Journals*, 21–28, 114, 147–48, 205–6. The *Judgement of Paris* is now in the National Gallery at London. There were at least two pictures of Mars and Venus by this artist. One is in the Fitzwilliam Museum at Cambridge, England, and another is in the Frick Collection at New York.

41. As part of the education of young ladies Jefferson recommended the reading of Corneille, Molière, and Racine, as well as Dryden, Pope, Shakespeare, and Thompson. See Jefferson to Nathaniel Burwell, Mar. 14, 1818, *Writings* (L&B), 15:165–66; and Thomas Jefferson, *Literary Commonplace Book*, ed. Douglas L. Wilson, in *The Papers of Thomas Jefferson*, 2d ser., ed. Charles T. Cullen et al. (Princeton: Princeton University Press, 1989), 146–47. For the works he owned by Beaumarchais, Corneille, Molière, and Racine, see Sowerby, *Jefferson's Library*, 4:542, 551, 555.

42. Piozzi and Johnson, *French Journals*, 96, 98, 137.

43. Jefferson to Abigail Adams, Dec. 27, 1785, and Jefferson to Humphreys, Jan. 5, 1785, *Papers*, 9:126, 152; and Young, *Travels*, 1:138–41, 187. Later, the Comédie Française took over the southwest wing of the Palais Royal.

44. Claude Nicholas Ledoux, *L'Architecture*, ed. Kevin C. Lippert after Daniel Ramée's 1847 Paris ed. (Princeton: Princeton Architectural Press, 1983), pls. 175–77.

45. Jefferson to Anne Willing Bingham, Feb. 7, 1787, *Papers*, 11:123.

46. Ledoux, *L'Architecture*, pls. 4, 10, 11, 32. See also Michel Gallet, *Ledoux et Paris*, 2d ed. (Paris: Rotonde de la Villette, 1979); Jean Marie Pérouse de Montclos, "Ledoux: L'Architecture," *Journal of the Society of Architectural Historians* 41 (Oct. 1982): 261–63; and Jacques Wilhelm, "Pavillons d'Octroi," *Dictionnaire de Paris*, 374–76. Ledoux proposed remarkable plans for industrial towns, one for the manufacture of salt and another for the manufacture of cannons. For an ideal farming village of Mauperthuis, he proposed a spherical guardhouse not dissimilar to Etienne Louis Boulée's 1784 project for a cenotaph to Isaac Newton.

47. Jefferson to Trumbull, June 1, 1789, *Papers*, 15:164.

48. Shackelford, *Jefferson's Adoptive Son*, 8–135 passim.

49. Thomas Lee Shippen to Dr. William Shippen, Feb.–Mar. 1788, ibid., 12:502–4.

50. Boyd, note, *Papers*, 9:364. They were students of Benjamin West, an expatriate American who was King George III's official painter of historical subjects.

51. Boyd, note on illustrations, ibid., 12:xxxv; Trumbull to Jefferson, Aug. 28, 1787, ibid., 60; Jefferson to Trumbull, Nov. 13, 1787, ibid., 358.

52. Jefferson to Francis Hopkinson, Aug. 14, 1786, ibid., 10:250.

53. Boyd, note on illustrations, *Papers*, 1:lvii, 2. See also Fiske Kimball, "The Life Portraits of Thomas Jefferson and Their Replicas," *Proceedings of the American Philosophical Society* 88 (1944): 499–505. Kimball points out that Trumbull's miniature of Jefferson painted for Mrs. Church shows him with his hair powdered and curled, while those for Maria Cosway and Martha Jefferson do not. Dorinda Evans in her *Mather Brown: Early American Artist in England* (Middletown, Conn.: Wesleyan University Press, 1982), 53, quotes favorable critical opinion of his historical painting and portraiture in the 1786 Royal Academy exhibition. See also Alfred L. Bush, ed., *The Life Portraits of Thomas Jefferson* (Charlottesville: Thomas Jefferson Memorial Foundation, 1963), 14–19.

54. Jefferson to James Barbour, Jan. 19, 1817, *Writings* (L&B), 9:242–43.

55. Short wrote Trumbull that "everybody" thought Brown's to be only "an étude, since it has no particular like him." Trumbull agreed in disliking his fellow student's picture, but he did not refer to Jefferson's clothes or hair. Jefferson thought enough of Brown to commission his portrait of John Adams, who donned a curled and powdered wig for the occasion. Short and Trumbull agreed that this was an excellent likeness.

CHAPTER 3. COURT AND COUNTRY: VERSAILLES, FONTAINBLEAU, AND LA ROCHE-GUYON

1. Boyd, Jefferson Chronology, *Papers*, 7:2; Malone, *Jefferson*, 2:9, 4. Franklin left Paris for America on July 11, 1785.

2. Young, *Travels*, 1:143–44; Piozzi and Johnson, *French Journals*, 125–29, 176.

3. Jefferson, "Autobiography," *Writings* (Ford), 1:85, 88; Marcel Manion, *Dictionnaire des institutions de la France au XVIIième et XVIIIième siècles* (1923; reprint, Paris: Editions A. and J. Picard, 1984), ix, 564, 346–56, 447, 502–4; Ingouf, "Ministry of Navy and Foreign Affairs at Versailles," *Papers*, 7:xxviii and plate opposite 453. The ministry is now the municipal library of Versailles and faces on the rue d'Indépendance Américaine.

There were four secretaries of state: the ministers of foreign affairs, war, marine, and the Maison du Roi. Upon the creation of the office of principal minister, Loménie de Brienne, archbishop of Toulouse (later of Sens), served in that capacity in 1788 and 1789. Jacques Necker served as director of finance in 1788 and 1790. Maréchal the Marquis de Ségur was secretary of war from 1780 to 1787, succeeded by the Comte de Brienne (the archbishop's brother) from 1787 to 1788 and by the Comte Puységur after 1788. The Marquis de Castries was secretary of marine from 1780 to 1787, followed by the Marquis de La Luzerne (the brother of the minister to the United States). As secretary of the Maison du Roi from 1783 to 1787, Baron de Tonnelier de Bréteuil held administrative authority over an area centered on the Ile-de-France; he was succeeded by Laurent du Villedeuil from 1787 to 1789.

4. Jefferson to Adams, Apr. 8, 1816, *Writings* (L&B), 14:468–69; Jefferson to Jay, Nov. 3, 1787, *Papers*, 12:314. Grimm helped Jefferson in the latter's unsuccessful plea that the tsarina permit the American pedestrian John Ledyard to cross Siberia. See Jefferson, "Autobiography," *Writings* (Ford), 1:94–95.

5. Thomas Lee Shippen to William Shippen, Feb. 14–Mar. 26, 1788, *Papers*, 12:502–4.

6. It is Jefferson's silences, rather than his words, that reveal his distaste for Versailles. See also Morris, *Diary of the French Revolution*, 1:16.

7. Young, *Travels*, 1:21.

8. Piozzi and Johnson, *French Journals*, 130–37, 177–78.

9. Jefferson to Short, Mar. 27, 1787, *Papers*, 11:246–47.

10. Jefferson, "Autobiography," *Writings* (Ford), 1:91; Carmichael to Jefferson, Mar. 25, 1787, *Papers*, 11:236.

11. Manion, *Dictionnaire des institutions*, 41, 346–51.

12. Jefferson, Jan. 1–2, 1787, Account Books, ViU.

13. Boyd, note, *Papers*, 18:547. These pictures followed the government from New York to Philadelphia to Washington but have been lost since 1790.

14. Jefferson to Adams, Aug. 30, 1787, ibid., 12:68.

15. "Autobiography," *Writings* (Ford), 1:140.

16. For the garden by Richard and Micque, see William Howard Adams, *The French Garden, 1500–1800* (New York: George Braziller, 1979), 112–13, 121–22.

17. Young, *Travels*, 1:142–44.

18. Madame de La Fayette to Jefferson, [Aug.] 26, [1786], *Papers*, 15:630. Madame de Tessé accompanied them.

19. Jefferson to the Reverend James Madison, Oct. 29, 1785, ibid., 8:681–83, 9:51n.

20. Piozzi and Johnson, *French Journals*, 125–28.

21. Young, *Travels*, 1:115.

22. Jefferson to the Reverend James Madison, Oct. 29, 1785, *Papers*, 8:681–83, 9:51n.

23. Piozzi and Johnson, *French Journals*, 125–28, 176.

24. Antoine Marie Eugène Philippe Boniface, Comte de Castellane, *Gentilshommes démocrates: Le Vicomte de Noailles, les deux La Rochefoucaulds, Clermont-Tonère, le vicomte de Castellane, le comte de Virieu* (Paris: Plon, 1891), 60–69. See also La Rochefoucauld, *Liancourt*, 42, 58–60, 67, 71, 148–49, 157, 162, 204–7, 214, 223, 442. The seigneury of Enville, located between Paris and Lyon, did not possess a château of consequence. The La Rochefoucaulds made periodic journeys to their châteaux La Rochefoucauld and Verteuil in Angoulème, where they were proud and responsible landlords, but in the 1780s they did not reside there for long periods.

25. Castellane, *Gentilshommes démocrates*, 60–110; Liancourt, *Voyages*, 1:2, 51, 131, 144–45; and La Rochefoucauld, *Liancourt*, 58, 78–79.

26. Philip Mazzei, "Memoranda concerning Persons and Affairs in Paris," *Papers*, 7:386.

27. Crevecoeur to Jefferson, July 15, 1784, *Papers*, 7:376.

28. La Rochefoucauld, *Liancourt*, 45, 63, 65.

29. [Louis Alexandre de La Rochefoucauld], *Constitutions des Treize Etats-Unis de l'Amerique* (Paris, 1783), 307–12; he gives the Virginia constitution of 1776 on pp. 313–28.

30. Coolie Verner, "Jefferson Distributes His *Notes*," *New York Public Library Bulletin* 56 (Apr. 1952): 172–73; Castellane, *Gentilshommes démocrates*, 69; Philip Mazzei, *Recherches historiques et politiques sur les Etats-Unis de l'Amerique Septentrionale*, 4 vols. (Paris: Froulle, 1788), 1:158–63. Jefferson also presented copies to Condorcet, La Fayette, and Mazzei.

31. Sotheby's International Auctions, *Bibliothèque du château de La Roche-Guyon* (Cowley: Nuffield, 1987); idem, *Tableaux et moblier et tapisseries ornant le chateau de la Roche-Guyon* (Alençon: Imprimerie Alençonnaise, 1987). The maternal grandfa-

ther of Marie Louise Nicole Elisébeth Le Tellier de Louvois (1716–97) was Jean Baptiste Louis Frédéric de La Rochefoucauld de Roye (1663–1728). For genealogical charts, see La Rochefoucauld, *Liancourt*, 442–45. La Roche-Guyon is on the north bank of the Seine between Mantes and Château Gaillard, about forty miles northwest of Paris.

32. Mazzei to Jefferson, [ca. July 1784], *Papers*, 7:386–87.

33. [Marie Jean Antoine Nicolas Caritat, Marquis de Condorcet], *Sur les fonctions des Etats-généraux et des autres assemblées nationales . . .*, 2 vols. ([Paris], 1789), 1, pt. 1:4, pt. 2:51; idem, "To a Young Frenchman in London, [1792]," in *Oeuvres de Condorcet*, ed. A. Condorcet O'Connor and M. F. Arago, 5 vols. (Paris: Firmin Didot Libraries, 1847–49), 1:33. Elected first a member of the French Convention and then its president, Condorcet became anathema to the La Rochefoucaulds after he countenanced the mob's invasion of the Tuileries on August 10, 1792, on grounds of circumscribing the "ability of the court to hatch plots against liberty and to exacerbate the fears of the people." He called for the suspension of the king's powers until a convention could "redefine" them. He took his own life in 1793 rather than be sent to the guillotine.

34. Malone, *Jefferson*, 2:194, 234; Peterson, *Jefferson*, 382–84; Marie Kimball, *Jefferson*, 3:91–94.

35. Condorcet to Jefferson, Feb. 12, 1789, Dec. 21, 1792, *Papers*, 5:419, 25:760–62; Condorcet, *Sur les fonctions des Etats-généraux*, 1, pt. 2:51. Condorcet said that he broke with La Fayette, a "hollow man," because the latter was plagued by "incertitude" and surrounded by intriguers. Although he knew that La Rochefoucauld was a "truly virtuous man and friend of liberty," Condorcet considered him "too weak."

36. Jefferson to Madison, written Sept. 6, 1789, sent Jan. 9, 1790, and Jefferson to Gem, [Sept. 9, 1789], *Papers*, 5:384–99. There is no evidence that receipt of this letter was acknowledged. Two decades ago Julian P. Boyd suggested in his editorial note, "The Earth Belongs In Usufruct to the Living," *Papers*, 15:387–91, that Jefferson intended La Fayette as the true recipient and that Jefferson's endorsement of Gem's revolutionary principles really pertained to France.

37. Liancourt, *Voyages*, 1:vi. Unlike his father, François de La Rochefoucauld-Liancourt returned to France (in 1799), where he served in civil and military capacities until he succeeded in 1827 as the Duc de La Rochefoucauld. See also La Rochefoucauld, *Liancourt*, 58, 443.

38. Mazzei, "Memoranda Regarding Persons and Affairs in Paris," [July 1784], *Papers*, 7:387.

39. Abbé de Morellet to Jefferson, Dec. 1785, ibid., 9:133–34.

40. Jefferson to Charles W. F. Dumas, Feb. 2, 1786, ibid., 9:293–94.

41. Jefferson to Carmichael, Dec. 15, 1787, ibid., 12:426.

42. Jefferson to Short, Apr. 6, 1790, July 28, 1791, ibid., 16:319, 20:691; Short to Jefferson, Sept. 9, 1790, ibid., 17:506.

43. Arnoux and Chalut to Jefferson, Apr. 19, June 28, Nov. 11, 13, 1785, ibid., 8:92, 256–57, 9:26, 28–29. Jefferson also knew Chalut's brother, the Comte du Chalut du Verin, who was a director of the French Farmers-General, the corporation that collected taxes in return for prepayment of a fee.

44. Jefferson to Chastellux, Apr. 4, 1787, ibid., 11:262.

45. John Adams, Apr. 16, 1778, *Diary*, 2:317, 4:59–60; Mrs. Adams to Mrs. Cranch, Sept. 5, 1784, *Letters of Mrs. Adams*, 189–90; Jefferson to Abigail Adams, July 7, 1785, *Papers*, 7:265; Jefferson to Chastellux, Apr. 4, 1785, ibid., 11:262. See also Abigail Adams Smith, *Journal Correspondence of Miss Adams*, 2 vols. (New York: Wiley Putnam, 1841–42), 1:37–38.

46. Jefferson to Arnoux and Chalut, Apr. 5, 1790, *Papers*, 16:305–6.

47. Jefferson, Feb. 5, 1787, Account Books, ViU; Jefferson to Arnoux and Chalut, Apr. 12, 1787, *Papers*, 11:287–88.

48. Arnoux and Chalut to Jefferson, Apr. 19, June 28, Nov. 11, 13, 1785, *Papers*, 7:92, 256–57, 265, 9:26, 28–29; Jefferson to Arnoux, July 19, 1789, Apr. 5, 1790, ibid., 15:282–83, 16:306.

CHAPTER 4. IN ENGLAND

1. John Adams to Jefferson, Feb. 21, 1786, *Papers*, 9:295.

2. Young, *Travels*, 1:12–13, 15–16; cf. Adams, *French Garden*, 27, 94, 101.

3. Jefferson, Mar. 6–8, 1786, Account Books, ViU; William S. Smith to Jefferson, May 21, 1786, *Papers*, 9:555. Jefferson entered memoranda concerning his travels in England for every day between Mar. 4 and Apr. 30, covering six pages.

4. Jefferson to Short, Mar. 28, 1786, *Papers*, 9:362; Abigail Adams to Mrs. Cranch, June 24, Oct. 1, 1785, *Letters of Mrs. Adams*, 294, 318–21; Abigail Adams to Mrs. Shaw, Aug. 15, 1785, ibid., 304.

5. Sir Walter Besant, *Eighteenth Century London* (1902; reprint, London: A. C. Black), 484–90.

6. Adams and Jefferson to Jay, Mar. 28, Apr. 25, 1786, *Papers*, 9:357–59, 406–7.

7. Jefferson to Jay, Mar. 12, 1786, ibid., 9:325; American commissioners to Lord Carmarthen, Mar. 31, Apr. 4, 1786, ibid., 9:375.

8. Horace H. Walpole to Horace Mann, Nov. 24, 1774, quoted in Wilmarth S. Lewis, *A Tour through London in the Years 1748, 1776, and 1797* (1951; reprint, Westport, Conn.: Greenwood, 1971), 82.

9. Bush, *Life Portraits of Jefferson*, 14–19.

10. Jefferson to Hopkinson, May 9, 1786, *Papers*, 9:482; Jefferson to Thomas Adams, Feb. 20, 1771, ibid., 1:62. Julian Boyd believed that Jefferson had this ring made "shortly after he went to Paris" (see ibid., 9:xxviii). For Jefferson's official complaint that his hotel had been robbed "for the third time," see Jefferson to Armand Marc, Comte Montmorin de Saint-Hérem, July 8, 1789, ibid., 15:260.

11. Lucy Necks to Jefferson, Apr. 17, 1786; Jefferson to Necks, Apr. 18, 1786; Jefferson to Eppes, Apr. 22, 1786; Jefferson to Henry Skipwith, May 6, 1786, *Papers*, 9:386, 395, 465.

12. St. Paul's Church, Shadwell Parish, Records, 1698–1736, Greater London Records Office, London. Jane Randolph was baptized there on February 25, 1720, but she lived with her widowed mother in Whitechapel Parish when she married "Isham Randolph, mariner" and moved back into Shadwell, a favorite residence of seafarers such as Captain James Cook. At that time a "ballast-man" named Henry Jefferson lived in New Crane Street, Shadwell.

13. Jefferson, "Autobiography," *Writings* (Ford), 1:89; Mrs. Adams to Mrs. Cranch, June 24, 1784, Oct. 1, 1785, *Letters of Mrs. Adams*, 294, 300–302.

14. Adams and Jefferson to Carmarthen, Apr. 4, 1786, *Papers*, 9:362–64; lists, ibid., 375; Jefferson to Short, Mar. 28, 1786, ibid., 405. Jefferson and Sinclair had met at one of La Fayette's dinner parties.

15. Edward Bancroft to Jefferson, Nov. 18, 1785, ibid., 9:40–41.

16. John C. Underwood, *The Rogers Family* (New York: Rudge, 1911), 23–26.

17. Jefferson to John Cartwright, June 5, 1824, *Writings* (L&B), 16:42–44.

18. Abigail Adams to Mrs. Shaw, Mar. 4, 1786, *Letters of Mrs. Adams*, 322–23; *London Gazetteer and New Daily Advertiser*, Mar. 13, 20, 22, 1786, quoted in Marie Kimball, *Jefferson*, 2:135–36, 329.

19. Jefferson, "An Interlude at Dolly's Chop House," *Papers*, 9:350–51; Morris, *Diary of the French Revolution*, 1:204; Besant, *Eighteenth Century London*, 334; Henry

C. Shelley, *Inns and Taverns of Old London, setting forth the historical and literary associations of those ancient hostelries,* 2d ed. (Boston: Page, 1923), 64–65, 192–93. Priestley emigrated to America in 1794.

20. Jefferson to Paradise, May 25, 1786, *Papers,* 9:578, 386, 395–96, 465. Jefferson did not go to the seat of the Isham family in Northamptonshire, for which see Sir Gyles Isham, *Lamport Hall* (Derby: English Life Publications, 1974).

21. John Adams, Mar. 30, 1786, *Diary,* 3:184; Abigail Adams to Lucy Cranch, Apr. 2, 1786, *Letters of Mrs. Adams,* 326–31; *London Chronicle,* Apr. 1–4, 1786, quoted in Archibald B. Shepperson, *John Paradise and Lucy Ludwell of London and Williamsburg* (Richmond: Dietz Press for Colonial Williamsburg, 1942), 203–6.

22. Helen D. Bullock, *My Head and My Heart: A Little History of Thomas Jefferson and Maria Cosway* (New York: Putnam's, 1945), 12; cf. Roof, *Colonel William Smith and Lady,* 151; and Shepperson, *John and Lucy Paradise,* 190. When Nabby met Maria, the American girl commented sourly on the beautiful artist's "singularity of taste."

23. Jefferson, Account Books, ViU; Bruce Gaeine [Graham M. Jeffries, pseud.], *A Century of Buckingham Palace, 1837–1937* (London: Hutchinson, 1937), 17–37, 49–53. The Duke of Buckingham built the house in 1703. The crown bought it in 1763 as a lifetime gift to Queen Charlotte. After living at St. James's Palace for two years, she and George III moved into the queen's house. It is probable that after its many renovations only the state apartments of the west wing remain from the eighteenth-century building. By 1789 Sir William Chambers had closed the upper windows of the salon, installed large mirrors, and sent the cartoons to Windsor.

24. Jefferson, "Notes of a Tour of English Gardens," *Papers,* 9:351n; John Adams to Abigail Adams, Nov. 8, 1783, *Letters of John Adams Addressed to His Wife,* ed. Charles F. Adams, 2 vols. (Boston: Charles C. Little and James Brown, 1841), 2:104; H. Clifford Smith, *Buckingham Palace: Its Furniture, Decoration, and History* (London: Country Life, 1931), 23–27, 30–32, 77, 80–83; Royal Academy of Arts, *The Exhibition of the King's Pictures* (London, 1946–47), xii–xiii; Ellis K. Waterhouse, *Painting in Britain, 1530–1790* (London: Penguin, 1954), 39, 85–86.

25. Jefferson, "Tour of English Gardens," *Papers,* 9:369–70; Jefferson, Account Books, ViU; John Adams, Mar.–Apr. 1786, *Diary* 3:184–87. Gouverneur Morris wrote that some of the paintings at Windsor were "good," that the views from the round tower were "truly magnificent and beautiful," but that St. George's Chapel was so "minced into minutiousness" with such whimsical carving as to be irreverent.

26. Sowerby, *Jefferson's Library,* 4:359–61, 381.

27. Thomas Whately, *Observations on Modern Gardening* (London: T. Payne, 1770), ed. John D. Hunt after the 1790 edition, also published by T. Payne (New York: Garland, 1980), 48–49; Jefferson, "Tour of English Gardens," *Papers,* 9:370; Jefferson, Account Books, ViU. Esher Place had been built for Thomas Holles Pelham and was then owned by Lady Frances Pelham.

28. Jefferson, "Tour of English Gardens," *Papers,* 9:370; Phyllis M. Cooper, *The Story of Claremont,* 7th ed. (London: West Brothers, 1979), 7–19; Robin Fedden and Rosemary Joekes, *The National Trust Guide,* 2d ed. (London: Jonathan Cape, 1977), 239–41. Claremont belonged successively to Vanbrugh; Thomas Holles Pelham, the first Lord Clare, who gave the place its name; the Duke of Newcastle in the time of the first two Georges; and then to Clive. Later Claremont was the residence of George IV's daughter Princess Charlotte and her husband, Prince Leopold, and then of Queen Victoria's youngest son, Leopold, Duke of Albany. Since 1931 it has been a Christian Scientist School.

29. Jefferson, "Tour of English Gardens," *Papers,* 9:370; John Adams, June 26, 1786, *Diary,* 3:191; Whately, *Modern Gardening,* 177–82; Giles Worsley, "A Garden

Reappears: Restoration of Painshill Park, Surrey," *Country Life* (London), Sept. 11, 1986, 802–5.

30. Whately, *Modern Gardening*, 177–82; John Burke et al., *Genealogical and Heraldic History of the Peerage and Knightage*, 103d ed., ed. Peter Townsend (London, 1963), 2097–98 (hereinafter cited as *Burke's Peerage*). Alexander Wedderburn (1733–1805) was created Earl of Rosslyn in 1805. His nephew Sir James Sinclair Erskine, Bart., succeeded to the title. Peter Jefferson paid William Randolph for his Shadwell estate in Albemarle County the biggest bowl of Henry Wetherburn's arrack punch. See Sarah N. Randolph, *The Domestic Life of Thomas Jefferson* (New York: Harper, 1871), 22.

31. Jefferson, "Tour of English Gardens," *Papers*, 9:371; Jefferson, Account Books, ViU; Whately, *Modern Gardening*, 84, 88; [William Gilpin], *A Dialogue upon the gardens of the Right Honorable the Lord Viscount Cobham at Stow[e], in Buckinghamshire* (London: Rivington, 1748); J. Seeley, *Stowe. A Description of the house and gardens of the most noble & puissant prince, George-Grenville-Nugent-Temple, Marquis of Buckingham* (London: Edwards & L. B. Seeley, [1797?]), 32.

32. Jefferson, "Tour of English Gardens," *Papers*, 9:374; Malone, *Jefferson*, 2:252–53.

33. John Adams, "Notes on a Tour of English Country Seats with Thomas Jefferson," *Diary*, 3:185; Jefferson, Account Books, ViU; Jefferson, "Tour of English Gardens," *Papers*, 9:374.

34. Jefferson to Bernard Moore, ca. 1764, *Writings* (Ford), 9:484; Jefferson to Robert Skipwith, Aug. 3, 1771, *Papers*, 1:77; Jefferson to Trumbull, Jan. 18, 1789, and Trumbull to Jefferson, Feb. 5, 1789, ibid., 14:467–68, 526.

35. John Adams, "Tour of English Country Seats," *Diary*, 3:184–87. Adams dismissed Stratford, saying that there was there "nothing preserved of this great genius which is worth knowing."

36. In 1786 a Mr. Horne owned Leasowes, concerning which I am indebted to Professor Eric Clements of the Polytechnic Institute at Wolverhampton, England, and to H. C. Newman, Esquire, secretary of the Halesowen Golf Club, Birmingham, England, which since 1909 has maintained sixty-eight acres of Shenstone's little estate. The club offers a golfing prize named for Shenstone's dog Rover.

37. Lyttleton also served as governor of Jamaica in 1760 and minister to Portugal in 1766. He was created Baron Westcote and Viscount Cobham in 1776. See *Burke's Peerage*, 2097–98.

38. Sir John Summerson, *Architecture in Britain, 1530–1830*, Pelican History of Art Series, ed. Nikolaus Pevsner (London: Penguin, 1953), 241.

39. Ottavio Bertotti Scamozzi, *The Buildings and Designs of Andrea Palladio*, ed. Francesco Modena, trans. Howard Burns (Trent: La Roccia, 1976), 59–60 and pls. 36 and 37.

40. Sowerby, *Jefferson's Library*, 2:217, 334; John Adams, Mar.–Apr. 1786, *Diary*, 3:186.

41. Jefferson, "Tour of English Gardens," *Papers*, 9:372; Gervase Jackson-Stops, *Hagley Hall* (Derby: English Life Publications, 1979), 1–17.

42. Jefferson, "Tour of English Gardens," *Papers*, 9:372; *Letters of Mrs. Adams*, 389–95.

43. Jefferson, "Tour of English Gardens," *Papers*, 9:372. Jefferson did not have a high opinion of Oxford at this time, preferring the more scientific and modern approach of the University of Edinburgh.

44. Although Jefferson did not refer to this expedition in his "Tour of English Gardens," he made an entry for it in his Account Books, ViU. See also D. O. Pam,

"The Rude Multitude: Enfield and the Civil War," *Occasional Papers of the Edmondton Hundred Historical Society* (Enfield, Eng.), n.s. 33 (1977): 10–13.

45. Arthur T. Bolton, *The Architecture of Robert & James Adam, 1785–1794*, 2 vols. (London: Country Life, 1922), 2:44, 54–55, 81.

46. Forty Hall was built for Sir Nicholas Raynton, who was Lord Mayor of London in 1632. See *Forty Hall, Enfield* (London: Curwen, [ca. 1980]).

47. Dorothy Marshall, ed., *Dr. Johnson's London* (New York: Wiley, [1968]), 154–55.

48. Jefferson, "Tour of English Gardens," *Papers*, 9:373; John Adams, Apr. 20, 1786, *Diary*, 3:190; Malone, *Jefferson*, 6:45–47.

49. Doren Yarwood, *Robert Adam* (New York: Charles Scribner's, 1970), 57, 59, based on Robert Adam's indirect quotation of Joseph Wilton.

50. John Adams, Apr. 20, 1786, *Diary*, 3:189–90; Horace Walpole to Lady Ossory, June 21, 1773, *Horace Walpole's Correspondence*, ed. W. S. Lewis et al., 48 vols. (New Haven: Yale University Press, 1937–83), 32:125–27; Walpole to William Mason, July 16, 1778, ibid., 28:413–14; Peter Thornton, *Osterley Park* (London: Victoria and Albert Museum, 1976).

51. John Adams, Apr. 20, 1786, *Diary*, 3:189–90.

52. Jefferson to Paradise, May 4, 25, 1786, *Papers*, 9:446, 578.

53. Morris, *Diary of the French Revolution*, 2:412. See also Shepperson, *John and Lucy Paradise*, 209.

54. Quotation from Abigail Adams to Mrs. Cranch, July 20, 1784, *Letters of Mrs. Adams*, 219; see also John Adams, Oct. 24, 1783, *Diary*, 3:147.

55. Jefferson to John Paradise, May 4, 1786, and Jefferson to Smith, May 4, 1786, *Papers*, 9:446–47.

56. Jefferson to Vergennes, May 3, 1786, and Jefferson to Paradise, May 4, 1786, ibid., 9:442, 446.

57. Jefferson to Page, May 4, 1786, ibid., 9:445–46.

58. Merrill D. Peterson, *Thomas Jefferson and the New Nation* (New York: Oxford University Press, 1970), 56–66, deals admirably with the "Saxon myth" and its ramifications.

59. Jefferson to Anne Mangeot Ethis de Corny, June 30, 1787, and Madame de Corny to Jefferson, July 9, 1787, ibid., 11:509, 570.

60. Jefferson to Page, May 4, 1786, ibid., 9:445–46. See also Jefferson to Jay, Apr. 23, 1786, ibid., 12:402. Cf. Robert E. Spiller, *The American in England during the First Half Century of Independence* (New York: Henry Holt, 1926), 107–10.

CHAPTER 5. MARLY AND MARIA COSWAY

1. Jefferson, July 31–Aug. 6, 1784, Account Books, ViU.

2. Jefferson, Sept. 4, 1786, ibid. The artist David instigated the moving of the Numidian Horses from Marly to what is now the Place de la Concorde in 1795. See Patrice Boussel, "Statues," *Dictionnaire de Paris*, 534–35.

3. Morris, *Diary of the French Revolution*, 1:53, 73–74.

4. Sotheby's International Realty, *Le Pavillon de Musique de la Comtesse du Barry at Louveciennes, Paris* (Cowley: Nuffield, 1968).

5. Morris, *Diary of the French Revolution*, 1:53, 73–74. After descending the hillside to see the villagers dance, he remarked that the pond at the termination of the cascade stank "abominably."

6. Adams, *French Garden*, 118–21. See also Nicole de Roffignac and Alain d'Albavie, *The Désert de Retz: A Brief Description* (Paris, ca. 1989, mimeographed), 1–2. Although Monville headed the Royal Office of Water and Forestry, he was not

considered to be "of the court." He was a rich, handsome widower who was reputed to conduct initiations of Freemasons at his estate.

7. Jefferson, entries for Sept. 5, 7, 16, 1786, and Jefferson to Cosway, July 1, 1787, *Papers*, 10:445, 454, 11:519–20; Sotheby's International Realty, *Le Pavilion de Musique;* Roffignac and Albavie, *Désert de Retz.*

8. Jefferson to Cosway, July 1, 1787, *Papers*, 11:520.

9. Jefferson to Jay, Jan. 11, 1789, and Jefferson to Madison, Mar. 15, 1789, *Papers*, 14:429–30, 662. From Dr. Gem, Jefferson learned that the prince's education consisted of "a little Latin . . . [and] not a single element of mathematics, of natural or moral philosophy, or any science on earth" and that "the society the prince kept was "of the lowest, the most illiterate and profligate . . . with whom the subject of conversation are only horses, drinking-matches, bawdy houses, and in terms most vulgar." Jefferson asserted to Jay that the future George IV had "not one single idea of justice, morality, religion, or of the rights of man."

10. Bullock, *My Head and My Heart.* Bullock charmingly avoids the question whether theirs was a passionate or platonic friendship.

11. Minutes of the Accademia di Firenze, Archivio di Stati, Florence.

12. George C. Williamson, "Maria Cosway," *Dictionary of Painters and Engravers*, ed. Michael Bryan, 5 vols., rev. ed. (London, 1913), 1:337–38; *Richard Cosway, R.A. and His Wife and Pupils: Miniaturists of the Eighteenth Century (1740–1821)* (London: George Bell & Sons, 1896).

13. Trumbull, *Autobiography, Reminiscences and Letters* (New Haven: Hamlin, 1841), 107–20.

14. Jefferson, Sept. 5, 7, 16, Account Books, ViU; Jefferson to Cosway, Oct. 12, 1786, *Papers*, 10:445, 454. Maria Cosway was a harpist as well as a pianist and organist. Krumpholtz was the most prominent teacher and composer for the harp in Paris. The Ruggieri firm has produced fireworks for French state occasions since the days of Louis XIV, examples of whose *feu d'artifices* delighted Jefferson and Cosway.

15. Jefferson broke his wrist on Sept. 17 or 18, 1786. See Jefferson, Sept. 18, 1786, Account Books, ViU; Jefferson to Maria Cosway, [Oct. 5, 1786], *Papers*, 10:431–32, 12:34; and Bullock, *My Head and My Heart*, 21, 135.

16. Evidently, he hoped to regain also his ability to play the violin, because he bought a small one in August 1788. To his disappointment, the bones of his wrist never mended well. See Jefferson, Aug. 15, 1788, Account Books, ViU.

17. Cosway to Jefferson, [Sept. 20, 1786], and Jefferson to Cosway, [Oct. 5, 1786], *Papers*, 10:393–94, 431–33.

18. Jefferson to Cosway, [Oct. 5], 12, 1786, ibid., 10:433, 443. Jefferson rode with the Cosways, while his own carriage followed them to St. Denis in order to bring him home.

19. Jefferson to Cosway, Oct. 12, 1786, ibid., 10:443–53.

20. Boyd, note, ibid., 10:453.

21. Their Lapland summer day enjoyed about fourteen hours and forty minutes of daylight.

22. Jefferson to Cosway, Oct. 12, 1786, ibid., 10:446, 450.

23. Referring to his broken wrist, he promised that his first letter with his right hand would be to her. See Jefferson to Cosway, Oct. 13, 1786, ibid., 10:458–59. See also Bullock, *My Head and My Heart*, 27. Boyd notes that *Dardanus* was produced at Paris on October 3, 1786, and suggests that it is "quite possible" that Jefferson and the Cosways attended it two days before the Cosways left Paris. The refrain to which Jefferson alludes is from act 2, scene 4:

Jour heureux, espoir enchanteur!
Prix charmant d'un amour si tendre!
Je vais la voir, je vais l'entendre,
Je vais retrouver le bonheur!

24. Boyd, note, *Papers*, 10:453.

25. Cosway to Jefferson, Oct. 30, 1786, ibid., 10:494–96.

26. Jefferson to Cosway, Nov. 19, 1786. Boyd notes that Jefferson had written with his right hand letters to Jay on Nov. 12 and to Washington on Nov. 14, 1786 (ibid., 10:542–43).

27. Cosway to Jefferson, Jan. 1, Feb. 15, 1787, ibid., 11:4, 148–50.

28. Jefferson to Cosway, July 1, 1787, and Cosway to Jefferson, July 9, 1787, ibid., 11:519–20, 568.

29. Jefferson to Trumbull, Nov. 13, 1787, ibid., 12:358.

30. Cosway to Jefferson, [Dec. 1, 1787], and Jefferson to Cosway, Apr. 24, 1788, ibid., 12:387, 13:104; Anthony M. Clark, *Pompeo Batoni and His British Patrons* (New York: New York University Press, 1985), 151–52; Edgar Petyers Bowron, *Pompeo Batoni* (London: Greater London Council, 1982). Princess Aleksandra Lubomirska, née Czartoriska, was the wife of the Prince Maréchal Alexander Lubomirski. Mazzei said that "her beauty [was] superior to any found at Paris and Versailles" (Philip Mazzei, *My Life and Wanderings*, ed. S. Eugene Scalia, trans. Margherita Marchione [Morristown, N.J.: American Institute of Italian Studies, 1980], 307; for her being guillotined in the spring of 1794, see Schama, *Citizens*, 827).

31. Armand Louis de Gontaud, Duc de Lauzun (later Duc de Biron), *Mémoires* (Paris: Barrois L'Ainé Librairie, 1822), xvi–xx, 238. As a member of the Estates General and the Constituent Assembly, Lauzun was the author of bills concerning the postal services, defense measures at the time of the Nootka crisis, and requiring the Duc d'Orléans to make an accounting. After a diplomatic mission to London with Talleyrand, he commanded troops in Alsace, the Alpes-Maritimes, and the Vendée. Denounced in July 1793 as a conspirator against foreign and domestic safety, he was condemned and executed on January 1, 1794.

32. Cosway to Jefferson, Aug. 19, 1788, *Papers*, 10:525. See also ibid., 10:xxix, 466. The bust is in the collection of the Cosway Foundation, Lodi, Italy. Lauzun did not mention Maria in his *Mémoires*.

33. Jefferson to Cosway, June 23, 1790, *Papers*, 16:550–51. After the birth of her daughter, Louisa Paolina Angelica Cosway (1790–96), Maria went to Italy. In 1794 she returned to Richard at London and exhibited in the Royal Academy shows of 1796 and 1800. She founded a girls' school at Lyons in 1805 and moved it to Lodi in 1819, the same year she returned to London to nurse Richard until his death in 1821. She returned to Lodi. In 1834 Emperor Francis I created her a baroness. In 1834 she died. See Bullock, *My Head and My Heart*, 134–95.

CHAPTER 6. FROM PARIS TO MARSEILLES

1. Jefferson to Jay, Feb. 14, 1787, *Papers*, 11:144.

2. During this portion of his travels Jefferson made entries every day between Feb. 28 and Apr. 10, 1787, covering about two pages; and he covered about a quarter of a page for the days between May 2 and May 10. In this chapter I follow the chronology and sequence of Jefferson's itinerary, but combine into his first visit to Marseilles descriptive details from his second visit. See Jefferson, Account Books, ViU; and Jefferson, "Tour through Southern France," *Papers*, 11:415–45.

3. Ferdinand Grand, Jefferson's letter of credit, [Feb. 28, 1787], and Jefferson to Short, Mar. 15, 1787, ibid., 11:184–85, 215. Grand's letter was sent in multiple copy to Messrs. Finguerlin Scherer at Lyon, J. L. Brethoul at Marseilles, Le Clerc Cie. at Nice, Feger Grammont Cie. at Bordeaux, and Burnet Durand De La Marche at Montpellier.

4. Jefferson's repairs at Fontainbleau cost 114 livres, 12 sous. Between Fontainbleau and Sens, he passed through the villages of Moret, Faussard, Villeneuve, Pont-sur-Yonne, and Villevalleux.

5. Liancourt, *Voyages*, 1:110–11. From Sens young Liancourt went to Estissac, the seat of the duchy that had been created in Périgord for his paternal grandfather. Between Sens and Auxerre, Jefferson passed through the villages of Villeneuve-le-roy, Villevalleux, Joigny, and Basson.

6. Jefferson to Short, Mar. 15, 1787, and Jefferson, "Tour through Southern France," *Papers*, 11:212–15, 415–16.

7. Jefferson, "Tour through Southern France," ibid., 11:415.

8. Piozzi and Johnson, *French Journals*, 210–13. Piozzi thought its inhabitants were so "happy with what Heaven has unsolicited shaken into their lap" that they did not bother to keep good inns. As a consequence, she declared, travelers had to pay at night "by lodging in wretchedness dirt for the pleasures" they enjoyed in the daytime.

9. Jefferson to Short, Mar. 15, 1787, *Papers*, 11:214–15. The tower of the château of Vermenton today houses the local fire department. Between Auxerre and Dijon, Jefferson passed through the villages of St. Bris, Vermenton, Lucy-le-bois, Cisy-les-forges, La Chalure, Pont-de-Paris, and La Cude.

10. Jefferson to Short, Mar. 15, 1787, and Jefferson, "Tour through Southern France," ibid., 11:214–16, 416–17; Liancourt, *Voyages*, 1:119–20, 123; Young, *Travels*, 1:314. The names of the wines are modernized.

11. Henry James, *A Little Tour in France*, intro. Leon Edel (New York: Farrar, Straus and Giroux, 1983), 237–38.

12. Jefferson, "Tour through Southern France," and Jefferson to Short, Mar. 15, 1787, *Papers*, 11:214–15, 416–17.

13. Short to Jefferson, Mar. 22, 1787, Jefferson to Arnoux and Chalut, Apr. 12, 1787, Arnoux and Chalut to Jefferson, Apr. 23, 1787, and Jefferson, "Tour through Southern France," ibid., 11:232, 287, 303, 418–20; Liancourt, *Voyages*, 1:123–24, 131–33.

14. Jefferson to Short, Mar. 15, 1787, and Short to Jefferson, Mar. 22, 1787, *Papers*, 11:214–15, 232, 287–38; Jefferson, "Tour through Southern France," ibid., 11:416–20, 462–63. See also Liancourt, *Voyages*, 1:123–24, 131–33; and Young, *Travels*, 1:323. Jefferson probably did not call on the three Lyonnais to whom Arnoux and Chalut had given him letters of introduction: M. Tournillon, a king's counsel and notary; a M. Pizay; and the Abbé Charrier de la Roche, the prévot of Ainay and vicar-general of Ainay and Lyon.

15. Piozzi and Johnson, *French Journals*, 210–13; Young, *Travels*, 1:545.

16. For a bridge of boats on the Po, see chapter 7, and for one on the Rhine, chapter 12.

17. Liancourt, *Voyages*, 1:161–71; Young, *Travels*, 1:545–49.

18. Jefferson to Tessé, Mar. 20, 1787, and Jefferson, "Tour through Southern France," *Papers*, 11:226, 420–21. Between Valence and Montilimar, he passed through the villages of La Paillasse, L'Oriol, and Laine. In the vicinity of Tain, he went through the villages of Donserre, La Polus, and St. Valier.

19. Jefferson, "Tour through Southern France," ibid., 11:420–23; Liancourt, *Voyages*, 1:192; Young, *Travels*, 1:357.

20. Jefferson, "Tour through Southern France," *Papers*, 11:420; Young, *Travels*, 1:361. Just before entering Orange, Jefferson passed through a village named Mornas.

21. Jefferson, "Tour through Southern France," *Papers*, 11:423; Liancourt, *Voyages*, 1:196–97; Young, *Travels*, 1:361–62; James, *Little Tour*, 221–22.

22. Jefferson, "Tour through Southern France," Short to Jefferson, Mar. 12, 1787, and Jefferson to Short, Mar. 27, 1787, *Papers*, 11:207–11, 247–48; Jefferson to Martha Jefferson, Mar. 28, 1787, ibid., 11:250; Short to Jefferson, Apr. 4, 1787, and Jefferson to Short, Apr. 7, May 5, 1787, ibid., 11:267, 280–81, 350, 427; Jefferson to Jay, May 4, 1787, ibid., 11:338; Liancourt, *Voyages*, 2:29. Between Aix and Marseilles Jefferson passed through Orgon and St. Cannat. At Aix he engaged a local valet named Flammand. The thermal spring of Aix was 90°F "at the spout."

23. Jefferson to Short, Mar. 27, 1787, *Papers*, 11:247; James, *Little Tour*, 180.

24. For both Mirabeaus, see François Furet, "Mirabeau," in *A Critical Dictionary of the French Revolution*, ed. François Furet and Mona Ozouf (Cambridge: Harvard University Press, 1989), 265–68.

25. Jefferson to Short, Mar. 29, 1787, *Papers*, 11:254.

26. Jefferson to Martha Jefferson, May 5, 1787, ibid., 11:348; Jefferson to Mazzei, Apr. 4, 1787, Jefferson to Arnoux and Chalut, Apr. 12, 1787, and Jefferson to Jay, Mar. 4, 1787, ibid., 11:266, 287–88, 338; Liancourt, *Voyages*, 2:3–14, 18–20; Young, *Travels* 1:372–73.

27. Arthur Young declared that the port of Marseilles was "only a horse pond" compared with Bordeaux. See Young, *Travels*, 1:372–78; and Liancourt, *Voyages*, 1:25.

28. Modern construction at the Château d'If dates from the sixteenth century (see Liancourt, *Voyages*, 1:25). Mirabeau was confined there in 1774. In the midnineteenth century the Château d'If was a principal locale for Alexandre Dumas's novel *The Count of Monte Cristo*.

29. Jefferson, "Tour through Southern France," *Papers*, 11:429; Liancourt, *Voyages*, 1:21–24; Michel Gallet, *Stately Mansions: Eighteenth-Century Paris Architecture* (New York: Praeger, 1972), 56–57. Today the château is a museum, while the estate is a municipal complex that includes a botanical garden, a pleasure park, and a racetrack.

30. Liancourt, *Voyages*, 1:215–16; Young, *Travels*, 1:379, 384. After leaving Marseilles, Jefferson passed through Aubagne, Cuges, and Beausset. Although he had letters of introduction, Young was not permitted to enter the dockyard of Toulon.

31. Liancourt, *Voyages*, 1:215.

32. Jefferson to Short, May 1, 1787, *Papers*, 11:326; Liancourt, *Voyages*, 1:211–14; Young, *Travels*, 1:387–88, 391. Jefferson was more fortunate than Young, who had to walk part of the way from Toulon to Antibes.

CHAPTER 7. NORTHERN ITALY

1. Jefferson to Cosway, July 1, 1787, *Papers*, 11:519.

2. See Jefferson to L'Enfant, Apr. 10, 1791, *Writings* (L&B), 7:162. Jefferson also recommended that tourists buy, in addition to the guidebooks he used, Joseph Addison's *Remarks on Italy*. See Jefferson, "Hints to Americans Travelling in Europe," *Papers*, 13:268; and Sowerby, *Jefferson's Library*, 4:128–33.

3. Jefferson to Jay, Oct. 23, 1786, and Jay to Jefferson, July 27, 1787, *Papers*, 10:484–85, 11:627–28.

4. Jefferson to Short, Apr. 7, 1787, ibid., 11:280–81.

5. Jefferson, "Tour through Southern France," ibid., 11:429–30, 463n; Jeffer-

son, Apr. 13, 1787, Account Books, ViU. In Italy Jefferson made an entry for every day between April 10 and May 1, 1787, covering one page.

6. Jefferson to Grand, and Grand to Jefferson, Feb. 28, 1787, *Papers*, 11:184–85.

7. De Scarnafis to the American commissioners, Feb. 2, 1785, Jefferson to John Adams, July 1, 1787, and Jefferson to Dumas, Dec. 9, 1787, ibid., 7:632–33, 11:516, 12:407. See also Malone, *Jefferson*, 2:40–49. Jefferson used the French version of the Sardinian minister's name, which in its Italian version was Filippo Ottone Ponte, Conte di Scarafiggi. He had been a student of Giambattista Beccaria at the University of Turin. See Antonio Pace, *Benjamin Franklin and Italy* (Philadelphia: American Philosophical Society, 1958), 95.

8. On Arnoux and Chalut, see chapter 6. On Mazzei, see Philip Mazzei, *Memoirs of the Life and Peregrinations of the Florentine, Philip Mazzei, 1730–1816*, trans. Howard Mararro (New York: Columbia University Press, 1942), 326. Mazzei was then at Paris supervising the publication of his *Recherches sur les Etats-Unis*.

9. Gaudenzio Clerici to Jefferson, Mar. 5, 1787, Jefferson to Clerici, Aug. 15, 1787, and Aug. 31, 1788, Clerici to Jefferson, Jan. 20, 1789, *Papers*, 11:199–200, 12:38–39, 13:553–54, 14:475.

10. Jefferson, Feb. 28, Apr. 10, 1787, Account Books, ViU.

11. Jefferson, "Tour through Southern France," *Papers*, 11:429–30, 463n; Jefferson, Apr. 10–13, 1787, Account Books, ViU. He visited the commandant, the director of the Royal Tobacco Factory, a banker, and two merchants. The quotation is from Joseph Addison, "A Letter from Italy to the Right Honorable Charles Lord Halifax," *Miscellaneous Works*, 1:65–67.

12. Jefferson to Short, Apr. 12, 1787, *Papers*, 11:287; Jefferson, Apr. 10–15, 1787, Account Books, ViU; *Guide pour le voyage d'Italie en poste*, 48–49; Young, *Travels*, 1:391–401. See also Karl Baedeker, *Italy: Handbook for Travellers . . . Northern Italy*, 9th rev. ed. (Leipzig: Baedeker, 1892), 80. Jefferson spent the night of the fourteenth at Sospello and on the fifteenth breakfasted at Ciandola before lodging at Tende.

13. Jefferson to Cosway, July 1, 1787, *Papers*, 11:520; Jefferson, "Tour through Southern France," ibid., 11:432; Young, *Travels*, 1:400. Jefferson's and Young's spelling "Saorgio" has been modernized. Earlier Jefferson had begged in his famous "My Head and My Heart" letter that Maria paint Niagara Falls, the junction of the Potomac and the Shenandoah, the Natural Bridge of Virginia, and Monticello (see Jefferson to Cosway, Oct. 12, 1786, *Papers*, 10:70). Arthur Young wrote that the town of Saorgo was "stuck like a swallow's nest" against the side of a cliff, while the fortresslike castle was almost "Oriental" in its wild setting on an equidistant triangular platform of about seventy yards. In 1792 the French destroyed the castle. See Baedeker, *Italy*, 80.

14. Cosway Collection, Cosway Foundation, Lodi, Italy.

15. Jefferson, "Tour through Southern France," *Papers*, 11:433; Jefferson, Apr. 15–16, 1787, Account Books, ViU; Jefferson, "Tour through Southern France," *Papers*, 11:433–34; *Guide pour le voyage d'Italie en poste*, 48–49; Young, *Travels*, 1:402–5; An American [Theodore Dwight], *A Journal of a Tour in Italy, in the year 1821 with a Description of Gibraltar* (New York: Paul, 1824), 466; Baedeker, *Italy*, 55.

16. Jefferson, Apr. 16–19, 1787, Account Books, ViU; Jefferson, "Tour through Southern France," *Papers*, 11:435; Young, *Travels*, 1:406; Charles Pinot-Duclos, *Voyage en Italie, ou Considérations sur l'Italie* (Paris: Buisson, 1791), 324. Young's visit was in the fall of 1789. Pinot-Duclos made his trip in 1767, when he was historiographer of France and *secrétaire perpétuelle* of the Académie française.

17. Jefferson, Apr. 17–18, 1787, Account Books, ViU; Jefferson, "Tour through Southern France," *Papers*, 11:435; Young, *Travels*, 1:407–8, 415. Professor Raimondo Luraghi kindly furnished me with comments on eighteenth-century Turin and the wines of Piedmont.

18. Jefferson, Apr. 17–19, 1789, Account Books, ViU; Cosway to Jefferson, July 9, 1787, *Papers*, 11:568–69, 464n; Sowerby, *Jefferson's Library*, 4:128–33; Pinot-Duclos, *Voyage*, 325. Jefferson visited two bankers and two or three merchants, whom he questioned concerning the potential market for American tobacco, whale oil, and fish products.

19. Young, *Travels*, 1:411. Addison's sightseeing at Turin was curtailed because the royal court was in mourning. See Addison, *Remarks on Italy*, 288.

20. Dwight, *Journal*, 466. Cf. Sigfried Giedion, *Space, Time and Architecture: The Growth of a New Tradition* (Cambridge: Putnam's, 1941), 55–61; and Richard Pommer, *Eighteenth-Century Architecture in Piedmont: The Open Structure of Juvarra, Alfieri, and Vittone* (New York: New York University Press, 1967), 7–11.

21. John Chetwoode Eustace, *A Classical Tour through Italy [in 1802]*, 3 vols., 8th ed. (London: T. Tegg, 1841), 3:166–69. Although marred by Francophobia, his book accurately reflects the distaste among most classicists for both the Gothic and the baroque.

22. Jefferson, "Tour through Southern France," *Papers*, 11:464n; Young, *Travels*, 1:410–11, 413; Pinot-Duclos, *Voyage*, 325.

23. Eustace, *Classical Tour*, 3:167–69. The academy also served as a preparatory school for civil and military service. Speculation that Jefferson became an honorary member of the academy does not rest on documentary evidence. Young's reception was warmer than Jefferson's, but he did not record becoming a member.

24. Clerici to Jefferson, July 14, 1787, *Papers*, 11:585–86.

25. Quoted in Paul Guichonnet, *Histoire de Savoie* (Annecy: Gardet, 1960), 105–10.

26. Jefferson, Apr. 18, 1787, Account Books, ViU; Jefferson, "Tour through Southern France," *Papers*, 11:435; Short to Jefferson, Oct. 18, 1788, ibid., 14:27. When Pinot-Duclos went to Superga, an accompanying carriage overturned and was dragged, but without human injury. Before riding to the basilica, Young walked from Turin to Moncalieri, which he called "the Windsor of Piedmont." The palazzo is now a military academy. See Pinot-Duclos, *Voyage*, 328–29; Young, *Travels*, 1:411; Eustace, *Classical Tour*, 3:167–69; and Baedeker, *Italy*, 38.

27. Jefferson, Apr. 18, 1787, Account Books, ViU; Hugh Thomas, "Stupinigi," in *Great Houses of Europe*, ed. Sacheverell Sitwell (London: Spring Books, 1970), 198–205; Pommer, *Architecture in Piedmont*, 61–78.

28. Eustace, *Classical Tour*, 3:106.

29. Short to Jefferson, Oct. 18, 1788, *Papers*, 14:27; and Addison, *Remarks on Italy*, 288.

30. Jefferson, Apr. 19–20, 1787, Account Books, ViU; Jefferson, "Tour through Southern France," *Papers*, 11:22–24; Young, *Travels*, 1:415–16.

31. Conte Francesco dal Verme (1758–1832) belonged to an ancient and wealthy family of Verona and Milan. He had friends in high places, such as Conte Ludovico di Belgiojoso (1728–1801), sometime Austrian ambassador at London, and his uncle by marriage, Giacomo d'Aquino, Principe di Caramanico, sometime Neapolitan ambassador at London. See Francesco dal Verme, *Seeing America and Its Great Men: The Journal and Letters of Count Francesco dal Verme, 1783–1784*, ed. and trans. Elizabeth Cometti (Charlottesville: University Press of Virginia, 1969), xi–xv, 97.

32. Jefferson, "Tour through Southern France," *Papers*, 11:437, 464; Dal Verme to Jefferson, Feb. 12, 1788, and Jefferson to Dal Verme, Aug. 15, 1788, *Papers*, 12:587–88, 13:42–43; and Jefferson, Apr. 20–23, 1787, Account Books, ViU.

33. Short to Jefferson, Oct. 28, 1788, *Papers*, 14:41–43.

34. Stendhal [Marie Henri Beyle], *Rome, Naples, and Florence*, trans. Richard N. Coe (New York: Braziller, 1960), 36–38, 337.

35. Jefferson, Apr. 20–24, 1787, Account Books, ViU; Jefferson, "Tour through Southern France," *Papers*, 11:437. The Casa Belgiojoso should not be confused with the present Gallery of Modern Art, formerly the Villa Reale and before that a different Villa Belgiojoso, which was built by Leopold Pollak in 1790 for Conte Ludovico Barbiano de Belgiojoso, who sold it to the Cisalpine Republic for Napoleon and Eugène de Beauharnais's use. See Baedeker, *Italy*, 95–96, 110; Ente Provinciale per il Turismo de Milano, *Tutta Milano* (Milan, 1969), 38.

36. Paolo D'Ancona and Francesca Leoni, *Tiepolo in Milan: The Palazzo Clerici Frescoes*, trans. Lucia Krasnik (Milan: Edizioni del Milione, 1956); see Ente Provinciale per il Turismo de Milano, *Tutta Milano* (Milan, n.d.), [9], 39; Young, *Travels*, 1:417, 419–20.

37. Jefferson to George Wythe, Sept. 16, 1787, *Papers*, 12:127; Young, *Travels*, 1:418. See also Baedeker, *Italy*, 97; and Touring Club Italienne, *L'Italie en une volume*, ed. Cesar Chiodi, Les Guides Bleus (Paris: Hachette, 1952), 45.

38. Addison, *Remarks on Italy*, 24.

39. Marie Kimball, *Jefferson*, 2:114. Calling the *Last Supper* "the most famous production of human genius," Arthur Young warned that it should be studied only by artists "who understand its merit, as it is not a picture for those who, with unlearned eyes, have only their feelings to direct them" (Young, *Travels*, 1:430).

40. Addison, *Remarks on Italy*, 18–22.

41. Jefferson, Apr. 23–24, 1787, Account Books, ViU; Jefferson to Cosway, July 1, 1787, *Papers*, 11:519–20; Eustace, *Classical Tour*, 3:11, 107–9; Baedeker, *Italy*, 141–44; *Guide pour le voyage d'Italie en Poste*, 33 and pl. 19.

42. Jefferson, "Hints to Americans Travelling in Europe," *Papers*, 13:272, 268; Young, *Travels*, 1:425–26; Eustace, *Classical Tour*, 3:125, 128–29; Marie Kimball, *Jefferson*, 3:114.

43. Jefferson to Cosway, July 1, 1787, *Papers*, 11:519–20; Addison, *Remarks on Italy*, 38–71; Young, *Travels*, 1:442–44.

44. Jefferson, "Tour through Southern France" and "Hints to Americans Travelling in Europe," *Papers*, 11:438, 13:272.

45. Addison, *Remarks on Italy*, 13, 16.

46. Jefferson, Apr. 24–28, 1787, Account Books, ViU; Jefferson, "Tour through Southern France," *Papers*, 11:440–41, 464; Jefferson to Short, Feb. 28, 1789, ibid., 14:598. See also Brusco, *Beautés de Gènes*, 11; Addison, *Remarks on Italy*, 7–8; and Eustace, *Classical Tour*, 3:82–97, 102. Jefferson presented letters of introduction from Le Clerc to the bankers Bertrand, Ricard, and Bramerel and from Jean Baptiste Guide to the merchant Régny.

47. Jefferson, "Hints to Americans Travelling in Europe," *Papers*, 13:268.

48. Boyd, note, *Papers*, 11:464.

49. Brusco, *Beautés de Gènes*, 51–56; Edwards, *Rubens*, 106; John Canaday, *The Lives of the Painters*, 4 vols. (New York: Norton, 1969). See also Editors of Réalités, *Great Houses of Italy* (New York: Putnam's, 1968), 128–31.

50. Eustace, *Classical Tour*, 82–87, 102.

51. Kimball, *Jefferson, Architect*, 38.

52. American commissioners to Pedro Pablo Abárca y Boléa, Count D'Aranda,

et al., Sept. 22, 1784, and papal nuncio to American commissioners, Oct. 15, 1784, *Papers*, 7:423–24, 575–76.

53. Addison, *Remarks on Italy*, 8.

54. George L. Gorse, "The Villa of Andrea Doria in Genoa: Architecture, Gardens, and Suburban Setting," *Journal of the Society of Architectural Historians* 44 (Mar. 1985): 18–36. Quotations from John Evelyn, *Diary of John Evelyn*, ed. Austin Dobson, 3 vols. (London: Macmillan, 1906), 1:131–33, and Richard Lasells, *The Voyage of Italy* (Paris, 1670), 91–94. Brusco, *Beautés de Gènes*, pl. 1 ff. See also Editors of Réalités, *Great Houses of Italy*, 124–27.

55. Jefferson to Short, Feb. 18, 1789, *Papers*, 14:598. Almost twenty years later President Jefferson asked Philip Mazzei to recruit for work on the U.S. Capitol Giuseppi Franzoni, son of the president of the Carrara Academy of Fine Arts, and a man named Giovanni Andrei. Jefferson and Latrobe reluctantly abandoned the possibility that Antonio Canova might undertake a commission for a marble or plaster statue of Liberty for this project. See Benjamin H. Latrobe to Mazzei, Mar. 6, 1805, and Latrobe to Jefferson, "Report," Mar. 23, 1808, quoted in Padover, *Jefferson and the National Capital*, 355–58, 400, 507, 510.

56. Jefferson to Martha Jefferson, May 4, 1787, *Papers*, 11:348; Jefferson, Account Books, Apr. 28–May 1, 1787, ViU; Jefferson, "Hints to Americans Travelling in Europe," *Papers* 12:270; Addison, *Remarks on Italy*, 3–4.

57. For quotations, see Jefferson, "Tour through Southern France," *Papers*, 11:441–43. See also Brusco, *Beautés de Gènes*, 7; and Pinot-Duclos, *Voyage*, 11–18. Twenty years before, Pinot-Duclos's boat had suffered somewhat the same fate. Spanish possession of the enclave of Albenga, between Genoa and Nice, from 1598 to 1713 had left a legacy of calculated insularity. Jefferson drew again on Grand's letter of credit at Nice.

58. Jefferson to La Fayette, Apr. 11, 1787, *Papers*, 11:284.

59. Geismar to Jefferson, Mar. 28, 1785, ibid., 8:63; Jefferson to Clerici, Aug. 15, 1787, ibid., 12:38; Malone, *Jefferson*, 2:234–35.

60. Jefferson to Short, Feb. 28, 1789, *Papers*, 14:598.

61. Short to Jefferson, Feb. 11, 1789, ibid., 14:540.

62. Short to Jefferson, Nov. 29, Dec. 23, 1787, Feb. 25, 1789, ibid., 14:312, 381–82, 591–92; Jefferson, "Hints to Americans Travelling in Europe" and enclosure to Rutledge, June 19, 1788, ibid., 13:269.

63. Frederick D. Nichols, *Thomas Jefferson's Architectural Drawings* (Boston: Massachusetts Historical Society, 1960), 8–9, pl. 27. Cf. Nichols and Bear, *Monticello*, 23 ff.

64. Randolph, *Domestic Life of Jefferson*, 334, designates the north and south porches as piazzi and the west and east porches as porticoes. See also William A. Lambeth and Warren H. Manning, *Thomas Jefferson: Architect and a Designer of Landscapes* (Boston: Houghton Mifflin, 1913), pl. 2. Cf. Kimball, *Jefferson, Architect*, 59, designating the north and south porches as loggias.

65. Jefferson to William Wirt, Nov. 12, 1816, *Writings* (Ford), 10:61; William B. O'Neal, *Jefferson's Buildings at the University of Virginia* (Charlottesville: University of Virginia Press, 1960). See also Nichols, *Jefferson's Architectural Drawings*, 8–9; and "The Rotunda," *University of Virginia Alumni News* 43 (Mar. 1953): 5–7.

66. Jefferson to Thomas Munroe, Mar. 21, 1803, quoted in Padover, *Jefferson and the National Capital*, 300; Malone, *Jefferson*, 4:47–48. See also Jefferson to Cosway, July 1, 1787, *Papers*, 11:519; and Victor Alfieri, *Memoir of the Life and Writings of Victor Alfieri*, 2 vols. (London: H. Colburn, 1810). The quivering of the leaves of this tree symbolized the prayers of those oppressed by despots.

1. Jefferson to Tessé, Mar. 20, 1787, *Papers*, 11:226. Jefferson was not unusual in viewing the Maison Carrée at night (see Liancourt, *Voyages*, 2:192–95; and Young, *Travels*, 1:70–74).

2. Jefferson, Mar. 19–25, 1787, Account Books, ViU; Jefferson to Short, Mar. 29, 1787, *Papers*, 11:254.

3. Jefferson, Apr. 18–21, 1787, Account Books, ViU.

4. Jefferson to Tessé, Mar. 20, 1787, *Papers*, 11:226–28. Cf. Clérisseau's statement that Rome does not have a perfect monument in Charles Louis Clérisseau, *Antiquités de la France* (Paris: Philippe-Denys-Pierres, 1778), vii.

5. Jefferson, "Tour through Southern France," *Papers*, 11:423–24, 443–44.

6. Ibid., 11:424–25.

7. Jefferson, June 2, 1786, Account Books, ViU; Sowerby, *Jefferson's Library*, 4:376.

8. Jean de Cayeux, *Hubert Robert* (Paris: Fayard, 1989), 380.

9. James Buchanan and William Hay to Jefferson, Mar. 20, 1785, Jefferson to Short, June 28, 1785, and Jefferson to Buchanan and Hay, Aug. 13, 1785, *Papers*, 8:48–49, 257, 366–67.

10. Jefferson to Page, May 4, 1786, ibid., 9:445.

11. Jefferson to Madison, Sept. 20, 1785, ibid., 8:534–35.

12. Tessé to Jefferson, Apr. 27, 1788, and Jefferson to Tessé, Aug. 27, 1789, ibid., 13:110, 15:363–64. The pedestal, or civic altar, was of dark marble with alternating putti, signs of the zodiac, and a fulsome inscription that Jefferson turned to the wall.

13. Jefferson to Tessé, Mar. 20, 1787, and Tessé to Jefferson, Mar. 30, 1787, ibid., 11:226–28, 257–58.

14. Kimball, *Thomas Jefferson, Architect*, 40–43; Jean Ch. Balty, *Études sur la Maison Carrée de Nîmes*, Collection Latomos, vol. 47 (Brussels: Revue D'Études Latines, 1960), 67–70.

15. Robert Adam to James Adam, Feb. 19, 1745, quoted in Thomas J. McCormick, *Charles Louis Clérisseau and the Genesis of Neo-Classicism* (Cambridge: MIT Press, 1990), 24.

16. John Fleming, *Robert Adam and His Circle in Edinburgh and Rome* (London: John Murray, 1962), 273.

17. Dazzled by Fiske Kimball's sumptuous reproduction of so many of Jefferson's architectural drawings in his great study *Thomas Jefferson, Architect*, 40–43, most subsequent writers have uncritically adopted his opinion that Jefferson's main sources of inspiration were the works of Andrea Palladio and his eighteenth-century English admirer James Gibbs. Even though Kimball stated that Jefferson's precedents in "Roman-classical" architecture were those "understood by Palladio and by the French of the Late eighteenth century," he deprecated Jefferson's employment of professional architects. He stated that the design of Virginia's Capitol was "essentially Jefferson's own" and that its plan was "wholly his," citing as evidence Jefferson's sketches of a floor plan for the legislature within a temple form that were on watermarked paper, most of which he used before he went to Europe (*Jefferson, Architect*, 2d ed., vi–viii, 40–43; idem, "Thomas Jefferson and the Public Buildings of Virginia," *Huntington Library Quarterly* 12 [1949]: 115–20, 303–10).

Kimball did not omit reference to Clérisseau, but he did not give him prominence. If Kimball had been able to study today's fullness of Jefferson's correspondence, he might well have given the Frenchman more credit for his part in the plan for the Virginia state capitol. Furthermore, in 1916 much of Clérisseau's works languished in Russian archives or suffered the obscurity of private collections. Now, thanks to Thomas McCormick's *Clérisseau*, 191–200, 272–74, that situation no longer obtains. Jefferson's recommendation of Palladio's book as "the Bible" to John Hartwell Cocke may only have meant that it was the most accessible reference work for the vocabulary of classical details (see Cocke to Isaac Coles, Feb. 23, 1816, quoted by Frederick D. Nichols in his introduction to Kimball, *Jefferson, Architect*, vii).

In the 1960s, James A. Bear, Jr., and Frederick D. Nichols in their *Monticello*, 23, and Nichols in his "Jefferson: The Making of an Architect," 163–67, made abundant reference to Clérisseau's and other French architectural books. Nichols slightly modified Kimball, saying that Jefferson's "Palladian vision was tempered by the Louis XVI style." Dumas Malone in his *Jefferson*, 2:91, did not depart from Kimball's emphasis on Jefferson's dependence on Palladio. Merrill Peterson in his *Jefferson*, 341, 538, denominated Clérisseau as "the consulting architect" for the design of the capitol. Jack McLaughlin in his *Jefferson and Monticello: The Biography of a Builder* (New York: Henry Holt, 1988), 25, 61, 64, credits Palladio as the architect who most inspired Jefferson and Clérisseau as Jefferson's "collaborator" on the capitol. Thomas J. McCormick in his definitive biography *Clérisseau*, 197, 199, concluded that while Jefferson may have desired a classic prototype for the Virginia state capitol as early as 1776, it was not while he was in Virginia that he selected the Maison Carrée for that purpose. McCormick delicately modified Kimball by concluding that while Jefferson may have had the basic idea for copying the Maison Carrée as a shell for the Virginia state capitol, Clérisseau's "architectural expertise entered into the design as a whole as well as the specific details."

Among other recent speculations, Mark R. Wenger in his "Thomas Jefferson and the Virginia State Capitol," *VMHB* 101 (Jan. 1993): 77–102, based his conclusion that Jefferson "contemplated a classical temple form for the Virginia Assembly at least as early as 1776" on the presence of Jefferson's words "Burgesses" and "Council" partially erased beneath "Delegates" and "Senate." Douglas L. Wilson speculated in his "Dating Jefferson's Early Architectural Drawings," *VMHB* 101 (Jan. 1993): 53–76, that Jefferson's calligraphy on this plan belongs to a period before 1784, when he used both a cursive and an open *s*.

CHAPTER 9. THROUGH LANGUEDOC AND GASCONY TO
TOULOUSE AND BORDEAUX

1. Grand to Jefferson, May 19, 1787, *Papers*, 11:364; Jefferson, "Tour through Southern France," ibid., 11:443.

2. Jefferson to Martha Jefferson, May 21, 1787, ibid., 11:369; Young, *Travels*, 1:362–67; Liancourt, *Voyages*, 1:200–203. When Young saw the famous fountain in August it was a stagnant pool.

3. "The Askos," *Papers*, 15:xxix–xxxiii, 280; Bear, *Reports*, 18:7–8.

4. Jefferson to Elénore François Elie, Comte de Moustier, July 24, 1787, *Papers*, 11:621; Young, *Travels*, 1:69.

5. Short to Jefferson, Apr. 4, 1787, and Jefferson to Short, May 5, 1787, *Papers*, 11:269–79, 349–50. See also Young, *Travels*, 1:131. Concerning his journey between Languedoc and Bordeaux, Jefferson made entries for every day between May 10 and 28, 1787, covering one page in all.

6. Jefferson to Jay, May 4, 1787, *Papers*, 11:339–42.

7. The St. Foin hay was of the sparsette variety. Simple clover was called *farouche*. See Jefferson to Jay, May 4, 1787, ibid., 11:339–45, 463–64. See also José da Maia to Jefferson, Oct. 2 and Nov. 21, 1786, ibid., 10:427, 546; and Jefferson to Da Maia, Dec. 26, 1786, and Mar. 19, 1787, ibid., 10:636, 11:225.

8. Liancourt, *Voyages*, 2:131.

9. Young, *Travels*, 1:69. Montpellier was known for its production of and market for wine, *eau de vie*, silk stockings, perfumes, woolen blankets, cotton toiles, leather goods, and verdigris coloring agents.

10. Jefferson, "Tour through Southern France," *Papers*, 11:444; Liancourt, *Voyages*, 2:50–54; Young, *Travels*, 1:64–68.

11. Jefferson, "Tour through Southern France," *Papers*, 11:446–47. See also Liancourt, *Voyages*, 2:65, 69; and Anna Francesca Craddock, *Voyage en France*, *1783–1786*, trans. Odalie H. Delphion-Bailleguier (Paris: Perrin, 1911), 167–72, concerning her trip from Béziers to Toulouse on May 22, 1785.

12. Jefferson, "Tour through Southern France," *Papers*, 11:444–46. See also Liancourt, *Voyages*, 2:59–63, 74, 76, 127, whose editor depends mainly on Antoine François, Comte d'Andréossy, *Histoire du Canal du Midi, ou Canal de Languedoc*, 2 vols., enl. ed. (Paris: Crapelet, 1807). Pierre Paul Riquet (1604–80) was from Béziers. The eastern terminus's name was spelled Cette in Jefferson's day. Sixty-two locks are of two or more chambers. Three of its fifty-four bridges are large ones.

13. Jefferson, Apr. 1788, Account Books, ViU; Jefferson, "Tour through Southern France," *Papers*, 11:449. See also Liancourt, *Voyages*, 2:56.

14. Jefferson, "Tour through Southern France," *Papers*, 11:446–47, 449. See also Liancourt, *Voyages*, 1:59–60, 66–67; and Young, *Travels*, 1:65, 67.

15. Liancourt, *Voyages*, 1:69.

16. Jefferson, Apr. 1787, Account Books, ViU.

17. Jefferson, "Tour through Southern France," *Papers*, 11:447–48. See also Liancourt, *Voyages*, 2:74–75, 78–79, quoting Jean Aimar Piganiol de La Force's *Nouvelle déscription de la France*, 6 vols. (Paris: T. Legras, 1718), 6:300. Construction of the branch canal to Carcassonne was suspended during the Revolution and was not finished until 1810. Arthur Young recorded that the town's woolens manufacturers suffered because they had to pay a 20 percent commission to merchants in Marseilles, who had the exclusive privilege of trading with the Levant. Young exclaimed: "These exclusive privileges are an odious thing and constrain commerce." See Young, *Travels*, 1:79.

18. Liancourt, *Voyages*, 1:65.

19. Jefferson, "Tour through Southern France," *Papers*, 11:448. See also Liancourt, *Voyages*, 2:81.

20. Liancourt, *Voyages*, 2:71–73, 17, 82–90, 107; Young, *Travels*, 1:43–46; Jacques Antoine Hyppolyte, Comte de Guibert, *Voyages dans diverses parties de France et en Suisse, faits en 1775, 78 et 85* (Paris: D'Hautel, 1806), 16; Piganiol de La Force, *Nouvelle déscription de la France*, 6:253; Craddock, *Voyage en France*, 171–91.

21. The large church in which the original Jacobin Club met had been the first Dominican monastery at Paris. It took its name from the rue St. Jacques. See Mazzei, *My Life and Wanderings*, 321, 420; see also François Furet, "Jacobinism," in Furet and Ozouf, *Critical Dictionary of the French Revolution*, 704, 710.

22. Jefferson, "Tour through Southern France," *Papers*, 11:454. See also Young, *Travels*, 1:92–93. There seems to have been no tobacco grown in France in 1787, although there is much grown there now.

23. Jefferson, "Tour through Southern France," *Papers*, 11:454–55; Jefferson to Barclay, May 5, 1787, Barclay to Jefferson, June 12, 1787, Jefferson to the commissioners of the treasury, June 17, 1787, ibid., 11:347–48, 466–67, 474–76.

24. Jefferson, "Tour through Southern France," *Papers*, 11:455. See also Liancourt, *Voyages*, 2:110–12, 114–16. The Trompette was demolished in 1818. Two small forts downstream, Fort Ha and Fort Royal, effectively blocked British amphibious operations in 1813. Since the Revolution the archepiscopal palace has been the Hôtel de Ville.

25. Jefferson, "Tour through Southern France," *Papers*, 11:454–55. The brick Roman remains now called the Palais Gallieni were then fully encrusted with buildings of later date.

26. Young, *Travels*, 1:95, 98.

27. Jefferson, "Tour through Southern France," *Papers*, 11:455–57; Liancourt, *Voyages*, 1:117–18, 120–21, quoting Craddock, *Voyage en France*, 206; Young, *Travels*, 1:94–98, 2:424–35.

CHAPTER 10. FROM BLAYE TO PARIS VIA BRITTANY AND THE LOIRE VALLEY

1. Concerning his journey from Blaye to Paris, Jefferson made entries for every day between May 28 and June 10, 1787. After Blaye he passed through six villages before dining: Etauliers, St. Aubin, Mirambeau, St. Gànis, Lajart, and Saintes. After dinner he went through St. Porchain and St. Hyppolite. See also Young, *Travels*, 1:101–2.

2. Liancourt, *Voyages*, 2:156–66. Château La Rochefoucauld stands on a bluff overlooking a prosperous town. As reconstructed in the eighteenth century, the château describes a quadrilateral with two fourteenth- or fifteenth-century towers, a Romanesque *donjon* thirty-five meters high, and two Renaissance wings. See Charles Louis Salch, *Dictionnaire des Châteaux et de Fortifications du Moyen Age en France* (Strasbourg: Editions Publitotal, 1979), 981–83. The Château de Verteuil is a fine but conventional eighteenth-century complex set in an English-style park above a modest town.

3. Nicole Charbonnel, *Commerce et cours sous la révolution et consulat à la Rochelle* (Paris: Presses Universitaires de France, 1977), 7, 132–33.

4. Liancourt, *Voyages*, 2:156–66; Young, *Travels*, 1:186.

5. Liancourt, *Voyages*, 1:186; James, *Little Tour*, 103–10. The Hôtel de Ville was built between 1535 and 1628. The present structure, which dates from 1873, occupies the same site and was intended to be a modern adaptation.

6. Liancourt, *Voyages*, 2:156–59; Young, *Travels*, 1:187–90; James, *Little Tour*, 103–10.

7. Young, *Travels*, 1:165–80.

8. Ibid., 1:184–86, 188–90.

9. Unlike Jefferson, Young traveled in northern and western Normandy. See ibid., 1:174–79, 184–86.

10. Liancourt, *Voyages*, 2:181.

11. Ibid., 2:173, 176–81; Young, *Travels*, 1:181–84.

12. Jefferson to Short, May 1, 1787, *Papers*, 11:327; Liancourt, *Voyages*, 1:88–90, 173; Young, *Travels*, 1:175–76, 191–93. The villages were Roudun, Brècharaye, Dérval, Nosay, Bout des Bois, and Gàsves.

13. Jefferson, June 5, 1787, Account Books, ViU; Jefferson to Short, May 1, 1787, *Papers*, 11:327.

14. Liancourt, *Voyages*, 1:181.

15. Ibid., 1:186–91.

16. Jefferson, June 8, 1787, Account Books, ViU; Young, *Travels*, 1:107–9; Roof, *Colonel William Smith and Lady*, 161; Liancourt, *Voyages*, 2:196–99, quoting Sir Nathaniel Wraxall, *A Tour through the Western, Southern and Interior Provinces of France*, first printed as an appendix to his *History of the Valois* (London, 1777), printed separately, London, 1784.

17. Two of the set of four paintings by Pannini are now in the Boston Museum of Fine Arts. Choiseul acquired these *vedute ideate* while he was the French ambassador to the Holy See and is depicted in them. See *Masterpiece Paintings from the*

Museum of Fine Arts, Boston (Boston: H. N. Abrams, 1986), 31; Rudolf Wittkower, *Art and Architecture in Italy, 1600 to 1750* (Baltimore: Penguin Books, [1958]), 325–26; Leandro Ozzola, *Gian Paolo Pannini* (Turin: E. Celanza, 1921); and Ferdinando Arisi, *Gian Paolo Panini* (Piacenza: Casa di Risparmio, 1961).

18. For the bridge over the Loire, see Karl Baedeker, *Northern France from Belgium and the English Channel to the Loire*, 4th ed. (Leipsig: Karl Baedeker, 1905), 269–78; and Georges Montmarché and Robert Doré, *La France automobile*, Les Guides Bleu (Paris: Hachette, 1938), 594, 601, 607.

19. Liancourt, *Voyages*, 2:203–5; Young, *Travels*, 1:113–14. Duhamel (1700–1782) was a noted botanist and meteorologist who was a member of the Académie française and the British Royal Society. M. Fougeroux owned Duhamel's estate in 1787.

20. Jefferson to Robert Skipwith, Aug. 3, 1771, *Papers*, 1:80. Sowerby, in *Jefferson's Library*, 1:330, cites Jefferson's ownership of four of Duhamel's works, including *Practical Treatise of Husbandry: wherein are contained, many Useful and Valuable Experiments and Observations in the New Husbandry*, 2d ed., trans. John Mills (London: C. Hitch and L. Hawes, 1762).

21. Jean Antoine Nicolas Caritat de Condorcet, "Eloge de M. [Henri Louis] Duhamel," in *Oeuvres de Condorcet*, 2:610–43, quotation from 616. See also Du Petit-Thouars, "Duhamel du Monceau," *Biographie Universelle* (Michaud ed.), 45 vols. (Paris: A. T. Desplaces, 1843–[1865]), 2:468–70. Duhamel's *Traité de la culture des terres*, 6 vols. (Paris: L. F. Delatour, 1750–61), was translated into English in an abridged edition (London: J. Whiston and B. White, 1759).

22. The botanical name for Venus flytrap is *Dionaea muscipula*; Jefferson also gave some seeds to Madam de Tessé. See Jefferson to Tessé, Feb. 28, 1787, and Jefferson to Short, Mar. 29, 1787, *Papers*, 11:187, 253; and Young, *Travels*, 1:184–86.

23. The villages were Chavilly, Arténay, and Toury; Angerville, Mondésir, Estampes, Estréchy, Arpajon, Longjumeau, and Croix de Bernis.

CHAPTER 11. THE NETHERLANDS

1. Jefferson, "Autobiography," *Writings* (Ford), 1:115. Concerning his trip to the Netherlands, Jefferson made an entry in his Account Books, ViU, for every day between March 4 and 31, 1788, except Mar. 11.

2. The status of the Dutch loan up to March 1788 and the ambiguous role of the Van Staphorsts, Willinks, and other brokers is found in Jefferson to Adams, Feb. 6, 1788, and Adams to Jefferson, Feb. 12, 1788, *Papers*, 12:566, 581–82. See also Jefferson to Jay, Mar. 16, 1787, Jefferson to Short, Mar. 13, 29, 1788, Jefferson to commissioners of the treasury, Mar. 29, 1788, and Jefferson to Van Staphorsts, Willinks, Mar. 29, 1788, ibid., 13:671–72, 698–701, 665, 697; and Short to Gouverneur Morris, Nov. 27, 1792, Short Papers. The best source concerning U.S. foreign loans is Rafael A. Bayley, *The National Loans of the United States* (Washington, D.C.: GPO, 1882), republished in *Tenth Census of the United States of America*, vol. 7 (Washington, D.C.: GPO, 1884), 295–520.

3. Adams to Jefferson, Feb. 12, 1786, *Papers*, 12:581.

4. Jefferson to Adams, Feb. 6, 1786, ibid., 12:566.

5. John Adams, July 27, 1780, *Diary*, 2:442–44.

6. John Adams, Aug. 1784, ibid., 4:265.

7. Smith to Jefferson, Feb. 22, 1786, Abigail Adams to Jefferson, Feb. 26, 1786, Jefferson to Adams, Mar. 2, 1786, *Papers*, 12:620, 624, 637–38. See also Jefferson, "Autobiography," *Writings* (Ford), 1:115; John Adams to Abigail Adams, Mar. 11, 14, 1788, *Letters of John Adams Addressed to His Wife*, 2:110–12; John Adams, *Diary*, 4:266.

8. Jefferson to Washington, May 2, 1788, *Papers*, 13:126.

9. Jefferson, Mar. 4, 17, 23, 1788, Account Books, ViU; Jefferson, "Notes of a Tour through Holland and the Rhine Valley" (hereinafter cited as "Holland and the Rhine"), *Papers*, 13:12, 8–36; Young, *Travels*, 1:148–49.

10. Jefferson, Mar. 17, 1788, Account Books, ViU; Young, *Travels*, 1:148–49; Barbara Tuchman, *A Distant Mirror: The Calamatous Fourteenth Century* (New York: Knopf, 1978), 3–4, 395–96. During the reign of Napoleon III the choice whether to restore the château at Coucy or the one at Pierrefonds was decided in favor of the latter. In 1917 General Ludendorff demolished what remained of the Château de Coucy with twenty-eight tons of explosives. Between Coucy and Cambrai, Jefferson passed through the villages of Royes, Fonches, Peronne, Fins, and Bonair. Between Valenciennes and Brussels he passed through the villages of Quisvrain, Quaregnon, Mons, Le Casteau, Braine-le-comte, and Hal.

11. Jefferson, "Autobiography," *Writings* (Ford), 1:116. John Adams and his sons had spent nights at Compiègne and Valenciennes. See John Adams, July 27, 1780, *Diary*, 2:442–44; J. Q. Adams, July 29–Aug. 3, 1780, *Diary*, 1:937–39; and Young, *Travels*, 1:150–51.

12. J. Q. Adams, Aug. 5–7, 9, 1780, *Diary*, 1:40–45, 48–52.

13. Jefferson, "Autobiography," *Writings* (Ford), 1:116; Jefferson to Short, Mar. 10, 1786, *Papers*, 12:659. See also J. Q. Adams, Aug. 9, 1780, and Aug. 7, 1783, *Diary*, 1:48–52, 177–78; and Abigail Adams to Mrs. Cranch, Sept. 12, 1786, *Letters of Mrs. Adams*, 344–48.

14. Jefferson to Short, Mar. 10, 13, 1788, and Jefferson to Jay, Mar. 13, 1788, *Papers*, 12:659, 661, 667; Jefferson, Mar. 10, 1788, Account Books, ViU.

15. Abigail Adams to Mrs. Cranch, Sept. 12, 1786, *Letters of Mrs. Adams*, 344–48.

16. Jefferson, "Autobiography," *Writings* (Ford), 1:102–7; John Adams, July 27, 1780, *Diary*, 1:442–44; Short to Alexander Hamilton, Dec. 2, 1790, *The Papers of Alexander Hamilton*, ed. Harold C. Syrett et al., 27 vols. (New York: Columbia University Press, 1961–81), 4:86–93; Shackelford, *Jefferson's Adoptive Son*, 70–71.

17. Boyd, note, *Papers*, 13:xxvii–xxviii, unnumbered pages after 16.

18. Abigail Adams to Mrs. Cranch, Sept. 12, 1786, *Letters of Mrs. Adams*, 345.

19. Short to Hamilton, *Papers of Hamilton*, 7:348–57.

20. Jefferson to commissioners of the treasury, Mar. 29, 1788, Jefferson to Trumbull, Mar. 27, 1788, Jefferson to Short, Mar. 29, 1788, and Jefferson to Washington, May 2, 1788, *Papers*, 12:698–700, 13:126–28, 693–94, 696–97. Concerning books, see Jefferson to Van Damme, Mar. 18, 21, 23, 1788, ibid., 13:678, 687–89.

21. J. Q. Adams, Aug. 11–13, 18, 1780, June 21, 30, July 10, 1781, *Diary*, 1:52–56, 84–85, 91–92; Dutens, *Itinéraire*, 179.

22. Musée Royal de la Haye (Mauritshuis), *Catalogue raisonnée des tableaux et des sculptures* (The Hague: Mauritshuis, Nijhoff, 1895), vii–ix passim.

23. Jefferson to Short, Mar. 29, 1788, *Papers*, 12:697.

24. Jefferson, "Holland and the Rhine," ibid., 13:11–12; J. Q. Adams, Aug. 13, 1780, June 21, 30, 1781, *Diary*, 1:54, 84–85; Dutens, *Itinéraire*, 175–76.

25. Jefferson, "Holland and the Rhine," "Hints to Americans Travelling in Europe," *Papers*, 13:12, 264.

CHAPTER 12. IN THE RHINELAND AND FROM STRASBOURG TO PARIS

1. Jefferson, Mar. 30–31, Apr. 5, 1788, Account Books, ViU. With reference to his journey in the Rhineland and back to Paris, Jefferson made entries for every day between Apr. 1 and Apr. 22, 1788, except Apr. 4, covering in all seven-eighths of a

page. See also Trumbull to Jefferson, Oct. 9, 1786, Jefferson to Short, Mar. 29, Apr. 9, 1788, and Jefferson, "Hints to Americans Travelling in Europe," *Papers*, 10:438–41, 13:48, 268–69, 696. See also Dutens, *Itinéraire;* and Sowerby, *Jefferson's Library,* 4:111–12.

2. Jefferson, Mar. 12, 1788, Account Books, ViU; Jefferson, "Hints to Americans Travelling in Europe" and "Holland and the Rhine," *Papers*, 13:12, 15, 264.

3. Jefferson, Mar. 30–31, Apr. 5, 1788, Account Books, ViU; Jefferson "Holland and the Rhine," *Papers*, 13:12, 15.

4. Jefferson, Apr. 1, 1788, Account Books, ViU; "Hints to Americans Travelling in Europe" and "Holland and the Rhine," *Papers*, 13:13, 264. Concerning Jefferson's interest in Ossian, see Jefferson to Charles McPherson, Feb. 25, 1773, and Jefferson to Peter Carr, Aug. 19, 1785, ibid., 1:96, 8:407. See also Jefferson, *Literary Commonplace Book,* 13; and Sowerby, *Jefferson's Library,* 4:464–66.

5. Jefferson, Apr. 2, 1788, Account Books, ViU; "Holland and the Rhine," Jefferson to Charles McPherson, Feb. 25, 1773, James McPherson to Charles McPherson, Aug. 7, 1773, and Charles McPherson to Jefferson, Aug. 12, 1773, *Papers*, 13:13, 1:96–97, 100–102. See also Thomas Jefferson, *An Essay on the Anglo-Saxon* (New York: John F. Trow, 1851), 7–8; and idem, *A Summary View of the Rights of British America,* ed. Thomas P. Abernethy (New York: Scholars' Facsimiles Reprints, 1943), 6, 19–20.

6. Jefferson, Apr. 2–3, 1788, Account Books, ViU; "Hints to Americans Travelling in Europe" and "Holland and the Rhine," *Papers*, 13:13–14, 264–65. Trumbull had left Paris for Strasbourg, Düsseldorf, and the Netherlands in early September 1786. See Jefferson to Hopkinson, Aug. 14, 1786, Abigail Adams to Jefferson, July 23, 1786, and Jefferson to Smith, Sept. 13, 1786, ibid., 10:160, 250, 262.

7. Trumbull to Jefferson, Oct. 9, 1786, ibid., 10:438–41. Dutens said that the Elector's gallery of paintings at Dusseldorff was "one of the greatest collections" in Europe. See Dutens, *Itinéraire,* 171. In 1788 there hung two of the half-dozen paintings by Adriaen van der Werff dealing with the Hagar story. Both were removed to Munich in 1805. See Barbara Gaehtgens, *Adriaen van der Werff* (Munich: Kunstverlag, 1987), 270, 277; Emmanuel Bénézit, *Dictionnaire critique et documentaire des peintres, sculpteurs, dessinateurs et graveurs de tous les pays et tous les temps,* 5 vols. (Paris: Librairie Gründ, 1966), 5:714.

8. Thomas Lee Shippen to Jefferson, July 31, 1788, *Papers*, 13:444–45.

9. Jefferson to Cosway, Apr. 24, 1788, ibid., 13:103–4; Trumbull, *Autobiography,* 137.

10. Jefferson, Apr. 4–5, 1788, Account Books, ViU; Jefferson, "Hints to Americans Travelling in Europe," "Holland and the Rhine," and Jean Jacques Peuchen to Jefferson, Apr. 25, 1788, *Papers*, 13:14–16, 107–8, 265–66. Dutens declared that the so-called Tomb of the Three Kings at St. Peter's, Cologne, was "one of the most beautiful works in gold and silver that exists." See Dutens, *Itinéraire,* 171. See also Karl Baedeker, *The Rhine from Rotterdam to Constance,* 7th ed. (Leipzig: Baedeker, 1880), 69–74.

11. Jefferson, Apr. 5–7, 1788, "Holland and the Rhine," "Hints to Americans Travelling in Europe," and Jefferson to Short, Apr. 9, 1788, *Papers*, 13:16–17, 48, 103, 265; Baedeker, *The Rhine,* 126. Bad Schwalbach was a fashionable watering place in the seventeenth and eighteenth centuries.

12. Jefferson to Richard Henry Lee, Apr. 21, 1779, and Lee to Jefferson, May 22, 1779, *Papers*, 2:255, 270.

13. Geismar to Jefferson, Feb. 26, Nov. 1780?, ibid., 2:304, 4:173.

14. Geismar to Jefferson, Mar. 28, 1785, ibid., 8:63. Professor Bellini of the College of William and Mary also addressed him thus (ibid.).

15. Jefferson to Geismar, Mar. 3, 1785, ibid., 8:10–11.

16. Geismar to Jefferson, Mar. 28, 1785, ibid., 8:63–64.

17. Jefferson to Geismar, Mar. 15, 1788, ibid., 12:680.

18. Geismar to Jefferson, Mar. 26, 1788, ibid., 12:691–92.

19. Jefferson, Apr. 6–10, 1788, Account Books, ViU; "Hints to Americans Travelling in Europe," "Holland and the Rhine," and Thomas Lee Shippen to Jefferson, Sept. 22, 1788, *Papers*, 13:17–18, 266, 628.

20. Jefferson, "Holland and the Rhine," and Jefferson to Short, Apr. 9, 1788, *Papers*, 13:17, 48.

21. J. Q. Adams, July 17–18, 1781, *Diary*, 1:97. Adams noted that the members of the very large Jewish community of Frankfurt were locked up in their ghetto on Sundays.

22. Jefferson, Apr. 11–12, 1788, Account Books, ViU.

23. Jefferson to Geismar, Mar. 3, 1785, Geismar to Jefferson, Dec. 6, 1785, and Jefferson, "Holland and the Rhine," *Papers*, 8:10, 9:81–82, 13:18, 26.

24. Jefferson, "Holland and the Rhine," and "Hints to Americans Travelling in Europe," ibid., 13:18–21, 265, and illustration facing 265.

25. Jefferson, Apr. 11–12, 1788, Account Books, ViU; Dutens, *Itinéraire*, 266; Baedeker, *The Rhine*, 247–51. Jefferson arrived at Worms in time for dinner on the twelfth and spent the night of April 13 at Mannheim. The bishop's palace at Worms became a Jacobin club in 1793.

26. Jefferson, Apr. 13–15, 1788, Account Books, ViU.

27. Ledoux, *L'Architecture*. See also Braham, *Architecture of the French Enlightenment*, 159–209.

28. Jefferson to Cosway, Apr. 24, 1788, "Hints to Americans Travelling in Europe," and "Holland and the Rhine," *Papers*, 13:22–25, 104, 266–67.

29. Jefferson to Geismar, July 13, 1788, and "Hints to Americans Travelling in Europe," ibid., 13:24, 35, 357. See also Lili Fehrle-Burger, *Die Welt der Oper in den Schlossgärten von Heidelberg und Schwetzingen* (Karlsruhe: Verlag G. Braun, 1977). Jefferson also intended to establish such paths for Mount Alto, as he often called Carter's Mountain, adjacent to Monticello.

30. Jefferson, "Holland and the Rhine" and "Hints to Americans Travelling in Europe," *Papers*, 13:22–24, 104, 267.

31. Jefferson, Apr. 15, 1788, Account Books, ViU; Jefferson, "Holland and the Rhine," *Papers*, 13:25.

32. Jefferson, "Holland and the Rhine," and "Hints to Americans Travelling in Europe," *Papers*, 13:25, 267.

33. Jefferson, Apr. 16–18, 1788, Account Books, ViU; "Holland and the Rhine" and "Hints to Americans Travelling in Europe," *Papers*, 13:xxvii–xxviii, illustration between 16 and 17, 25–26, 267.

34. For the extent to which Jefferson was aware of the facts and fictions concerning the Affair of the Queen's Necklace, see Jefferson to Humphreys, Jan. 5, 1785, and Jefferson to Smith, May 4, 1786, *Papers*, 9:152, 447, 578, 634. See also Baedeker, *The Rhine*, 254–62.

35. Jefferson, Apr. 15–18, 1788, Account Books, ViU; Jefferson, "Holland and the Rhine" and "Hints to Americans Travelling in Europe," *Papers*, 13:xxvii–xxviii, illustration between 16 and 17, 25–26, 267.

36. Jefferson to Geismar, July 13, 1788, and "Hints to Americans Travelling in Europe," *Papers*, 13:24, 35, 357.

37. Jefferson to Short, Apr. 9, 1788, ibid., 13:48.

38. Jefferson to Geismar, July 13, 1788, ibid., 13:357.

39. Jefferson, "Holland and the Rhine," ibid., 13:23, 27, 34; Betts, *Thomas Jefferson's Garden Book*, 47–56.

40. Jefferson, "Holland and the Rhine," *Papers*, 13:28–36. Between Strasbourg and Phalsbourg Jefferson stopped at relays in Sternheim, Wiltenheim, and Savèrne; between Phalsbourg and Nancy, at those in Dieuse, Moyenvic, and Champernons; between Nancy and St. Dizier, in Velaine, Toul, Laye, Voie, St. Aubin, Ligny-en-Barrois, and Bar-le-Duc; between St. Dizier and Epernay, in Longchamp, Vitry, La Chausée, Châlons-sur-Marne, and Jalons; and between Epernay and Paris, in Port-à-Bainson, Dormans, Parois, Château-Thierry, La-Fèrme-de-Paris, La Ferte, Meaux, Claye, and Bondy.

41. Ibid.; Jefferson, Apr. 21–22, 1788, Account Books, ViU.

42. Jefferson, Apr. 24, 1788, Account Books, ViU.

EPILOGUE: APOSTLE OF EUROPEAN CULTURE

1. Jefferson, Account Books, ViU. Short later sold Jefferson's three horses on a collapsing market. The old carriage and cabriolet were later shipped to Philadelphia.

2. Nathaniel Cutting, Sept. 29, 1789, "Extract from Diary," *Papers*, 15:490; Young, *Travels*, 1:160–62.

3. Cutting, Sept. 28–Oct. 8, 1789, "Extract from Diary," *Papers*, 15:490–96.

4. Jefferson, Aug. 19, 1789, Account Books, ViU.

5. Jefferson, Oct. 7, 1789, ibid.

6. Cutting, Oct. 8, 1789, "Extract from Diary," *Papers*, 15:496.

7. Cutting, Oct. 8–12, 1789, "Extract from Diary," ibid., 15:496, 499.

8. See Trumbull to Jefferson, Sept. 22, 1789, *Papers*, 15:468.

9. Short to Jefferson, Nov. 7, 1790, ibid., 18:35–39; Jefferson to Trumbull, Sept. 16, 24, 1789, ibid., 15:435–36, 471; Trumbull to Jefferson, Sept. 7, 11, 18, 22, 1789, ibid., 15:400, 417–18, 453–54, 467–69.

10. Short to Jefferson, Nov. 3, 1790, ibid., 18:30–39.

11. William Gilpin, *Observations on the Western Parts of England Relative Chiefly to Picturesque Beauty, to which are added A Few Remarks On . . . The Isle of Wight* (London: Cadell and Davies, 1798), 301–4.

12. Jefferson, Oct. 11, 1789, Account Books, ViU.

13. Gilpin, *Observations on the Western Parts of England*, 313–18.

14. Jefferson, Oct. 9–22, 1789, Account Books, ViU.

15. Cutting, Sept. 28–Oct. 12, 1789, "Extract from Diary," *Papers*, 15:490–99.

16. Jefferson to William Shippen, May 8, 1788, *Papers*, 13:146; Jefferson to Trumbull, Nov. 25, 1789, ibid., 15:559–60.

17. Jefferson to Short, Oct. 23, Nov. 21, 1789, ibid., 15:527, 552–53.

18. Jefferson to Mazzei, Aug. 2, 1791, ibid., 20:715.

19. Jefferson made entries for every day between Sept. 26 and Nov. 23, 1789, covering in all three and one-quarter pages, including the estimated noon positions of the *Clermont*. See Account Books, ViU. See also Jefferson to Trumbull, June 1, 1789, and Short to Jefferson, Nov. 7, 1790, *Papers*, 15:164, 18:35–39.

20. Jefferson to Nathaniel Cutting, Aug. 30, Sept. 10, 15, 17, 1789, *Papers*, 15:373, 411–12, 419–21, 428–29, 436; Nathaniel Cutting to Jefferson, Sept. 3, 12, 26, 1789, ibid., 15:380–81, 477–78; John B. Cutting to Jefferson, Sept. 18, 1789, ibid., 15:440–41; and Jefferson to John B. Cutting, Sept. 24, 1789, ibid., 15:469.

21. Young, *Travels*, 1:vi–vii.

22. Jefferson to Joseph Fay, Mar. 18, 1793, *Papers*, 25:402; Malone, *Jefferson*, 2:84. For Franklin's title of doctor, see Jefferson to François Soulés, Sept. 13, 1786, *Writings* (Ford), 4:308.

23. Jefferson to Thomas Mann Randolph, Sr., Aug. 11, 1787, *Papers*, 11:20–22. After a prolonged stay at Paris, Jefferson said, one should spend a month each at Rome and Naples, two weeks at Florence, a week each at Genoa, Milan, and Turin, four days each at Lyons, Nantes, and Nîmes, and one day each at Nice and Pisa.

24. This conclusion is based on a compilation of chronologies, counting as a month in a city each month in which any day was spent there. See the introductions to *Papers*, vols. 1–8, 15–20; and Malone, *Jefferson*, introductions to vols. 2–5.

25. Kimball, *Jefferson, Architect*, 45; Malone, *Jefferson*, 2:214–41, 486–87, 3:39–44.

26. Jefferson to Jay, July 29, Aug. 12, 27, 1789, Jefferson to Madison, Sept. 6, 1789, and Jefferson to Gem, Sept. 9, 1789, *Papers*, 15:314, 340, 358, 384–99.

27. Jefferson to Jay, Nov. 3, 1787, ibid., 12:314; Malone, *Jefferson*, 2:47–49; Peterson, *Jefferson*, 322–28.

28. Chinard, *Jefferson*, vii, ix, 215–41. He makes no mention of Jefferson's correspondence with Dr. Gem. See also chapters 6 and 15 above.

29. Jefferson, "Autobiography," *Writings* (Ford), 1:148–49.

30. Malone, *Jefferson*; Peterson, *Jefferson*, 389; idem, *Jefferson Image*, 417.

31. Jefferson, "Hints to Americans Travelling in Europe," *Papers*, 13:267.

32. Jefferson to Madison, Sept. 20, 1785, *Papers*, 8:534. There are extant only four letters between Jefferson and Clérisseau: Jefferson to Clérisseau, and Clérisseau to Jefferson, both June 2, 1786, Clérisseau to Jefferson, Dec. 4, 1787, and Jefferson to Clérisseau, June 7, 1789, ibid., 9:602–3, 12:393, 15:172–73.

33. McCormick, *Clérisseau*, 191–99.

34. Malone, *Jefferson*, 4:37, 44–45, 367, 5:530–40, 6:258–66; Adams, *Eye of Jefferson*, 242–43, 254–55, 259–62, 268, 272.

35. Desgodets, *Les Edifices antiques de Rome, mesurés et dessinés exactement sur les lieux*. See Sowerby, *Jefferson's Library*, 4:371–72.

36. Jefferson, "Hints to Americans Travelling in Europe," *Papers*, 13:269.

37. Marie Kimball states that Clérisseau was a "consultant rather than designer" of the Virginia capitol (*Jefferson*, 3:74). She does not comment on Jefferson's not seeing a work by Palladio. Nor did Gilbert Chinard, Bernard Mayo, or Henry S. Randall.

38. Geismar to Jefferson, Mar. 28, 1785, *Papers*, 8:64.

39. Starobinski, *1789*, 5–9. See also Thomas Crow, *Painters and Public Life in Eighteenth Century Paris* (New Haven: Yale University Press, 1985).

40. Jefferson to Tott, Feb. 28, 1787, Trumbull to Jefferson, Aug. 28, 1787, and Jefferson to Trumbull, Aug. 30, 1787, *Papers*, 10:553–54, 12:xxiv, 60, 69.

41. Evans, *Mather Brown*, 53. Evans has reestablished Brown's reputation by quoting critical opinion of his historical painting and portraiture in the 1786 Royal Academy show. See also Kimball, "Jefferson and the Arts"; and Bush, *Life Portraits of Jefferson*, 15–19; Adams, *Jefferson and the Arts*, 21–26; Bear, *Reports*, 4:6–7; and Roof, *Colonel William Smith and Lady*, 190. Quotation from Jefferson to Smith, Feb. 21, 1825, *Writings* (Ford), 10:341.

42. Jefferson to Trumbull, Jan. 18, Feb. 15, 1789, *Papers*, 15:xxxv–xxxvi, 467, 561; Bear, *Reports*, 3:7, 4:8, 5:19–20, 21:12, 22:12–13; Kimball, *Furnishings of Monticello*, 7–13.

43. Short to Trumbull, Sept. 10, 1788, *Papers*, 14:365.

44. Jefferson to Cosway, Apr. 24, 1788, ibid., 13:104.

45. Jefferson to Trumbull, Jan. 18, Feb. 15, 1789, ibid., 15:467, 561.

46. Jefferson to Tott, Feb. 28, Apr. 5, 1787, and Tott to Jefferson, Mar. 4, 1787, ibid., 11:187–88, 270–73, 198–99.

47. Short to Jefferson, Nov. 7, 1790, *Papers* 18:30–39; Bear, *Reports*, 4:8, 5:9, 11;

7: facing 12, 10:10; Julian P. Boyd, "The Comtesse de Tessé's Parting Gift to Jefferson, 1788," *Papers*, 18:xxxiii–xxxiv, 37, facing 269. See also Bush, *Life Portraits of Jefferson*, 27–29. Jefferson paid Houdon a thousand francs for the busts on July 3, 1789 (Account Books, ViU).

48. Boyd, notes, *Papers*, 15:xxxv–xxxvi; Bear, *Reports*, 3:7, 4:8, 5:19–20, 21:12, 22:12–13; Marie Kimball, *Jefferson*, 3:114–20; idem, *The Furnishings of Monticello* (Charlottesville: Thomas Jefferson Memorial Foundation, 1940), 7–13; Marie Kimball, *Jefferson*, 3:114–15, 326–27, says that Jefferson bought fourteen items between the Billy sale in October 1784 and the Saint-Séverin sale of February 1785.

49. Jefferson to Thomas Mann Randolph, Jr., Feb. 24, 1791, *Papers*, 19:330; Jefferson to James Barbour, Jan. 19, 1817, *Writings* (L&B), 9:242–43.

50. Short to Jefferson, Jan. 14, 1789, *Papers* 14:449–51; Jefferson, Jan. 8, Feb. 16, 1789, Account Books, ViU; Jefferson to Mazzei, Oct. 17, 1787, Jefferson to Trumbull, Feb. 15, 1789, *Papers*, 12:245, 14:561; Boyd, notes, ibid., 15:xxxv–xxxvi; Bear, *Reports*, 3:7, 5:19–20, 6:14–16, 7:17–19, 20:12–13. See also Marie Kimball, *Jefferson*, 3:56, 115.

51. Jefferson, *Notes on the State of Virginia*, 149; Jefferson, "A Bill for the More General Diffusion of Knowledge" and "A Bill for Establishing a Public Library," *Papers*, 2:526–35, 544–45.

52. Latrobe to Jefferson, Aug. 13, 1807, *The Journal of Latrobe, Being the Notes and Sketches of an Architect, Naturalist and Traveller in the U.S. from 1796 to 1820* (New York: D. Appleton-Century, 1905), 141–44.

BIBLIOGRAPHY

For Jefferson's account and memorandum books and major editions of his writings, see the headnote to the notes, which give complete information on the works I relied on in my research. Here follow the most pertinent published primary sources and secondary sources on the subject.

PRIMARY WORKS

Adams, Abigail S. *Letters of Mrs. Adams, the Wife of John Adams*. Edited by Charles F. Adams. Boston: Little, Brown, 1840.

Adams, John. *The Diary and Autobiography of John Adams*. Edited by Lyman H. Butterfield. 4 vols. Cambridge: Belknap, 1961.

———. *The Papers of John Adams, 1755–1778*. Edited by Robert J. Taylor et al. 6 vols. to date. Cambridge: Belknap, 1961–.

———. *The Works of John Adams*. Edited by Charles F. Adams. 10 vols. Boston: Little, Brown, 1886.

Adams, John Quincy. *The Diary of John Quincy Adams*. Edited by David G. Allen. 2 vols. to date. Cambridge: Belknap, 1981–.

Andréossy, Antoine François, comte d'. *Histoire du Canal du Midi, ou Canal de Languedoc*. 2 vols. 1804. Enl. ed. Paris: Crapelet, 1807.

Bertotti Scamozzi, Ottavio. *The Buildings and Designs of Andrea Palladio*. Edited by Francesco Modena. Translated by Howard Burns. Trent: La Roccia, 1976.

Clérisseau, Charles Louis. *Antiquités de la France*. Paris: Philippe-Denys-Pierres, 1777.

Condorcet, Marie Jean Antoine Nicolas Caritat de. "Eloge de M. [Henri Louis] Duhamel" and "To a Young Frenchman in London, [1792]." In *Oeuvres de Condorcet*, edited by A. Condorcet O'Connor and M. F. Arago. 5 vols. Paris: Firman Didot Libraries, 1847–49.

———. *Sur les fonctions des Etats-généraux et des autres assemblées nationales. . . .* 2 vols. [Paris], 1789.

Craddock, Anna Francesca. *Voyage en France, 1783–1786*. Translated by Odalie H. Delphion-Bailleguier. Paris: Perrin, 1911.

Eustace, John Chetwoode. *A Classical Tour Through Italy [in 1802]*. 3 vols. 8th ed. London: T. Tegg, 1841.

Gilpin, William. *Dialogue upon the gardens of the Right Honorable the Lord Viscount Cobham at Stow[e], in Buckinghamshire*. London: Rivington, 1748.

———. *Observations on the Western Parts of England Relative Chiefly to Picturesque Beauty, to which are added a Few Remarks On . . . The Isle of Wight*. London: Cadell and Davies, 1798.

Guide pour le Voyage d'Italie en poste. New ed. Genoa: Yvres Gravier Librairie, 1793.

Hogarth, William. *Analysis of Beauty: A Reprint including the Plates*. Chicago: Reilly and Lee, [ca. 1908].

Hyppolyte, Jacques Antoine, comte de Guibert. *Voyages dans diverses parties de France et en Suisse, faits en 1775, 78 et 85*. Paris: D'Hautel, 1806.

Lauzun, Armand Louis de Gontaud, duc de. *Mémoires*. Paris: Barrois l'Ainé Librairie, 1822.

Ledoux, Claude Nicholas. *L'Architecture*. Edited by Kevin C. Lippert after Daniel Ramée's edition, 1847. Princeton: Princeton Architectural Press, 1983.

Liancourt, François de La Rochefoucauld. *Voyages en France (1781–1783)*. Edited by Jean Marchand. 2 vols. Paris: Librairie Ancienne Honoré Champion, 1932–38.

Mazzei, Philip. *My Life and Wanderings*. Edited by S. Eugene Scalia. Translated by Margherita Marchione. Morristown, N.J.: American Institute of Italian Studies, 1980.

Morris, Gouverneur. *A Diary of the French Revolution*. Edited by Beatrix C. Davenport. 2 vols. Boston: Houghton Mifflin, 1939.

Pinot-Duclos, Charles. *Voyage en Italie, ou Considerations sur l'Italie*. Paris: Buisson, 1791.

Piozzi, Hester Lynch, and Samuel Johnson. *The French Journals of Mrs. Thrale and Doctor Johnson*. Edited by Moses Tyson and Henry Guppy. Manchester: Manchester University Press, 1932.

Trumbull, John. *Autobiography, Reminiscences and Letters*. New Haven: Hamlin, 1841.

———. *The Autobiography of Colonel John Trumbull, Patriot-Artist, 1756–1843*. Edited by Theodore Sizer. New Haven: Yale University Press, 1953.

Verme, Francesco dal. *Seeing America and Its Great Men: The Journal and Letters of Count Francesco dal Verme, 1783–1784*. Edited and translated by Elizabeth Cometti. Charlottesville: University Press of Virginia, 1969.

Whately, Thomas. *Observations on Modern Gardening*. London: T. Payne, 1790. Edited by John D. Hunt. New York: Garland, 1982.

SECONDARY WORKS

Adam, Robert, and James Adam. *The Works in Architecture of Robert and James Adam*. Edited by Robert Oresko. London: St. Martin's, 1975.

Adams, William Howard. *The French Garden, 1500–1800*. New York: George Braziller, 1979.

———, ed. *The Eye of Thomas Jefferson*. Washington, D.C.: National Gallery of Art, 1976.

———. *Jefferson and the Arts: An Extended View*. Washington, D.C.: National Gallery of Art, 1976.

Bear, James A., Jr. "The Furniture and Furnishings of Monticello." *Magazine Antiques* 105 (July 1972): 118–20.

———. *Report[s] of the Curator to the Trustees of the Thomas Jefferson Memorial Foundation*. 30 vols. Charlottesville: Thomas Jefferson Memorial Foundation, 1954–84.

Bear, James A., Jr., and Frederick D. Nichols. *Monticello*. Charlottesville: Thomas Jefferson Memorial Foundation, 1967.

Beard, Geoffrey W. *The Work of Robert Adam*. Edinburgh: John Bartholomew, 1978.

Berman, Eleanor D. *Thomas Jefferson among the Arts*. New York: Philosophical Library, 1947.

Besant, Sir Walter. *Eighteenth Century London*. 1902. Reprint. London: A. C. Black, 1925.

Betts, Edwin M. *Thomas Jefferson's Garden Book, 1766–1824*. American Philosophical Society Memoirs, vol. 22. Philadelphia: American Philosophical Society, 1944.

Bolton, Arthur T. *The Architecture of Robert & James Adam, 1785–1794*. 2 vols. London: Country Life, 1922.

Braham, Allen. *The Architecture of the French Enlightenment*. Berkeley and Los Angeles: University of California Press, 1980.

Bullock, Helen D. *My Head and My Heart: A Little History of Thomas Jefferson and Maria Cosway*. New York: Putnam's, 1945.

Bush, Alfred L., ed. *The Life Portraits of Thomas Jefferson*. Charlottesville: Thomas Jefferson Memorial Foundation, 1963.

Castellane, Antoine Marie Eugène Philippe Boniface, comte de. *Gentilshommes démocrates: Le vicomte de Noailles, les deux La Rochefoucaulds, Clérmont-Tonnère, le vicomte de Castellane, le comte de Virieu*. Paris: Plon, 1891.

Charbonnel, Nicole. *Commerce et cours sous la révolution et consulat À La Rochelle*. Paris: Presses Universitaires de France, 1977.

Chinard, Gilbert. *Les Amitiés américaines de Madame d'Houdetot d'après sa correspondence inédite avec Benjamin Franklin et Thomas Jefferson*. Paris: Champion, 1924.

———. *Thomas Jefferson: Apostle of Americanism*. Boston: Little, Brown, 1939.

———. *Trois amitiés françaises de Jefferson d'après sa correspondence inédite avec Madame de Bréhan, Madame de Tessé et Madame de Corny*. Paris: Société d'Edition, 1927.

———, ed. *The Letters of La Fayette and Jefferson*. Baltimore: Johns Hopkins Press, 1929.

Connelly, James L. "The Grand Gallery of the Louvre and the Museum Project: Architectural Problems." *Journal of the Society of Architectural Historians* 31 (May 1972): 120–32.

Constans, Marie, and Claude Ducourtail-Rey. *La Rue de Lille [et l'] Hôtel de Salm*. Paris: Institut Néerlandais for Délégation À L'Action Artistique de la Ville de Paris, Musée de la Légion d'Honneur and Société d'Histoire et de l'Archéologie de VIIe Arondissement, 1983.

Cripe, Helen. *Thomas Jefferson and Music*. Charlottesville: University Press of Virginia, 1974.

Deitz, Paula. "The Desert de Retz." *Magazine Antiques* 135 (Mar. 1989): 718–31.

Desgodets, Antoine Babuty. *Les Edifices antiques de Rome, mesurés et dessinés exactement sur les lieux*. Paris: Jombert, 1779.

Dickson, Harold E. "Th. J. Art Collector." In *Jefferson and the Arts: An Extended View*, edited by William Howard Adams, 105–32. Washington, D.C.: National Gallery of Art, 1976.

Evans, Dorinda. *Mather Brown: Early American Artist in England*. Middletown, Conn.: Wesleyan University Press, 1982.

Fehrle-Burger, Lili. *Die Welt de Oper in den Schlossgarten von Heidelberg und Schwetzingen*. Karlsruhe: Verlag G. Braun, 1977.

Fleming, John. *Robert Adam and His Circle in Edinburgh and Rome*. London: John Murray, 1962.

Forty Hall, Enfield. London: Curwen, [ca. 1980].

Gaehtgens, Barbara. *Adrian van der Werff*. Munich: Kunstverlag, 1993.

Gaeine, Bruce [Graham M. Jeffries, pseud.]. *A Century of Buckingham Palace, 1837–1937*. London: Hutchinson, 1937.

Gallet, Michel. *Demures Parisiennes: L'Époque de Louis XVI*. Paris: Le Temps, 1964.

———. *Ledoux et Paris*. 2d ed. Paris: Rotonde de la Villette, 1979.

———. *Stately Mansions: Eighteenth-Century Paris Architecture*. New York: Praeger, 1972.

Gorse, George L. "The Villa of Andrea Doria in Genoa: Architecture, Gardens, and Suburban Setting." *Journal of the Society of Architectural Historians* 44 (Mar. 1985): 18–36.

Gottschalk, Louis. *Lafayette between the American and the French Revolutions, 1783–1789*. Chicago: University of Chicago Press, 1950.

Gottschalk, Louis, and Margaret Maddox. *Lafayette in the French Revolution through the October Days*. Chicago: University of Chicago Press, 1969.

Guehenno, Jean. *Jean Jacques Rousseau*. Translated by John Weightman and Doreen Weightman. 2 vols. New York: Columbia University Press, 1966.

Hood, Graham. *The Governor's Palace in Williamsburg: A Cultural Study*. Williamsburg: Colonial Williamsburg Foundation, 1991.

Howard, Seymour. "Thomas Jefferson's Art Gallery for Monticello." *Art Bulletin* 59 (Dec. 1977): 583–600.

Isham, Sir Gyles. *Lamport Hall*. Derby: English Life Publications, 1974.

James, Henry. *A Little Tour in France*. Introduction by Leon Edel. New York: Farrar, Straus and Giroux, 1983.

Kimball, Fiske. "Clérisseau and Adam." *Architectural Review* 97 (Apr. 1955): 272–73.

———. "Jefferson and the Arts." *Proceedings of the American Philosophical Society* 137 (July 1943): 241–43.

———. *Thomas Jefferson, Architect*. 2d ed. Introduction by Frederick D. Nichols. New York: Da Capo, 1968.

———. "Thomas Jefferson and the Public Buildings of Virginia." *Huntington Library Quarterly* 12 (1949): 303–10.

Kimball, Marie. *The Furnishings of Monticello*. Charlottesville: Thomas Jefferson Memorial Foundation, 1940.

———. *Thomas Jefferson*. 3 vols. New York: Coward-McCann, 1943–50.

La Rochefoucauld, Jean Dominique de. *Le Duc de La Rochefoucauld-Liancourt, 1747–1827*. Paris: Librairie Académique Perrin, 1980.

Lewis, Wilmarth S. *A Tour through London in the Years 1748, 1776, and 1797*. 1951. Reprint. Westport, Conn.: Greenwood, 1971.

McCormick, Thomas J. *Charles Louis Clérisseau and the Genesis of Neo-Classicism*. Cambridge: MIT Press, 1990.

———. "Virginia's Gallic Godfather." *Arts in Virginia* 4 (Winter 1964): 2–13.

Malone, Dumas. *Jefferson and His Time*. 6 vols. Boston: Little, Brown, 1948–81.

Manion, Marcel. *Dictionnaire des institutions de la France au XVIIième et XVIIIième siècles*. 1923. Reprint. Paris: Editions A. and J. Picard, 1984.

Mauritshuis. *Catalogue raisonné des tableaux et des sculptures*. The Hague: Nijhoff, 1895.

Montclos, Jean Marie Pérouse de. "Ledoux: L'Architecture." *Journal of the Society of Architectural Historians* 41 (Oct. 1982): 261–63.

Nichols, Frederick D. "Jefferson: The Making of an Architect." In *Jefferson and the Arts: An Extended View*, edited by William Howard Adams, 159–85. Washington, D.C.: National Gallery of Art, 1976.

———. *Thomas Jefferson's Architectural Drawings*. Boston: Massachusetts Historical Society, 1960.

Nichols, Frederick D., and Ralph E. Griswold. *Thomas Jefferson: Landscape Architect*. Charlottesville: University Press of Virginia, 1978.

Pam, D. O. "The Rude Multitude: Enfield and the Civil War." *Occasional Papers of the Edmonton Hundred Historical Society* (Enfield, Eng.), n.s., 33 (1977).

Peterson, Merrill D. *The Jefferson Image in the American Mind*. New York: Oxford University Press, 1960.

———. *Thomas Jefferson and the New Nation*. New York: Oxford University Press, 1970.

Pommer, Richard. *Eighteenth-Century Architecture in Piedmont: The Open Structure of Juvarra, Alfieri, and Vittone*. New York: New York University Press, 1967.

Rawlings, Mary. *The Albemarle of Other Days*. Charlottesville: Michie, 1925.

Rice, Howard C., Jr. *L'Hôtel de Langeac: Thomas Jefferson's Paris Residence, 1785–1789*. Paris: Lefebvre; Monticello: Thomas Jefferson Memorial Foundation, 1947.

———. *Thomas Jefferson's Paris*. Princeton: Princeton University Press, 1976.

Roffignac, Nicole de, and Alain d'Albavie. *The Désert de Retz: A Brief Description.* Paris, ca. 1989. Mimeographed.

Roof, Katharine M. *Colonel William Smith and Lady: The Romance of Washington's Aide and Young Abigail Adams.* Boston: Houghton Mifflin, 1929.

Sahut, Marie Catherine. *Le Louvre d'Hubert Robert.* Paris: Editions de la Réunion des Musées Nationaux, 1979.

Seeley, J. *Stowe. A Description of the house and gardens of the most noble & puissant prince, George-Grenville-Nugent-Temple, Marquis of Buckingham.* London: Edwards & L. B. Seeley, [1797?].

Shelley, Henry C. *Inns and Taverns of Old London, setting forth the historical and literary associations of those ancient hostelries.* 2d ed. Boston: Page, 1923.

Shepperson, Archibald B. *John Paradise and Lucy Ludwell Paradise of London and Williamsburg.* Richmond: Dietz Press for Colonial Williamsburg, 1942.

Sotheby's International Auctions. *Bibliothèque du château de La Roche-Guyon.* Cowley: Nuffield, 1987.

———. *Tableaux et moblier et tapisseries ornant le chateau de la Roche-Guyon.* Alençon: Imprimerie Alençonnaise, 1987.

Sotheby's International Realty. *Le Pavillon de Musique de la Comtesse du Barry at Louveciennes, Paris.* Cowley: Nuffield, 1968.

Sowerby, E. Millicent, ed. *The Catalogue of the Library of Thomas Jefferson.* 5 vols. Washington, D.C.: Library of Congress, 1952–59.

Starobinski, Jean. *1789: The Emblems of Reason.* Translated by Barbara Bray. Charlottesville: University Press of Virginia, 1982.

Summerson, Sir John. *Architecture in Britain, 1530–1830.* Pelican History of Art Series. Edited by Nikolaus Pevsner. London: Penguin, 1953.

Swarbrick, John. *Robert Adam and His Brothers.* London: Batsford, 1916.

Thomas, Hugh. "Stupinigi." In *Great Houses of Europe*, edited by Sacheverell Sitwell, 198–205. London: Spring Books, 1970.

Toritti, Piero, and Franco Sborgi. *La Pittura a Genova e Liguria.* 2 vols. Genoa: Sagep Editrice, 1971.

Underwood, John C. *The Rogers Family.* New York: Rudge, 1911.

Vliegenhart, Adriaan W. *Bildersammlung de Fursten zu Salm.* Apledoorn, The Netherlands: Walburg, 1981.

Walton, Guy. *Louis XIV's Versailles.* Chicago: University of Chicago Press, 1985.

Worsley, Giles. "A Garden Reappears: Restoration of Painshill Park, Surrey." *Country Life* (London), Sept. 11, 1986, 802–5.

ACKNOWLEDGMENTS

How few are alive now of those to whom I am indebted for guidance and help since I began my research on Thomas Jefferson's travels in Europe almost fifty years ago. I can never adequately acknowledge my debt to my academic mentors at the University of Virginia and Columbia University: Bernard Mayo, Thomas Perkins Abernethy, and Dumas Malone. My essential source has been the bound photostatic copies of Jefferson's Account Books in the Alderman Library of the University of Virginia, concerning which I appreciate the advice of James A. Bear, Jr. I am grateful for aid from my former colleagues in the Department of History at Virginia Polytechnic Institute and State University. Virgil P. Randolph III was good enough to provide valuable advice concerning diplomacy. At the Johns Hopkins University Press Robert J. Brugger has given me an invaluable combination of criticism and encouragement, while Joanne Allen and Kimberly Johnson have been incomparable editors.

Too often I have put aside this project. Although my punishment for delay has been the necessity of substituting printed sources for the manuscripts that were for me a lure to explore the past, Julian P. Boyd's erudite volumes in *The Papers of Thomas Jefferson* expanded my knowledge and have been a stylistic inspiration.

For many courtesies I thank the staffs of the Manuscripts Division of the Library of Congress, the American Philosophical Society, the Archives Etrangères de France, the Bibliothèque Nationale de France, the Butler Library of Columbia University, the Newman Library of Virginia Polytechnic Institute and State University, the Swem Library of the College of William and Mary, and the Alderman and Fiske Kimball Libraries at the University of Virginia. Individuals who have aided my research have been W. Howard Adams, Helen D. Bullock, Lester J. Cappon, Comte Réné de Chambrun, Oron J. Hale, John Melville Jennings, Marie Kimball, Mrs. Theodore Murphy, Mrs. Barbara Short Price, Howard C. Rice, Duc Louis de La Rochefoucauld, and William E. Runge.

Finally, I must acknowledge the long-suffering patience of my family and friends, but especially that of my wife, Grace Howard McConnell Shackelford, to whom I dedicate this book.

SOURCES

Frontispiece: Courtesy of Museé de la Marine and Museé du Louvre, Paris.

Pg. 7: For *Déscription historique de Paris, et ses plus beaux monuments*, vol. 1 (Paris, 1779), pl. 11. Courtesy of Bibliothèque Nationale, Paris.

Pg. 15: Courtesy of Thomas Jefferson Memorial Foundation, Charlottesville.

Pg. 17: From *Voyage pittoresque de la France*, ed. Jean Etienne Guettard, Jean Benjamin de La Borde, and Edme Beguillet, 12 vols. (Paris: Lamy, 1784-1802), *Isle de France*, pl. 8. Courtesy of Boston Athenaeum, Boston.

Pg. 18: After Jean-Baptiste Lallemand, "Vue du Portail de la Nouvelle Eglise de St. Philippe du Roule," *Voyage pittoresque de la France*, vol. 10, pl. 60. Boston Atheneum.

Pg. 19: Courtesy of Musée Carnavalet, Paris.

Pg. 20: Courtesy of Massachusetts Historical Society, Boston.

Pg. 21: Courtesy of Bibliothèque Nationale, Paris.

Pg. 22: Courtesy of Bibliothèque Nationale, Paris.

Pg. 23: George Nixon Black Fund; courtesy of Museum of Fine Arts, Boston.

Pg. 24: Courtesy of Metropolitan Museum of Art, New York.

Pg. 26: Courtesy of Thomas Jefferson Memorial Foundation.

Pg. 27: *Top*, Reprinted by permission from *L'Architecture, Edition Ramee*, C. N. Ledoux, Princeton Architectural Press, New York, pl. 4; *bottom*, reprinted by permission from *L'Architecture, Edition Ramee*, C. N. Ledoux, Princeton Architectural Press, New York, pl. 176.

Pg. 28: *Right*, Courtesy of College of William and Mary, Williamsburg; *left*, courtesy of Bibliothèque Nationale, Paris.

Pg. 31: Courtesy of Bibliothèque Nationale, Paris.

Pg. 33: Courtesy of Musée du Louvre, Paris.

Pg. 39: *Top*, Courtesy of Bibliothèque Nationale, Paris; *bottom*, for *Jardins à la Mode et Jardins Anglo-Chinois*, 2d. ed., vol. 2 (Paris: Jacomet, 1978), portfolio 2, pg. 14.

Pg. 40: Courtesy of Musée des Beaux Arts, Rouen.

Pg. 44: Courtesy of Paul Mellon Collection, Upperville, Virginia.

Pg. 46: *Left*, Courtesy of Boston Athenaeum, Boston; *right*, courtesy of Mr. Charles Francis Adams, Boston.

Pg. 49: Courtesy of Victoria and Albert Museum, London.

Pg. 50: For *Jardins à la Mode et Jardins Anglo-Chinois*, 2d. ed., vol. 2 (Paris: Jacomet, 1978), portfolio 6, pl. 8.

Pg. 53: For Thomas Whately, *Observations on Modern Gardening*, 6th ed., ed. Horace Walpole, Earl of Orford (London: West and Hughes, 1801), 30.

Pg. 54: For Thomas Whately, *Observations on Modern Gardening*, 6th ed., ed. Horace Walpole, Earl of Orford (London: West and Hughes, 1801), 98.

Pg. 55: For *Jardins à la Mode et Jardins Anglo-Chinois*, 2d. ed., vol. 1 (Paris: Jacomet, 1978), portfolio 4, pl. 20.

Pg. 57: After drawing (ca. 1770) by James Gandon from Colin Campbell, John Woolfe, and James Gandon, *Vitruvius Brittanicus*, 5 vols. (London: 1715-71), vol. 5, pl. 15.

Pg. 61: Courtesy of Paul Mellon Collection, Upperville, Virginia.

Pg. 65: Hermitage Museum, St. Petersburg. Photograph courtesy of Courtauld Institute, London.

Pg. 66: From [Nicholas de Malézieu], *Elémens de géometrie de monseigneur le duc de Bourgogne*, 3d ed. (Paris: E. Ganeau, 1729), bk. 1, pl. 125.

Pg. 67: Reprinted by permission from *L'Architecture, Edition Ramee*, C. N. Ledoux, Princeton Architectural Press, New York, pl. 270.

Pg. 68: For *Jardins à la Mode et Jardins Anglo-Chinois*, 2d. ed., vol. 4 (Paris: Jacomet, 1978), portfolio 1, pl. 3.

Pg. 69: Courtesy of Cosway Foundation, Lodi, Italy.

Pg. 71: Courtesy of Thomas Jefferson Memorial Foundation, Charlottesville.

Pg. 72: Courtesy of Bibliothèque Nationale, Paris.

Pg. 74: Courtesy of Thomas Jefferson Memorial Foundation, Charlottesville.

Pg. 76: Courtesy of Musée nationale de la Voiture et du Tourisme, Compiègne, France.

Pg. 83: For Florence Ingersoll-Smouse, *Joseph Vernet, Peintre de Marine, 1714-1789*, vol. 2 (Paris: Etienne Bignou, 1926), pl. 113. Musée Fabre, Montpellier, France.

Pg. 84: Courtesy of Thomas Jefferson Memorial Foundation, Charlottesville.

Pg. 85: Courtesy of Musée de la Marine and Musée du Louvre, Paris.

Pg. 86: Courtesy of Musée Borély, Marseilles.

Pg. 87: For Florence Ingersoll-Smouse, *Joseph Vernet, Peintre de Marine, 1714-1789*, vol. 1 (Paris: Etienne Bignou, 1926), pl. 63. Musée de la Marine and Musée du Louvre, Paris.

Pg. 91: After Carlo Randoni, Archivio Storico della Citta di Torino, Collezione Simeon, serie D, 558, from Giorgio Vaccarino, *I Giacobini Piemontesi, 1794-1814*, vol. 2 (Rome: Ministerio per beni culturali e ambientali, 1979), 569-70.

Pg. 93: From Michele Ruggiero, *Storia del Piemonte* (Turin: Piemonte in Bancarella, 1979), fig. 24.

Pg. 94: From Geoffrey Symcox, *Victor Amadeus II* (Berkeley and Los Angeles: University of California Press, 1983), fig. 20.

Pg. 96: From Alessandro Visconti, *Storia di Milano* (Milan: Cescina, 1967), 560.

Pg. 98: From Clemente Fusero, *I Doria* (Milan: Dall' Oglio, 1973).

Pg. 101: From Edmund Howard, *Genoa: History and Art in an Old Seaport*, 2d ed. (Genoa: Sagep, 1978), pl. 23.

Pg. 103: Courtesy of Musée du Louvre, Paris.

Pg. 105: Courtesy of British Museum, London.

Pg. 107: Courtesy of Virginia State Library, Richmond.

Pg. 110: From *Voyage pittoresque de la France*, ed. Jean Etienne Guettard, Jean Benjamin de La Borde, and Edme Beguillet, 12 vols. (Paris: Lamy, 1784-1802), *Provence*, pl. 76.

Pg. 113: For Florence Ingersoll-Smouse, *Joseph Vernet, Peintre de Marine, 1714-1789*, vol. 1 (Paris: Etienne Bignou, 1926), pl. 66. Musée de la Marine and Musée du Louvre, Paris.

Pg. 118: For Florence Ingersoll-Smouse, *Joseph Vernet, Peintre de Marine, 1714-1789*, vol. 1 (Paris: Etienne Bignou, 1926), pl. 75. Musée de la Marine and Musée du Louvre, Paris.

Pg. 120: For *Voyage pittoresque de la France*, ed. Jean Etienne Guettard, Jean Benjamin de La Borde, and Edme Beguillet, 12 vols. (Paris: Lamy, 1784-1802), vol. 12, *Gironde*, pl. 1.

Pg. 122: Courtesy of Musée de la Marine and Musée du Louvre, Paris.

Pg. 127: For *Jardins à la Mode et Jardins Anglo-Chinois*, 2d ed., vol. 2 (Paris: Jacomet, 1978), portfolio 7, pl. 10.

Pg. 136: Courtesy of Gemeentarchif, Harlem, The Netherlands.

Pg. 142: For the *Catalogue Raisonné et Figuré de la Galerie Electorale de Düsseldorff* (Basel, 1778). Courtesy of Stadtmuseum, Düsseldorf, Germany.

Pg. 143: Originally in Kurfürstliche Sammlung, Düsseldorf, now in Rheinisches Landesmuseum, Bonn, Germany, by whose courtesy it is reproduced.

Pg. 145: From *Deutscher Jacobiner: Mainzer Republik und Cisrehenanen, 1792-1798*, ed. Hans Bruns (Mainz: Bundesarchiv und Stadt Mainz, 1981), pl. 10.

Pg. 146: From Friedrich Bothe and Bernard Müller, *Bilderatlas zur Geschichte der Stadt Frankfurt am Main*, 2d ed. (Frankfurt-am-Main: Wolfgang Weidlich, 1976), 70.

Pg. 147: From Friedrich Bothe and Bernard Müller, *Bilderatlas zur Geschichte der Stadt Frankfurt am Main*, 2d ed. (Frankfurt-am-Main: Wolfgang Weidlich, 1976), 47.

Pg. 148: From Daniel Meissner, *Thesaurus Philopoliticus Politisches Schatzkastelin*, 2 vols. (Heidelberg: C. Winters Universitatsbuchhandlung, 1927).

Pg. 149: German print, reproduced and copyrighted by Dr. Hans Peters Verlag, Hanau.

Pg. 152: For *Jardins à la Mode et Jardins Anglo-Chinois*, 2d ed., vol. 5 (Paris: Jacomet, 1978), portfolio 2, fig. 19.

Pg. 167: Courtesy of Musée Carnavalet, Paris.

INDEX

215

Library of Congress Cataloging-in-Publication Data

Shackelford, George Green.
    Thomas Jefferson's Travels in Europe, 1784–1789 /
George Green Shackelford.
            p.   cm.
    Includes bibliographical references and index.
    ISBN 0-8018-4843-1 (alk. paper)
    1. Jefferson, Thomas, 1743–1826—Journeys—
Europe.   2. Europe—Description and travel.   I. Title.
      E332.745.S53   1995   94-34705

Portsmouth

Cowes

Le Havre

Paris

Calais

Dover

London

Birmingham

Oxford

Dijon

Lyons

Nîmes

Aix

Marseilles

Nice

Turin

Milan

Genoa

Noli

Sète

Toulouse

Bordeaux

La Rochelle

Rennes

Blois

Brussels

Antwerp

The Hague

Amsterdam

Nijmegen

Dusseldorff

Frankfurt

Hanau

Heidelberg

Schwetzingen

Strasbourg

Nancy

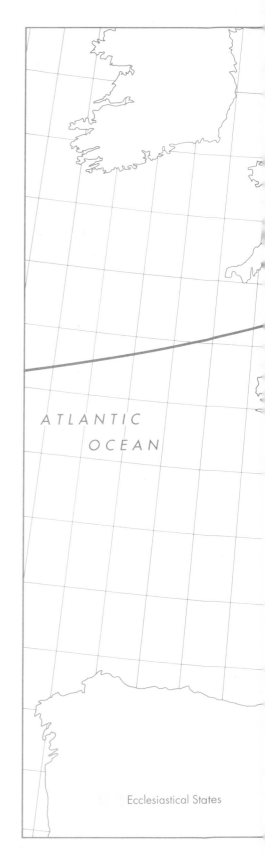

ATLANTIC OCEAN

Ecclesiastical States

923 J35sh
Shackelford, George Green.
Thomas Jefferson's travels
 in Europe, 1784-1789

DATE DUE
